THE COMPLETE IDIOT'S GUIDE® TO

Selling Your Home

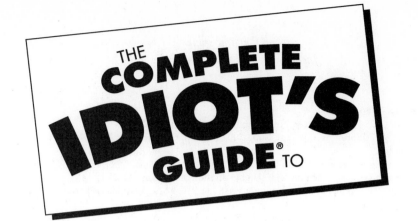

THE COMPLETE IDIOT'S GUIDE® TO

Selling Your Home

by Katie Severance and Nancy Gentile

ALPHA

A member of Penguin Group (USA) Inc.

For Bob and John
Jack, Jessica, Maddie, and Julie

ALPHA BOOKS

Published by the Penguin Group

Penguin Group (USA) Inc., 375 Hudson Street, New York, New York 10014, USA

Penguin Group (Canada), 90 Eglinton Avenue East, Suite 700, Toronto, Ontario M4P 2Y3, Canada (a division of Pearson Penguin Canada Inc.)

Penguin Books Ltd., 80 Strand, London WC2R 0RL, England

Penguin Ireland, 25 St. Stephen's Green, Dublin 2, Ireland (a division of Penguin Books Ltd.)

Penguin Group (Australia), 250 Camberwell Road, Camberwell, Victoria 3124, Australia (a division of Pearson Australia Group Pty. Ltd.)

Penguin Books India Pvt. Ltd., 11 Community Centre, Panchsheel Park, New Delhi—110 017, India

Penguin Group (NZ), 67 Apollo Drive, Rosedale, North Shore, Auckland 1311, New Zealand (a division of Pearson New Zealand Ltd.)

Penguin Books (South Africa) (Pty.) Ltd., 24 Sturdee Avenue, Rosebank, Johannesburg 2196, South Africa

Penguin Books Ltd., Registered Offices: 80 Strand, London WC2R 0RL, England

Copyright © 2010 by Katie Severance and Nancy Gentile

International Standard Book Number: 978-1-59257-863-4
Library of Congress Catalog Card Number: 2008935072

12 11 10   8 7 6 5 4 3 2 1

Interpretation of the printing code: The rightmost number of the first series of numbers is the year of the book's printing; the rightmost number of the second series of numbers is the number of the book's printing. For example, a printing code of 10-1 shows that the first printing occurred in 2010.

Printed in the United States of America

Most Alpha books are available at special quantity discounts for bulk purchases for sales promotions, premiums, fundraising, or educational use. Special books, or book excerpts, can also be created to fit specific needs.

For details, write: Special Markets, Alpha Books, 375 Hudson Street, New York, NY 10014.

Publisher: *Marie Butler-Knight*
Editorial Director: *Mike Sanders*
Senior Managing Editor: *Billy Fields*
Acquisitions Editor: *Michele Wells*
Development Editor: *Ginny Bess Munroe*
Production Editor: *Kayla Dugger*
Copy Editor: *Amy Borrelli*

Cartoonist: *Steve Barr*
Cover Designer: *Bill Thomas*
Book Designer: *Trina Wurst*
Indexer: *Johnna VanHoose Dinse*
Layout: *Chad Dressler*
Proofreader: *John Etchison*

Contents at a Glance

Part 1:   **Getting Ready to Sell**   1

    1   Create a Master Plan   3
Major decisions that need to be made before you sell; preparing for it and understanding the stages of a sale.

    2   Renovations That Make You Money When You Sell   19
The do's and don'ts of profit-driven renovations.

    3   How to Find and Hire a Top-Notch Realtor   37
How to compare real estate agents and agencies, as well as how to negotiate the listing agreement and commission.

    4   To For-Sale-By-Owner … or Not   55
How to find the buyers and price, show, and market your home when you're going it alone.

    5   How to Price Your Home Properly   67
All the tools you need to come up with a great list price for your home. Also, when to do price reductions.

    6   Staging Your Home to Get Top Dollar   83
Hundreds of how-to's and tips to make your home more valuable.

Part 2:   **It's Showtime: When Your Home Is on the Market**   101

    7   Putting Your Home on the Market   103
Everything you'll need to do, including photography, brochures, open houses, signs, and Multiple Listing Services.

    8   How Your Home Gets Shown   117
This is it! Critical things to do before and during a showing to guide the buyers while in your home.

    9   How to Sell Your Home in Any Type of Market   131
What sells a home every time, no matter where you live.

   10   How Buyers Behave When Home Prices Are Down   145
Getting into the minds of the buyers, including their most common traits and their biggest fears.

   11   How Buyers Behave When Home Prices Are Up   155
Leveraging the buyers' mindset to drive your sale price up.

12 Relocations and Estate Sales   169
    Negotiating a relocation package for yourself and how to
    cope with and execute an estate sale.

13 Selling Income-Producing Properties   179
    How to sell a home with rental income for the highest
    dollar amount, including how to calculate potential income
    for interested buyers.

14 Flipping Homes   191
    A comprehensive guide to finding, buying, and selling a
    property in a short period of time with the goal of mak-
    ing a profit.

Part 3:   Negotiating and Closing the Deal   209

15 Evaluating and Accepting an Offer   211
    The four elements of an offer and how to evaluate them.

16 The Inspection and Environmental Issues   233
    What happens on an inspection and what you are
    required to fix. Also, understanding some of the most
    common environmental issues.

17 The Final Walk-Through   245
    What a seller is responsible for in a walk-through, along
    with the things you are not allowed to take and those
    that you should take to avoid problems.

18 At the Closing Table and After   257
    A seller's major responsibilities at closing. How to calcu-
    late your profit and loss in the sale.

19 Packing and Moving Made Simple   273
    Everything you need to know about packing and hiring
    movers, whether you're moving locally or out-of-state.

Appendixes

A Glossary   285

B Resources   293

C Closing and Moving Checklists   299

   Index   301

Contents

Part 1: Getting Ready to Sell   **1**

1 Create a Master Plan   **3**

Reasons for Selling Your Home 4

Where Are You Going? 5

Is It the Right Time to Sell? 6

Selling in a Buyer's Market 6

How to Recognize a Buyer's Market 8

How to Recognize a Transitional Market 9

Selling in a Seller's Market 9

How to Recognize a Seller's Market 9

Preparing to Sell 11

Setting Your Time Line 11

Getting Your Papers in Order 11

Getting Your Home Ready 13

Doing a Presale Inspection 14

The Stages of a Sale 15

Offer Accepted 15

Attorney Review 15

The Deposits 15

The Inspection 16

The Appraisal 16

The Final Mortgage Commitment 16

The Walk-Through and Closing 16

2 Renovations That Make You Money When You Sell   **19**

Increasing Value Through Renovating 20

Good Renovations 20

Bad Renovations 24

Don't Overimprove! 25

Expensive Additions 25

Upgrading Rooms with Super-Expensive Materials 26

A Step-by-Step Plan for Renovating 26

Having a Realtor Evaluate Your Idea 26

Finding and Interviewing Contractors 27

Creating a Renovation Schedule..28
 Creating a Renovation Budget 29
 Cost-Saving Strategies...30
Renovating to Save Energy, or "Going Green"..........................32
 Energy Star Appliances and Materials 34

3 How to Find and Hire a Top-Notch Realtor   37

Finding the Best Realtors 38
 How to Begin...38
 What to Do If Your Friend or Relative Is a Realtor 39
Targeting the Best Real Estate Companies 40
 Agencies That Claim to Be the Market Leader 40
 Agencies with a Global Reach 41
Interviewing Real Estate Agents 42
 Your Realtor's First Walk-Through 42
 The Realtor's Listing Presentation 42
What a Realtor Does..46
 Educating Sellers 47
 Pricing Your Home Properly 47
 Presenting Your Home Well 47
 Exposing Your Property to the Marketplace................................48
 Managing Showings 48
 Managing the Deal When an Offer Comes In.............................48
The Commission 49
 How It Is Paid..49
 What Your Realtor Makes 49
The Listing Agreement...51
 Types of Listing Agreements 51
 The Commission Section of the Listing Agreement.......................52
 The Term: When a Listing Agreement Begins and Ends..............52
 Other Sections of a Listing Agreement..52
Selling to Someone You Know Without Paying
 a Commission 53

4 To For-Sale-By-Owner ... or Not   55

What Is a FSBO? 56
Pricing Your Own Home...56
 Where to Get Information About Comps 57
 Using the Internet to Help You Price Your Home.........................57
 Hiring an Appraiser to Help You Price Your Home.....................58

Showing Your Own Home 58
   Appointments and Preinformation..............................*59*
   Security *59*
   When a Realtor Knocks on Your Door *60*
   Follow-Through with Buyers..*60*
How to Describe Your Home and Its Features............................61
   The Big Three: Size, Condition, and Location *61*
   The Architecture *62*
   The Amenities *62*
Where to Find Buyers 62
   Online Multiple Listing Services..................................*62*
   Reach Out to Buyers' Real Estate Agents......................*63*
   Canvass Neighbors..*63*
   Hold Public Open Houses *64*
   Put a Sign on the Property *64*
Professional Guidance on Managing a Deal 65

5 How to Price Your Home Properly   **67**
The Difference Between Price and Value 68
   The Price..*68*
   Creating Value *69*
Setting Your List Price..69
Relevant Data 70
   Comparables *70*
   Local Market Trends..*71*
   Appraisals and Tax Assessments *72*
Insider Access 73
Basic Instinct...74
   Knowing What Buyers Will Pay....................................*74*
   Hard-to-Comp Homes *75*
Reductions 77
   How Overpriced Is Your Home?....................................*77*
   Tracking Showings..*78*
   When to Do a Reduction *79*

6 Staging Your Home to Get Top Dollar   **83**
The First Impression..84
Room-by-Room Staging 84
   The Living Room..*85*
   The Dining Room..*86*

The Kitchen *88*
The Bathroom *90*
The Bedroom *91*
Closets *92*
Windows and the Importance of Light *93*
Basements, Attics, and Garages *94*
The Exterior and Curb Appeal 94
Shaping Up the Lawn and Garden *94*
Decks, Porches, and Patios *96*
Vacant Homes 98
Professional Stagers for Hire 98

Part 2:   It's Showtime: When Your Home Is on the Market   101

7   Putting Your Home on the Market   103

How to Describe Your Home 104
Location *105*
Size *105*
Condition *106*
Photographing Your Home 107
The Purpose and Importance of Good Photographs *107*
Biggest Photography Mistakes and How to Avoid Them *108*
Brochures and Handouts 110
Lawn Signs 111
Seller's Disclosures 111
Choosing the Date to Introduce Your Home 112
Entering Your Home on the Multiple Listing Service 113
The Realtor Open House 113
Running Ads 114
The Real Reason Agencies Run Ads *114*
An Advertising Plan *114*
The Public Open House 115

8   How Your Home Gets Shown   117

Showing Guidelines 118
Scheduling Appointments 118
How Buyers Get Inside Your Home 119
Lockboxes *120*
Picking Up the Key *120*
Listing Realtor Hosts and Supervises Showings *121*

If You Must Be Home During Showings 121
What to Do Right Before a Showing 122
   Things to Do When a Buyer Is on the Way 122
   Things Not to Do When a Buyer Is on the Way...................124
How to Control Showings Without Being There...................125
   Demonstrate the Potential of Your Home Through Blueprints....125
   Reveal Hidden Hardwood Floors 126
   Direct the Eye Toward Hidden Appliances and Fixtures............126
   Point Out Captive Attics...126
   Show Off Your Pool, Garden, and Landscaping with Photos.......127
   Point Out Neighborhood Amenities 127
Multiple Showings at the Same Time 127
   Conducting Multiple Showings......................................127
   Multiple Showings as a Positive 128
Rallying the Neighbors 128
Tracking Showings 128

9 How to Sell Your Home in Any Type of Market   **131**
Why Some Homes Sell and Others Do Not 132
What Sells Your Home Every Time 132
   Stage Your Home..133
   Aggressively Price 133
   Lead the Deal..138
   Expose Your Home to the Whole Buyer Pool 139
What to Do When Your Home's Been on the Market
  Too Long 143

10 How Buyers Behave When Home Prices Are Down   **145**
Predicting Buyer Behavior in a Down Market.......................146
The Buyer's Most Common Trait: A Low Sense
  of Urgency...146
The Buyer's Biggest Fear: Paying Too Much.........................147
Why a Buyer Won't Make an Offer When Your Home
  Is Overpriced...148
   Fighting the "What's Wrong with It?" Perception.................148
Lowball Offers..149
   Trying to Define a Lowball Offer...................................149
   Responding to Lowball Offers 149
   How to Negotiate a Lowball Offer..................................150

The Myth That Buyers Have Gone Away 152
    Cycle-One Buyers Never Go Away 152
    The Buyer's Best Talent 152

11 How Buyers Behave When Home Prices Are Up   **155**

Buyers' Most Common Trait: A Strong Sense of Urgency 156
Buyers' Greatest Fear: Missing the Market 157
    How Buyers Miss the Market When Prices Are Rising 157
    The Incredible Shrinking Home 157
Driving Your Sale Price Up 158
    When Buyers Don't Mind Paying a Premium 158
    How to Inspire a Bidding War on Your Home 159
How to Nurture and Handle Bidding Wars 160
Receiving and Reviewing Multiple Offers 162
    Highest and Best, or the One-Step Bidding Process 162
    Beware of the Escalation Clause 164
    The Two-Step Bidding Process 164
    Presenting Offers in Person vs. Sealed Bids 165
Choosing the Best and Handling the Rest 165
    The Importance of Backup Offers 166
    Buyer's Remorse 166

12 Relocations and Estate Sales   **169**

Selling When an Employer Relocates You 170
Employee Relocation Packages 171
    Relocation Package 171
    Listing Your Home with a Relocation Clause 172
Estate Sales 173
    Marketing a Home as Part of an Estate 174
    Family Roles and the Division of Labor 174
    Dispersing the Proceeds of the Sale to Heirs 174
    Tax Implications for You in an Estate Sale 175
    Calculating the Value of an Estate 176
Power of Attorney 177

13 Selling Income-Producing Properties   **179**

Types of Investment Properties 180
Deciding to Sell a Home with Rental Income 180
    Pros of Selling 180
    Cons of Selling 181

Selling Homes with Pre-Existing Renters..................................182
   Obstacles to Selling a Home Occupied by Renters.......................182
   Overcoming the Obstacles...183
The Powerful Key to Marketing Income-Producing
   Homes..185
   Calculating Property Income for Your Buyers.........................186
   What Really Attracts Buyers to Investment Properties?.............187
   Attached Rental Units, Mother/Daughter, and Boarder
     Apartments...188
   Showing Rental Properties 189

14 Flipping Homes   **191**

What Is Flipping?..192
   Should You Get into the Business of Flipping?..........................192
   The Necessary Skills to Flip Homes 192
The Formula for Successful Flipping.....................................194
   Location..194
   Upgrades...195
   Contractors and Partners...199
   Kickoff and Timeline..202
   Yardsticks for Success 204
How to Market a Flipped Home...206
   Lead with the Best...206
   Sell the Contractor..206

Part 3: Negotiating and Closing the Deal   **209**

15 Evaluating and Accepting an Offer   **211**

Price..212
   Below the List Price 212
   Full-Price Offers...213
   Above the List Price 214
Terms 214
   If the Buyer Needs to Sell Property Before Buying Yours............215
   Closing Date..215
   Deposit Monies 216
   Mortgage Contingency 217
   Inspection Contingency 219
The Source of the Offer 220

The Presentation 221
  Cover Letter 221
  The Actual Contract 223
  Financing Letter 230
  Disclosure Forms 230
  Copy of Earnest Money Check 230
Accepting an Offer 231
  What to Do After You Have Accepted 231
  When Other Offers Come in After You Have Accepted 231

16 The Inspection and Environmental Issues   233

What Gets Inspected and When Is It Done? 234
What You Are Required to Fix 235
  Items Mandated by Law 235
  Items Listed in the Contract 235
  Items Negotiated 236
How to Negotiate Inspections 236
  Receiving the Buyer's Request for Repairs 237
  Responding to a Buyer's Request for Repairs 237
Environmental Issues 238
  Asbestos 239
  Radon 239
  Underground Oil Tanks and Septic Tanks 240
  Lead-Based Paint 241
  Water Wells 241
  Wet Basements 242
  Mold 242
  Carpenter Bees 242
  Carpenter Ants 243
  Termites 243
  Other Pest and Rodent Infestations 243

17 The Final Walk-Through   245

The Walk-Through 246
The Condition of the Property 246
  Floors 247
  Walls and Ceilings 247
  Dishwasher, Washer, and Dryer 247
  Stoves and Ovens 248
  Toilets, Sinks, Tubs, and Showers 248

The Lawn..248
Broom Clean..249
No Debris...249
What You Are Not Allowed to Take 249
Wall and Ceiling Light Fixtures 249
Built-In Appliances..250
Replacing Appliances...250
Doorknobs and Cabinet Hardware.......................250
Shutters and Flower Boxes 251
Porch Swing..251
Swing Sets...251
Mailboxes, Flag Poles, and Sheds........................251
What You Should Take in Order to Avoid Problems 252
Paint Cans, Stains, and Epoxy............................252
Air Conditioners 253
Firewood...253
Second Refrigerators and Freezers.......................254
Garden and Workshop Tools, Lawn Mowers, and Trash Cans 254
Hangers...254
Nice Things to Do for the New Homeowners.......254

18 At the Closing Table and After   **257**
What Happens at the Closing Table 258
The Seller's Responsibilities at the Closing 258
Certificates for Use...258
Pay Off the Mortgage and Other Liens 260
Pay Taxes 261
Read and Sign the Settlement Statement..............266
Pay Credits to the Buyer (Inspection Issues)........266
Receive Credits from the Buyer 267
Pay Commission and Other Fees 267
Other Documents...268
Calculating Profit and Loss on the Sale 268
Keys...269
Seller Liability After Closing...................................269
Money Held in Escrow 269
Civil Claims or Lawsuits......................................270
Use and Occupancy Agreements...........................271

19 Packing and Moving Made Simple   **273**

   Moving Out of State vs. Within the State..................274
     Local Moving 274
     Out-of-State Moving 275
   Your Packing Plan 275
   Packing Materials 277
     Moving Boxes 277
     Other Materials 277
   Finding the Right Mover 278
   Getting Moving Estimates 278
     Guidelines for Estimates 279
   Insurance 280
   Moving Day 280
     Your Role 280
     Paying the Movers 281
   Moving Terminology 281

Appendixes

  A Glossary   **285**

  B Resources   **293**

  C Closing and Moving Checklists   **299**

    Index   **301**

Introduction

This book is about getting your home sold in any type of market. We show you how, through strategic thinking, to understand real estate as well or better than many of the professionals working in the business. You will be able to directly apply what you learn here to the sale of your home. You will sell it successfully and will minimize your stress while doing it.

We will also guide you through all of the stages of a sale, discussing what truly motivates buyers and specifically what gets you top dollar for your home.

Selling your home is not just about hitting all your marks and completing checklists. What it's really about is the understanding of the process and the people involved in it. There is a huge element of psychology in the sale of real estate. Knowing how to use it your advantage is what makes you more money than another seller who does not. We're going to teach you how to do it.

Part 1, "Getting Ready to Sell," is a comprehensive guide to all the decisions you need to make and the things you need to do before you put your home on the market. It starts with creating a plan of action and then screening and hiring the best Realtor that you can find. You may have decided to sell your home on your own, without the aid of a professional. We have dedicated an entire chapter to selling a FSBO (For-Sale-By-Owner). The two most important things you must do before you put it on the market are to price it properly and stage it well. These two things are of paramount importance.

Part 2, "It's Showtime: When Your Home Is on the Market," talks about how your home will actually be put on the market, how to manage showings to your home's greatest advantage, and the power of the Internet for maximum exposure. Also in this section are some very important chapters for getting top dollar. We discuss buyer behavior patterns in both a rising and falling market as well as devoting an entire chapter to selling your home anywhere, anytime, and in any type of market. There are also some special kinds of sales that we address in Part 2: estate sales, relocation for a job, selling income-producing properties, and flipping homes. While the basic approach to marketing these homes is the same as any other, they have their own special set of considerations and challenges to deal with.

Part 3, "Negotiating and Closing the Deal," is all about keeping the deal together, which is as important as receiving the offer in the first place. After all, what good is a fabulous offer if it never makes it to the closing table? We will show you how to scrutinize and evaluate an offer before you accept it, how to negotiate, and what happens at an inspection, the final walk-through, and the closing table. We'll show you how to calculate your profit and reduce your liability. And we've concluded the book with all the ways to make packing and moving simple.

On a personal note, we hope that you enjoy reading this book as much as we enjoyed writing it. We feel strongly about every single chapter and hope that they give you all the information and guidance that you'll ever need to sell a home.

Extras

We've added a few helpers to define terms used in the main text and to provide you with additional tips and warnings. You'll find these located in boxes throughout this book.

Trick of the Trade

Through the years in which we've been practicing real estate, we have picked up a million tips and tricks to make things easier, better, stronger, and worth more. We share them all over this book and hope you find them as useful as we have.

def•i•ni•tion

There are so many terms and phrases associated with a real estate transaction, and they can be confusing. You'll know them all after reading this book.

Seller Alert

These are our version of red flags. Their purpose is to warn you about anything that requires extra care, safety, or precaution.

Acknowledgments

We'd like to thank our families for being instrumental in the writing of this book—mostly our husbands, John Gentile and Bob Severance, whose love and support made it all possible. Our children: Katie's little Jack; Nancy's Jessica, Maddie, and Julie, who were all supportive in so many special ways. A special thank you to our literary agent, Janet Rosen, at the Sheree Bykofsky agency—the catalyst for it all. Without her tremendous support and guidance, this book would not exist.

We'd also like to thank some of our professional friends who gave of their time and advice so generously: Tom Conk (CPA), David Rubenstein and Joanne Cabe (mortgage brokers), Melanie Factor (attorney), Kate Pruim (home renovator), Dan Casella (Goman's Moving Company), Charles Mabee (May-Pan Moving), Roy Scott and Deborah Campbell (our brokers), and our friend Jay who gave us our start in the real estate business.

Thank you to our parents, Jerry and Marge Rubacky and Bill and Gloria Lawrence. And finally, to the others whose feedback was so appreciated: Maggie Chess, Anthony and Donna Gentile, Carol Garcia, Jerry Rubacky Jr., Susan Kempton, Maryanne Rubacky, Frank Pita, Frank Rubacky, Susan Severance, Sandy Neville, Barbara Lawrence, Nora Keefe, Denise Brown, Maeve Walsh, and Mike Rubacky.

Special Thanks to Our Editors at Penguin

We'd like to thank the editors of *The Complete Idiot's Guide to Selling Your Home* for all the ways they guided, collaborated, and inspired us: Mike Sanders, Michele Wells, Ginny Bess Munroe, Kayla Dugger, and Amy Borrelli. Every suggestion and edit made the book better.

Trademarks

All terms mentioned in this book that are known to be or are suspected of being trademarks or service marks have been appropriately capitalized. Alpha Books and Penguin Group (USA) Inc. cannot attest to the accuracy of this information. Use of a term in this book should not be regarded as affecting the validity of any trademark or service mark.

Part 1

Getting Ready to Sell

If you are thinking about selling your home, you have some big decisions to make and things to do before you actually put the house on the market. If you take the time to go through these steps, not only will you be more knowledgeable and in control than you ever thought you would be, but you will make a lot more money than you expected to, as well. You can actually increase the sale price of your home by making some strategic moves through good planning.

The decision to sell a home begins with a thought or an idea in your head. Making it a reality and a success depends on how well you plan it out and then how well you execute. We help you to do both.

In Part 1 of this book, we cover everything that should happen before you put your home on the market.

Create a Master Plan

In This Chapter

- ◆ Creating your plan
- ◆ The big decisions you need to make
- ◆ Getting everything in place for the sale
- ◆ The stages of a sale

When you sell your home, it can be that one chance in your lifetime to make a huge financial profit. Good planning saves you money. It also *makes* you money—and a lot of it! On the other hand, mistakes and delays could cost you a lot. You may surround yourself with professionals, or you may try to go it alone. Either way, for you to maximize your profit when the deal is complete, it is crucial to take an active role from the beginning.

The more prepared you are from the start, the smoother the process of selling your house. The entire experience is much less stressful and much easier on you and your family.

In this chapter, we help you to create that plan. Some of the things you need to do are: understand why you're selling, establish a personal time frame, know where you're going after you sell, determine if it's the right time to sell, determine whether or not to use a Realtor or sell it yourself, get paperwork organized, physically prepare the home, and understand the stages of a sale.

Reasons for Selling Your Home

To create a good plan for selling your home, start with becoming clear about the reason that you are selling. Not only will it help focus you, it will also have a big impact on the next home you choose to buy, and that will affect your financial bottom line. Now, your reason for selling may be obvious to you, but in reading on, you may see that you possibly have more than one reason. Keeping all of the reasons in mind will help you make good decisions.

Having clarity about why you are selling is important for the rest of your family, too. You're all leaving this home together. When everyone rallies for a common cause, the result is always better.

Here are some common reasons why homeowners sell:

- ♦ Lifestyle change (death, divorce, marriage, retirement, youngest child is graduating from high school)

- ♦ Job relocation

- ♦ Taxes are too high

- ♦ Personal bankruptcy

- ♦ Testing the market to see what the home is worth

- ♦ Unhappy with the location or neighborhood

- ♦ Unhappy with the school system

- ♦ Bored with or no longer love the property

- ♦ Need a bigger kitchen

- ♦ Need more bedrooms

- ♦ Need more bathrooms

- ♦ Want a finished basement

- ♦ No room for an addition

- ♦ Want to scale down and have less living space

- ♦ Cannot keep up with the maintenance; ownership is too much work

Seller Alert _____

If you put your home on the market and then find that you've changed your mind or feel that you're selling for the wrong reasons, you have the legal and ethical right to withdraw it from the market at any time, provided that you have not signed a contract with a buyer.

Where Are You Going?

There is a saying in residential real estate circles that "there is no such thing as performing just one transaction." This is almost always true. The minute you buy your first home, the odds are that you will always be a homeowner, until your old age. It's true that some homeowners will sell and then rent, or move into assisted living. But the majority of sellers always buy another home. This means that you are likely to conduct two transactions in approximately the same window of time.

While most of us understand this idea in theory, we still tend to judge each purchase or sale alone, as an individual transaction. But they're not really individual transactions when you have made them in the same time period. We forget that, while we may have lost money on the sale, we may have made it up on the purchase of the next home.

To illustrate the point, think of boats in a harbor, rising and falling with the tides. No matter how big or small the boat, they all move up and down at the same rate. Now, think of your community as the harbor. All the homes in it will rise and fall with the market at about the same percentage.

Let's say that you are looking for a larger home (or "trading up") in your community. At the moment, the market has fallen 10 percent. You actually stand to make a tidy profit after selling the smaller one and buying an even bigger one. The following shows you how.

The Home You Are Selling	The Home You Are Buying
Smaller House	Larger House
Original Value: $300,000	Original Value: $600,000
–10% Drop in Home Value	–10% Drop in Home Value
————————————	————————————
= $30,000 Loss	= $60,000 Loss
New Value: $270,000	**New Value = $540,000**

You lost $30,000 in value on the home that you sold, but the seller of the home you bought lost $60,000 in value. By making two transactions, you made $30,000 after both trades were completed. Not a bad return when all you could think about was losing $30,000 in the sale of your current home.

Trick of the Trade _____

If you are thinking of "trading down" to a smaller house because you feel that your current one is "too much work," consider the possibility that you may still want a lot of space but are just growing weary of yard work and all the outdoor maintenance required. An alternative could be a townhouse or very large condo that has all exterior upkeep included in the monthly maintenance fees.

Is It the Right Time to Sell?

This is perhaps the biggest question that homeowners ask themselves. It's a valid one because everybody is worried about losing money if they sell at the wrong time. But what is the wrong time or the right time?

Let's talk about the three different types of markets in which you may be selling your home and how to spot them.

Selling in a Buyer's Market

A buyer's market is also known as a falling market. In a falling market, home prices are coming down and it therefore favors buyers.

There is an understandable perception that you will lose money selling your home in a buyer's market. You don't have to! With the exception of some extraordinary circumstances, like an environmental or economic disaster in your community, there are only a few reasons why you would actually lose money when selling. These reasons include:

◆ You've made too many expensive upgrades.

This is also known as *overimproving*. The result is that your home now costs more than all the homes around it, and buyers are fearful of buying the most expensive home in a building or in a neighborhood. They want to know that their home is among its peers and not among the smaller, less valuable homes. For more information on strategic renovations and home improvements, see Chapter 2.

◆ You've owned it a short time and the market has fallen since your purchase.

If the market goes down right after you bought it and then you found yourself needing to sell after a short period of time owning it, you could lose money. Short-term ownership is always risky. If you must move and prices have fallen dramatically, try to keep the property and rent it out until the market bounces back enough for you to sell without loss.

def•i•ni•tion

Overimproving is when the owner has put a substantial amount of money into improvements on the home, such as an addition or expensive kitchen, and the size or location of the home cannot support the expense. The outlay of dollars does not come back to the homeowner when it's sold.

Seller Alert

If renters are in your home when you do finally put it up for sale, it is like a double-edged sword. You will get monthly income to offset your mortgage and taxes, but beware: renters can have a negative impact on the sale price. Homes that are "owner-occupied" tend to show much better than homes with renters in them because the owner always has a much deeper and vested interest in its appearance, condition, and how much it sells for. Renters don't care because they aren't making any money from the sale. Further, they can be uncooperative, as they may be frustrated about the inconvenience of showings and the possibility of having to find a new place to live. This often comes across to buyers viewing the home and can be a turn-off.

◆ You owe too much on the home.

This means that the amount of money that you borrowed is simply more than what the home is now worth. In order to sell, you must make up that difference to the bank. If you've ever heard of a seller needing to "bring cash to the closing table," this is what it means. The amount of money that the buyer borrowed in order to purchase the home was probably too high in the first place. If the homeowner went on to borrow even more against the home during ownership and then the home's value falls, disaster strikes. The sale price will not cover the debt to the bank.

How to Recognize a Buyer's Market

When the real estate market is coming down and beginning to favor buyers, it's usually pretty clear to most homeowners. But how can you tell which way the market is headed when it's not so obvious? The answer is by looking at the speed at which homes are selling.

Sometimes, you just have to count. To measure the speed, you want to count the number of days that it takes for the majority of homes in your area to receive an offer and go under contract. This is a real measurement called days on market (DOM), and it is a powerful tool used by all real estate professionals. What you're looking for is the average DOM among all the homes that are similar to yours in size, style, condition, and price.

Calculating the Average Days on Market

Properties	Days on Market
10 Smith Road	96
21 Elm Street	89
5 Oak Street	101
52 Blueberry Lane	125
19 Main Street	106
16 Wood Avenue	145
21 Ocean Avenue	172
Total: 7	**834**

834 ÷ 7 properties = 119 Avg DOM

Take the total number of days on market (834) and divide by the total number of properties (7) to find the average DOM. In this case, it is taking about four months for homes in the area to sell.

This statistic may sound familiar to you. In the news and on TV, it is referred to as the *absorption rate*, which is another fancy term for how fast homes sell. While our measurement talks about "days" on the market, absorption rates usually get reported when they are measured in "months" and the market is in some trouble. For example, a news headline might read, "The current absorption rate in the United States is $8\frac{1}{2}$ months."

def•i•ni•tion

The **absorption rate** is the average length of time it takes for homes to sell. It can be reported for all homes in the United States or for homes in a certain region.

How to Recognize a Transitional Market

What if some homes are selling quickly and others are taking months to sell? The trends are all over the place and you're not really sure what kind of market we're in. That's a sign of a transitional or changing market. But sooner or later, the market will choose which way it's going—up or down.

If you are selling in this type of market, you could be a big winner because you sold just before the market tanked—or you could regret having sold your home just before the market took off. The patterns that reveal which way the market is about to go are what economists and financial analysts on Wall Street spend all day trying to figure out. It's extremely difficult to predict, and anyone who could would make billions of dollars.

Selling in a Seller's Market

A seller's market, also known as a rising market, is when home prices are going up. These types of markets can get crazy and seduce you into selling even when you are not ready. Some homeowners want to test the waters by putting their home on the market just to see how much they could get. They may not have thought through where they are going or that it will be expensive to buy in that kind of market as well. When they do get a terrific offer, suddenly they are scrambling to find a new place to live.

How to Recognize a Seller's Market

Most homeowners know pretty quickly when their community has moved into a seller's market. Good news travels fast! When the market shifts over to favoring sellers, it usually begins in fits and starts. There are stories and anecdotes that go around about how this home or that home received multiple offers and got 10 percent or more above the list price.

If the market continues in this manner, the stories become more common. The local media may report on the trend. The Realtors in your community will begin to talk about it with their buyers. They'll point out homes and quote the big sale prices. The buyers who understand the market in your area will realize what they need to do in order to buy a home there. Suddenly, the big sale prices are the norm because the buyers—for the moment—don't mind paying them.

Now the supply seems to be getting smaller and the buyer pool appears to be getting bigger. The buyers begin to get competitive with each other—which only makes them want a home even more. They want to win.

Seller Alert

Be careful when trying to time the top (or bottom) of any market cycle. There is only one way to know when we've hit the top, and that is when the moment is behind us—and usually not until it is weeks or months behind us.

Many sellers assume that they will automatically make a profit in a rising market. Much of the time, they will. But again, how much money you walk away with depends also on what you are buying. If you are moving to another, more expensive community, your bottom-line profit will clearly be smaller after you purchase the new home.

But let's look at an example of selling and then buying within the same community in which you now live. Perhaps you've been in your home for 35 years. Your last child is about to go to college and the house is too big to keep up, but you want to stay in town. You are looking to buy a smaller home or to scale down.

Now, let's assume that it's a seller's market, where prices have risen 10 percent. That cute little craftsman bungalow you had your eye on is now more expensive than you anticipated. You were hoping to have a much smaller mortgage to go with your much smaller home. After considering the cost of moving and taking on a still sizeable monthly mortgage payment, you may conclude that it is not worth it to sell and trade down.

Yet, even in this scenario, you will likely come out ahead after making both the sale and the purchase in the same community.

The following shows how it works:

You're Selling …	You're Buying …
(Draw Big House)	(Draw Small House)
$600,000 Original Value	$300,000 Original Value
+ 10% Rise in Home Values	+ 10% Rise in Home Values
———————————	———————————
= $60,000 Gain in Value	= $30,000 Gain in Value
New Value = $660,000	**New Value = $330,000**

You are paying $30,000 more than you planned to pay on the small house, but you have received $60,000 more than expected on the home you are selling.

What appears to be a bad time to sell can actually be a good time when you consider where you're going and what your "net" will be after the two transactions are completed. The first thing to do, always, is to decide where you are going and how much it will cost you to get there.

Preparing to Sell

Selling a home is about a lot more than just staging and pricing. The process begins weeks or months before that. The following sections discuss some things to consider when you are getting ready to sell.

Setting Your Time Line

When you are at the stage of simply contemplating the sale of your home, it is smart to take out a calendar and estimate the month or week that you would like to have your home come on the market, how long it will take to prepare it properly, when you would like to close on a sale, and when you'd like to move.

These dates might not coincide with when a buyer actually makes an offer on your home. But estimating target dates is helpful when you make decisions along the way. For example, if your home is not selling and you want to be out of it by a certain date, you may be more motivated to make a strategic price reduction early on. Without a time line, you're sort of adrift and hoping for things to just "work out" in line with your needs.

Getting Your Papers in Order

Paperwork is a necessary evil when selling real estate. When it is not in order, it will cause delays and probably money. For example, let's say that you have misplaced your survey and there is some question as to whether the neighbor's fence is encroaching on your property. The bank, title company, and/or attorneys will not close until there is legal proof of the boundaries of your lot. You have to order a new survey and have your property staked and measured. This can take a few days or a few weeks.

The documents that you need in order to sell your home depend on the laws in your state. In any state, the more documents you have and can share with the buyer, the better. But you may only be required to provide one or two. Following is a checklist of some common types of paperwork that could be helpful to have at the ready.

❏ **Your mortgage:** When you sell, your mortgage will be paid off with the proceeds from the buyer. Whoever is conducting your closing (an attorney or a title
company) will be in contact with your bank or lender and will therefore need
that information.

❏ **The deed:** This is the written document that allows you to transfer ownership
of real estate.

❏ **The survey:** This is the precise measuring of the boundaries of your property
and is used as a legal description of it.

❏ **Homeowner's insurance:** This covers major perils to the property, like fire. It
is required by banks and lenders to protect their loan on the property, but it also
protects your investment in the property.

❏ **Home warranty insurance:** You may want to offer this to a buyer. It covers the
new homeowner and insures major components of your home, such as electrical,
plumbing, heating, and major appliances. It is not required of you. It can, however, be attractive to a buyer, particularly in a difficult market.

❏ **Environmental remediation documents:** Some environmental hazards include
underground oil or septic tanks, radon, asbestos around piping, termites, mold,
and more. If you have remediated any of these problems, the paperwork will be
needed by the buyers—and their attorney, if they are using one.

❏ **Closed permits for upgrades and additions:** Buyers will want to be sure that
all permits you pulled for work on the home were closed. This means that the
township or municipality where you live was notified that you were doing major
work and it was inspected by them when the work was finished.

 Seller Alert _____

When you do work on your home and pull the appropriate permits, the local
municipality will automatically become aware that you have made capital
improvements, which means that it has the right to raise your property taxes.

Additionally, your property taxes may have needed to be adjusted after the
work was complete. If you don't have closed permits, then your work was not
inspected and your property tax amount may not be up-to-date, as well.

❑ **Instruction manuals and warranties:** It is not legally required that you provide instruction manuals and warranty paperwork for appliances that will remain in the home after you sell. It is, however, a nice thing to pass on to the new home-owners.

Getting Your Home Ready

When you make the decision to sell your home, it's amazing how fast the big day arrives when you actually put it on the market. Your to-do list can get long in a hurry! Suddenly, there are a million little repairs to be made and clearing out to be done.

The more organized you are up front, the less stress you will feel once your home is on the market. Repairs can take a long time to get done because you are either doing them yourself and need time to accomplish all of it, or you are hiring a handyman or contractor and they tend to be booked a few weeks in advance. Allow enough time for all the work to be done.

If you choose to sell your home in as-is condition, with all its flaws unattended to, they will be reflected in a lower sale price—usually significantly lower. If it does sell, some repair issues may still come up in the inspector's report. You may have to make them in order to keep the deal together.

Consider making repairs like the following before putting your home on the market:

◆ Leaking roof, faucets, and pipes

◆ Backed-up drains and running toilets

◆ Faulty stoves, furnace, or hot-water heaters

◆ Loose railings

◆ Ripped screens

◆ Debris-filled or broken gutters

◆ Carpet stains

◆ Uneven sidewalks

◆ Loose or broken fire escapes

◆ Doors that creak or won't close

◆ Broken sash cords in windows

◆ Cracked window panes

Doing a Presale Inspection

Many sellers today are conducting inspections on their own homes before putting them on the market to help them determine what repairs to make in advance, possibly getting them a better sale price. It also gives buyers a higher level of comfort when it comes time for the inspection of the property.

If you perform an inspection, you might also be able to share the report if the buyer asks for a particular repair that you may not agree with.

When you speak with an inspection company, following are some questions to consider asking:

- Are they licensed in the state where my home is located?

- Are they certified with any national organizations such as ASHI (American Society of Home Inspectors)?

- How long has the company been in business?

- How many inspections has the individual inspector performed?

- How long will the inspection take?

- What will be inspected at the property?

- What environmental tests will they perform?

- How will the systems be evaluated and rated?

- May I see a sample report?

- How soon will I receive a written report?

 Seller Alert _____

If you live in an area where they use oil heat (even if your home is not heated with oil), it is a smart thing to have your property scanned for evidence of old, abandoned underground oil tanks. Do this well before you put it up for sale. The cost is nominal. Most buyers have a search performed before they will close and, if they find one, it can seriously jeopardize the deal through delays and/or the buyer backing out altogether. We cover this and many other environmental issues in Chapter 16.

The Stages of a Sale

Every sale has certain stages that a buyer and seller must pass through on the way to closing. The sequence varies from state to state, and some of them don't even apply in certain states. We discuss them individually and what your role is in each.

Offer Accepted

Most real estate contracts are in writing. In some states, they are required to be in writing. The buyer (or the buyer's Realtor) draws up the offer and signs it. It then comes to you for consideration. If you accept it, you then sign it. It is typical for there to be some money put into *escrow* at this early stage. It can be $100, $1,000, $5,000, or much more. This is called *earnest money*.

def•i•ni•tion

Holding money in **escrow** means that a disinterested third party holds it until all the terms and conditions of the agreement are met. It is typically held by a title company or an attorney and it will be held in a trust bank account. Sometimes a real estate agency will hold it until closing. The money itself is called **earnest money** and represents the good faith of the buyer to proceed with the purchase.

Attorney Review

Some states have a legally imposed period of time wherein a buyer has the right to have an attorney review the contract that you have both signed. It could be a three-day period or more. In that period, the buyer often has the right to back out of the deal without giving a reason. This law is designed to protect buyers. You, on the other hand, also have the right to back out of the transaction and not sell to that buyer or to sell it to another buyer.

The Deposits

As we said in the previous section about when the offer is accepted, the first part of a buyer's deposit comes along with the offer itself—the earnest money. The next portion of his deposit money, according to the contract, may come anywhere from 10 days to a few weeks later. The final portion of the deposit money comes on closing day.

The Inspection

Depending on the state, the inspection is done either before the buyer makes an offer or after the offer has been signed and accepted. If it is done after the offer has been accepted, then the buyer has the right to ask you to make certain repairs. If you decline to make them, the buyer has the right, once again, to back out of the deal. This portion of the contract is called the *inspection contingency*.

def•i•ni•tion _____

> An **inspection contingency** in a real estate contract usually states that the buyer will only go through with the sale if an inspection is done to the satisfaction of the buyer. The sale is literally contingent upon the inspection happening and any needed repairs being successfully negotiated by the buyer and seller. If the buyer requests repairs and the seller refuses to make them, the contract is voidable and the buyer may back out of the deal with no penalties.

The Appraisal

The buyer's bank, or lender, will send an appraiser out to your home to appraise the value of your home. He will decide if the buyer paid too much or more than he thinks your home is worth. This is what happens when a home "does not appraise." The appraisal is always a condition of the loan, and the bank will not lend money on a home that it has not evaluated. The appraisal happens soon after you have signed the buyer's offer.

The Final Mortgage Commitment

When a buyer is prequalified or even preapproved, he is only partway through the process of getting a loan. Once you have accepted his offer and the lender sends out the appraiser to your home, the lender also sends the buyer's file to what's called its "underwriting department" for a final stamp of approval. This is the department that determines if the buyer is ultimately qualified to borrow. It is only then that the buyer truly has final approval for the loan.

The Walk-Through and Closing

Either on the day of the closing, or perhaps the day before, the buyer will do a final walk-through of your home to be sure that it is in the same condition that it was in when he last viewed it. He also wants to be sure that you have vacated the property without leaving behind any belongings or debris. Most real estate contracts stipulate that you are to leave the premises in "broom-clean" condition. If there is anything that comes up during the walk-through, it must be settled and negotiated immediately in order for the closing to take place.

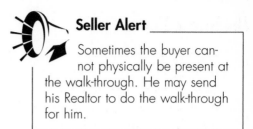

Seller Alert

Sometimes the buyer cannot physically be present at the walk-through. He may send his Realtor to do the walk-through for him.

The Least You Need to Know

◆ Your master plan and knowing where you are going will have an enormous impact on your financial bottom line.

◆ Buying a bigger home is often a smart move when the market is coming down.

◆ To figure out which way the market is headed, study the speed at which homes in your area are going under contract.

◆ Do not underestimate how important it is to have your paperwork in order before putting your home on the market.

◆ Consider performing a presale inspection to establish necessary repairs and to be in a stronger negotiating position with your buyer.

Chapter 2

Renovations That Make You Money When You Sell

In This Chapter

- How to make money on a renovation
- Good and bad renovation ideas
- Step-by-step plan for renovating
- Loads of cost-saving tips
- Energy-saving costs and "green" renovation ideas

A renovation can have a powerful impact on your sale price. However, renovations made specifically for the purpose of selling, and not just for your own enjoyment, should be done strategically and with careful thought. It is possible to make expensive upgrades that do not translate into actual dollars. If the purpose of your renovations is solely to make money on a sale, you want to be sure that they will do just that. If you make poor choices when renovating and the buyers don't see the value in the upgrade, you could take a big financial hit. It's also disappointing when you create something that you feel is valuable only to find out that others do not agree.

In this chapter, we discuss all kinds of renovations, good and bad. We share tips and cost-saving strategies that will increase your profit upon selling and help you to avoid costly mistakes.

Increasing Value Through Renovating

Renovating a home is complicated, but there is nothing more rewarding and fun than transforming something shabby or old into something new and valuable—and making a lot of money in the process! However, there are financial dangers. When you renovate simply for your own enjoyment, there is less riding on it because you have only yourself to please. But keep in mind that you may pay a price down the road if your renovations are too specific to your taste or too trendy.

Too often, homeowners simply assume that whatever they put into a home will come back to them. When you are renovating strictly for the purpose of selling, your motive is entirely profit driven. Consider every possible angle before you begin. If you misjudge, you could take a loss. Let's begin with a discussion of good and bad renovations and how to tell the difference between them.

Good Renovations

The definition of a good renovation is one that is appropriate to the size and style of the home, one that clearly adds value and that is universally appealing. After all, what good is a renovation when a significant portion of the buyer pool may not want it or like it?

Here are some good renovations for the interior:

Seller Alert

Be careful not to spend a great deal of money on vibrantly colored countertops, tiles, or other expensive materials that may not appeal to a wide audience. Stick with neutral colors and classic lines that never go out of style.

Updating the kitchen: The kitchen is the room with the most power to affect value because it is the most expensive to keep up-to-date. Hence, it is usually the most effective renovation to increase your profit in a sale. You will almost always make a big profit by redoing a kitchen—typically in the tens of thousands of dollars on a medium-size house.

Cost-Saving Tip: If money is limited, try just replacing the countertops and appliances. Paint the cabinets and add new hardware to them, and the whole room will look newer.

Updating the bathroom(s): A bathroom is the second most important room to upgrade because it is also expensive to renovate, and buyers will pay a solid premium if they are updated. Your return will be strong, but it is hard to quote a range here because it depends on which and how many bathrooms you renovate. In general, master baths are important as well as main-floor powder rooms.

Cost-Saving Tip: Try to replace the countertops, sink, and toilet, and paint the walls. Other minor upgrades include replacing the mirror, faucets, showerhead, and towel racks.

Adding a main-floor *powder room:* If your home does not have one, then create one and it will become more valuable by thousands of dollars. You may be able to convert a coat closet, storage room, food pantry, or part of a vestibule into a powder room. Some homes simply don't have the space and require a small addition to accommodate a powder room.

Cost-Saving Tip: If you choose to put a tiny addition on, it is more cost effective to add something else in the process, such as a mud room. You'll get a lot more bang for your buck as long as you already have the contractors on your property.

def•i•ni•tion

A **powder room** has only a sink and a toilet. It does not have a shower or bath tub. It is also known as a half-bath.

Finishing the basement: This is a fantastic renovation to make because it adds another level of useable living space without the expense of putting an addition onto your home. This strategy almost always pays off in thousands and thousands of dollars on a sale.

Cost-Saving Tip: Save money on furniture and cabinetry. As you design the basement, put closets or built-in shelving anywhere and everywhere that you can fit them. Because you're losing storage space by finishing that room, you'll need them. Plus, they're great for holding children's toys and games.

Installing central air-conditioning: In some parts of the country, central air-conditioning is considered a necessary system of a home. But there are many regions where it is considered an upgrade—and even a luxury. It's worth more money than a similar home without central air.

 Seller Alert

Check with your insurance carrier or insurance agent to make sure that you can get additional coverage for basement upgrades. In some areas, insurers will cover only furnaces, heaters, washers, and dryers.

Cost-Saving Tip: Most average-size houses require two condensers (an apparatus that cools a portion of a home) to cool the entire structure. If money is tight, install central air in the upper floors only. Cool air falls (as opposed to heat, which rises). The main floor will benefit from cool air coming down from the upper levels. Your energy costs will also be lower. Another way to save money is, if you live in a region with seasonal climate changes, to have it installed in the fall or winter. Contractors will charge you less then because they are not as busy.

Refinished original (or install) hardwood floors: Refinishing original floors is an upgrade with a wonderful return on investment because it maximizes an existing and expensive feature in a home. It would be extremely costly to install, today, the quality of wood that they used decades ago, so leverage that feature and make a nice profit. If you can afford to install new hardwood floors, then we encourage that as well.

Cost-Saving Tip: If a complete refinishing is not in your budget, do something called screening, which is a light sanding and staining of the floor. It costs much less but still looks great.

Installing French drains: If you live in an area that has a high water table or where you and many of your neighbors get water in the basement during heavy rain, a French drain is a very valuable renovation. They cost a few thousand dollars, but this renovation is well worth it if you have a water problem that can knock a huge amount of money off your sale price.

A French drain is a trench that is dug along the perimeter of your basement floor. If the floor is concrete, it must be jackhammered apart first. The trench can be as deep as 18 inches. It is filled with gravel and then the concrete floor is repoured within a couple of inches of the wall. If water ever comes in again, it will drain out through this gravel lip along your basement walls—although most well-constructed French drains should keep the water from ever coming inside again.

Cost-Saving Tip: If you cannot afford a French drain, opt for a sump pump (or two). They are far less expensive than French drains. They do not always keep water from coming into the basement, but they do take the water out of the basement. A sump pump is a 3- or 4-foot circular hole which is usually dug into a corner of your basement floor with an electric pump inside. It literally pumps water out of the room and into the earth.

Seller Alert

If you lose electrical power in a storm, the sump pump will not work unless you have a battery back-up system. This will add a few hundred dollars to the installation cost, but is well worth it if your area is subject to power outages.

Here are some good renovations for the exterior:

Adding a dormer to the roof to create a new room: If you have an attic with a sloped roof that inhibits head room, add a dormer to create enough height to finish the room. Like a finished basement, this adds a whole new level of living space, which is worth tens of thousands of dollars.

Cost-Saving Tip: If your roof is old, plan the dormer construction to coincide with replacing the roof. This will save you even more money.

Creating a portico: If your home does not have a vestibule or covered porch at the entrance, and the front looks a little bland, then building an architecturally interesting portico over the front door is not only functional but it can add a lot of value in terms of curb appeal.

Cost-Saving Tip: If you have a *pediment* above the door, try just extending it over the stoop and adding two columns.

def•i•ni•tion

A **pediment** is a low-pitched triangular gable over an entrance. It is part of the Greek revival style of architecture.

Building a deck or patio: This is a fantastic strategy for small homes with a limited amount of square footage on the main floor. It gives the illusion of more livable and usable space without having to build an expensive addition.

Cost-Saving Tip: Building decks and patios can actually be do-it-yourself jobs. But pay close attention to the transition from the inside to the outside by making sure to create a nice finished look with a natural flow.

Seller Alert

If you live in an area with some historic homes, check with the local planning board about restrictions on changes made to the exterior of your home. Even if your home is not specifically designated as historic, it could still be in a historically designated zone and therefore subject to some rules.

Commissioning a landscape design: Landscaping itself is often a do-it-yourself project, but dramatic landscape design is not. If you want to significantly increase the sale price of your home, call in a genuine landscape design architect to really make an impact on the value of the exterior of your home.

Cost-Saving Tip: Ask the designer what perennials or annuals he wants to use and then buy them yourself, as opposed to being forced to use the plants that he sells to you directly. When he's done, tell him to leave the mulching to you and you'll save a few hundred dollars more. If you need to remove trees, hire that contractor in the cool months—in their off season—and get a discount.

Installing shutters and flower boxes: It's amazing what these two items can do in terms of helping a buyer to fall in love with your home from the curb. They are relatively inexpensive to buy, and buyers will pay a lot more for storybook-type curb appeal.

Cost-Saving Tip: Flower boxes and shutters are items that can be comparison shopped and ordered online. We have found that there is a huge variety to view, easy-to-understand descriptions of materials, wonderful photos, and periodic offerings of discounts.

Bad Renovations

Bad renovations are ones that do not add value, are too specific in taste, are inappropriate to the size or style of a home, or may not be universally appealing to buyers. If you spend the sort of time and energy and money required for a renovation, the last thing you want is for it to be unprofitable.

Here are some examples of bad renovations:

Converting a bedroom: Some homeowners will turn a bedroom into something else, like a giant walk-in closet. Unless the home is extremely large with an excessive number of bedrooms, this is usually a mistake. There is a strong relationship between sale price and number of bedrooms. When you lose one of them, you could be losing 10 to 20 percent on the sale.

Building a second kitchen: You may have in-laws, boarders, or a nanny living with you; or you may have a "summer kitchen," which is often on the lower level and used for outdoor entertaining. The majority of home buyers do not want or need a second kitchen. Even if they could overlook it for the sake of the purchase, it will still cost money to have it ripped out.

 Seller Alert

Don't be afraid to renovate and create a state-of-the-art kitchen in an old-world-style home. Every buyer appreciates and wants an updated kitchen, no matter what the style of home.

Changing the style of a home: Homes that have maintained their architectural integrity are more valuable than those that have been changed. They are considered "true to the period" in which they were built. If you change the style that the home was intended to be, the home is no longer "authentic." It would need to be "restored," which everyone knows is an expensive word! When you try to sell a home with a style that has been compromised, it will cost you a great deal of money in the sale.

Modifying the use of the home: If you turn a single family home into a multifamily structure or a "mother/daughter" (which is a single family with a wing that has a bath and kitchen in it), then you have reduced your buyer pool by a huge percentage. Again, if the purpose of the renovation was expressly to sell, then you will likely have fewer interested buyers, which usually translates into a lower sale price.

Poorly executed renovations: Buyers are much more knowledgeable than ever before. They will notice if you used cheap materials or if the labor was shoddy, and it will be reflected in the offers that you receive. The savings you were after may be washed away by the loss of dollars in the sale price.

Paving over or converting a yard: Some families will convert the entire rear yard (or a very large portion) into a basketball court, skateboard park, dog run, tennis court, or even a pool. When you create a facility that takes up most or all of the yard, you're taking away open land, which is a major motivating factor in buying. If your child got terrific use out of it, then it was worth it. But it is not a renovation to make in order to get a higher price.

Don't Overimprove!

Overimproving a home is when you spend money on improvements and the money does not come back to you when you sell. You may have gotten enjoyment from them while you lived in the house, but they can literally rob you of profit when selling.

The two most common examples of overimprovement are expensive additions and upgrading rooms using super-expensive materials.

Expensive Additions

Additions, on their own, are not bad renovations. They can add great value to a home. But it is crucial that you analyze what you will be spending compared to what the home will be worth when the work is done.

Let's say that your home is worth $600,000 today, and most of the homes on your street are worth between $550,000 and $700,000. The addition that you want to put on will cost $150,000. That means that you would need to get $750,000 on the sale just to break even. As the average value of homes on your street demonstrates, you are not likely to break even, let alone make a profit.

We have clients who call us constantly to discuss their ideas for an addition. They are very smart to do that because they know that when you're spending that kind of money (sometimes in the hundreds of thousands), you don't want to bet on the market automatically giving you a profit in return. If you bet wrong, you can be in big trouble.

Upgrading Rooms with Super-Expensive Materials

Good materials are always a good idea. But top-of-the-line materials are sometimes a bad idea when you are getting ready to sell. When you upgrade rooms, particularly kitchens and baths, it is possible to overspend and not get your money back.

A typical example of this type of overimprovement is when you see a million-dollar kitchen or master bathroom in either a very tiny home or in a home located in a less expensive neighborhood. By "million-dollar kitchen," we mean a kitchen with the most expensive countertops, appliances, flooring, light fixtures, tile, millwork, and cabinetry that you can buy. When you're trying to make a profit, it's all about the best return on your investment—not necessarily the best materials that you can buy. Save the million-dollar materials for the million-dollar home.

Again, the only way to know if you are going too far with materials is to find out what the approximate value of your home is before you renovate. Then add to it the cost of all of your materials and labor. If the number is higher than what most of the other homes on the street are worth, consider cutting back on the level of materials you've chosen. If the cost is greater than average values on the street, the addition is probably not a good way to make money on the sale.

A Step-by-Step Plan for Renovating

Planning is everything when it comes to renovations. The main reason you should plan is to save money. Another reason is that you do not want to be inconvenienced any longer than you have to. Ask anyone who has lived through a renovation. It is stressful, messy, and expensive, and it can take a long time! If you do not have a good plan in place, it will take even longer, you may make mistakes, and your costs will go up. The following sections guide you through a plan that will help you execute your renovation.

Having a Realtor Evaluate Your Idea

Most people think that the first person you should call when renovating is a contractor. But the first person you should actually call is a Realtor, because she can tell you how the renovation is going to impact your sale price. Have the Realtor come over to your home and physically walk the area that will be renovated. Share your ideas with her. Then ask her to share her thoughts about the profitability of the renovation. Will the renovation allow you to make a bigger profit when you sell or not? She may need to go look at some comparables and do some research in order to give you an intelligent answer, or she may know instantly that it is a risky move. Either way, this simple and cost-free act could save you untold thousands or even tens of thousands of dollars.

Finding and Interviewing Contractors

To find a good contractor, begin with personal referrals from your friends. They will likely have firsthand experience with a contractor, or know of someone who has. And Realtors usually keep lists of the good ones and what their specialties are. A referral is the best way to find a good professional.

If you only have the yellow pages at your disposal, then the questions you ask and the way that you screen them will be even more important. You may also ask to speak to their last three clients. If the contractor refuses, then move on to the next candidate immediately. That's a red flag.

Questions to Ask a Contractor

- ◆ Are you licensed and insured?

- ◆ Who will be the dedicated on-site person with whom I will communicate each day? Can I meet him before I hire the company? If I hire you, would I be able to have his cell phone number so that I have access to him when I need it? (If he says no, that's an interesting answer and should tell you a lot about his accessibility.)

- ◆ What is the payment schedule? How much money down do you require and when? When do you require the balance of the payment?

 Seller Alert

Any contractor who asks for more than 50 percent up front before the work has begun—other than for purchasing materials—is someone you may not want to hire. A possible reason that he asks for this is that his company is not financially solvent and may be operating "in the red" on a day-to-day basis. Proceed with caution.

- ◆ When can you begin the job? When will it be completed?

- ◆ How often do your jobs come in on schedule and on budget?

- ◆ How many other jobs will you be working on at the same time as mine?

- ◆ Can you provide me with referrals?

Creating a Renovation Schedule

Time is money! It's never truer than in a renovation. Okay, maybe it's a little truer on a movie set. But we're not talking about a film studio's money; we're talking about your money! Delays are costly, not to mention inconvenient when your home is in ruins (and possibly your marriage), or when you're eating fast food every night and everything is covered in a film of plaster dust.

Kitchen renovations are especially tough. When you're eating in, you may be doing dishes in the bathroom, and eating out can be expensive and tough on your health.

To make a tight but realistic renovation schedule, begin with the estimated duration of the job given to you by the contractors whom you have interviewed. It's prudent to add two weeks—at the minimum—to that estimate. Some people add a month or more.

Work with the contractor to create a list of things that you are responsible for doing and establish when they need to be done in order to stay on schedule. A big responsibility of yours will be purchasing materials in order for them to be at your home on the day the contractor plans to install them. Another is providing access and scheduling inspections by the local municipality, which may need to witness certain stages of the renovations. Also, you need to determine when to have vendors come in for carpeting, appliances, and so on.

The time of year is important because, depending on when you launch the renovation, utilities may need to be rerouted or even shut down for a period. No water in the summer or no heat in the winter could present problems.

And finally, consider the family's schedule. If there is a trip, camp, or even sleepovers on the horizon, leverage those as convenient windows to work with.

Typical delays on a home renovation include the following:

- ◆ The permits are filed too late or take longer than expected to be ready for your contractor to legally begin work.

◆ Some corroded pipes or dangerous electrical wires are revealed after opening up walls. They need to be addressed before proceeding with work.

◆ Sometimes workers actually hit a buried gas pipe. Trust us, nothing stops work faster than a ruptured gas line! This happens more often than you'd think, yet it is entirely avoidable.

Seller Alert _____

Before any major renovation that may include digging on the exterior of your home, call the gas utility company to come over and flag the main gas line so workers can clearly see where it runs across your property. It's usually a free service and it is worth its weight in gold when it comes to peace of mind, avoiding dangerous accidents, and staying on schedule.

◆ Parts or materials were not ordered early enough to arrive on time, or the wrong thing was ordered and must be exchanged.

◆ The homeowner changes his mind about a material or design choice and switches to another option.

◆ Measurements were miscalculated by either the homeowner or the contractor, causing a delay because there were not enough materials on hand.

◆ Prolonged rain, high wind, frigid temperatures, or other weather conditions make work impossible.

◆ The contractor is working on more than one job at a time and the attention is deflected from one job.

Creating a Renovation Budget

If you are renovating specifically for the purpose of selling, then you will have a sale price in mind that you would like to get. The first thing to do is to make sure that you will, in fact, get that price when your home goes on the market. You will have this information if you consulted a Realtor at the beginning of this process.

For example, let's say that your home is currently worth approximately $410,000 and you hope to get $450,000 after making the renovation. That's a profit of $40,000. Your contractor has given you an estimate of $25,000 for the job. You stand to make $15,000 in profit. But will you really get that $15,000 if the job goes over budget?

There are always hidden costs in a renovation. Good contractors will advise you that their estimates do not cover all your out-of-pocket costs. But they will not necessarily point out for you every single cost that is outside their domain on the job.

The contractor estimate should include the cost of materials such as Sheetrock, plaster, and moldings, as well as permit fees and labor, including the installation of appliance and fixtures, painting, and electrical and plumbing work.

But there are many items that may not be on the contractor's estimate. Some of them are …

- ◆ Cost of paint.

- ◆ Cost of carpeting, tile, and other flooring.

- ◆ Cost of appliances such as stoves, refrigerators, and dishwashers.

- ◆ Cost of fixtures such as cabinets, chandeliers and sconces, faucets, toilets, sinks, and shower and tub inserts.

- ◆ Unforeseen repairs and preexisting code violations that appear in the process of demolition.

As you can see, that $15,000 profit could be eaten up by these items. It is important for you to sit down and do a complete budget. Leverage your contractor's experience. Have him look it over and advise you as to what items you may be missing.

Cost-Saving Strategies

We have a number of cost-saving strategies for renovations:

Keep the original footprint of the home. If you are able to work in the existing structure of your home—without putting on an addition—right away you will have saved an enormous amount of money. After you make the decision to expand a home, the costs begin to pile up. To begin, it usually requires some sort of variance or zoning approval from the town in which you live. You will need to present a plan and blueprints. This delays the start of the job for weeks or even months. Then there are the costs associated with pouring or building a new foundation; adding to and rerouting electrical and plumbing service; installing a new roof over the addition (and perhaps the whole house), as well as new exterior siding or exterior paint; and providing new landscaping and possibly irrigation or drainage work. The final major cost comes when the work is complete and your taxes are reassessed based on more square footage. This is why we are such big fans of finishing basements and attics. The comparative costs are much lower.

General contracting your own renovation. When renovating, there are workers in your home doing all sorts of different jobs: electricians, plumbers, carpenters, painters, masons, and more. The boss, or the general contractor (also know as the GC), will often be the point person who oversees all of the work and the timing. There is a built-in fee for this role, and it could be as much as 15 percent of the total cost of the job.

If you have the time and energy, you can assume this role yourself. It requires your being on-site most days, making sure that everything is happening on the day it is supposed to happen, ensuring that all the materials you have chosen (appliances, fixtures, paint) are on-site when the workers need them, being available for inspections by the town, making phone calls and doing any necessary research, as well as communicating directly with the workers on the job. Sometimes, the renovation can actually go smoother when you are your own GC. After all, you've only got one client and it's you—so you have your full attention!

 Seller Alert _____

Let your contractor (and even your community's building or engineering department) educate you about what needs to be done in terms of permits, inspections, and materials. This will help you to run a safe, legal, and efficient renovation but will also have the added benefit of giving you ample warning when you are falling behind schedule.

Being able to stay in the home throughout the renovation. Unless you own more than one home, one of the biggest costs of a renovation is the rent you'll pay to live elsewhere during the process. And while you are renting, you continue to make mortgage payments on the home you are renovating! These costs can mount to extraordinary heights. Find a way to reside in one portion of your home and close off the portion that is being renovated. If your kitchen is under construction, create a makeshift temporary one in another corner of the home. Move your microwave and refrigerator to that area and try to have some fun with it. (We said "try"!) When it begins to overwhelm you, remind yourself of the thousands you are saving by roughing it.

Making more than one renovation simultaneously. A small-scale example of this is when you wait to call a plumber or electrician until you have at least two or three things for him to fix. It costs money just for him to show up, so you want to get as much bang for your buck as possible. With a renovation, there are costs associated simply with setting up a job. If you're going to have workmen crawling all over your property, it's cheaper to have them renovate more than one thing. But more importantly, when you have a room that is gutted and the walls are open, that is the time to consider a renovation in a nearby space or adjacent room.

Renovating without having to move appliances. If you can keep the appliances in the same general location, it saves a lot of money. Keeping the main electrical, water, and plumbing lines intact, and avoiding the rerouting or creation of new ones, can save up to 50 percent on the costs.

Plan, plan, plan. As we've said, good planning is everything. But on a renovation, it is particularly important and can be the difference between making a profit and suffering a loss. If you have a clear timeline (with some wiggle room built in) and a detailed budget (also with some padding built in), then you can survive curve balls along the way and still make money.

Supervise, supervise, supervise. Even if you do not choose to GC your own renovation, it is imperative that you are present, at some point, during the course of each day. Ask anyone who has ever done a renovation before: the one day that you don't show up, something will get installed, hung, or affixed in the wrong manner. Every day find out from the contractor what project he will be working on. Maybe it is a task for which you do not need to be present and you can take a worry-free day off. Also, you may not be a contractor yourself, but if something looks wrong, it very well may be. Ask a lot of questions. Don't be afraid to ask the contractor to explain to you what he is doing, if you are unclear. Try to keep your interruptions to a minimum, however, as work often stops when the homeowner walks into the room with questions.

Weekend warriors. More and more homeowners around the country are making big renovations quickly with the help of family and friends. If you have the skill and know-how to oversee a project like this, then good for you. Do yourself a favor and make the turnaround as quickly as possible so you don't lose your workers after time. And don't forget to reward them with a big barbecue when it's done!

Renovating to Save Energy, or "Going Green"

The types of renovations described in this section have two fantastic benefits. They save energy, which is something that we all must look to do. But they also save you a lot of money on your energy costs. True, there is an up-front cost associated with these renovations, but those costs are offset rapidly by the money that you immediately begin to save in heating, cooling, and lighting your home.

If you are not already familiar with these renovations and terms associated with them, you will be in the coming months and years. They're going to become more and more common. Here are some of them:

♦ **Geothermal heat**—Geothermal heat pumps do not burn fossil fuel. They have no emissions. They also enable you to use 30 percent less heat. Liquid is pumped through pipes or coils in the ground beside your home. When the liquid goes through the pipes, it picks up heat from the ground in the winter and delivers heat back into the ground in the summer.

♦ **Tankless water heaters**—Gas-fired tankless water heaters are also known as *demand water heaters*. Traditional water heaters keep your water heated at all times, in reserve, so that it is there when you need it. Tankless water heaters heat water only when you need to use it and then the heater shuts down automatically after you've stopped using it.

♦ **Solar energy panels**—Solar energy panels are also known as photovoltaic technology. This means that it turns sunlight into electricity to cool, heat, and light your home. The sunlight is captured through panels installed on your roof. It's a nice feature because you have little reliance on the local utility company and, when you capture an overflow of energy, it can be stored and used when you need it or even sold back to the utility company at a profit to you.

♦ **Radiant heat**—A radiant heating system is usually more efficient than baseboard and forced-air heat because there are no ducts from which energy can escape. The heat is delivered directly to floors, walls, or even ceilings. As opposed to delivering heat through air, it is a water-based delivery system (also known as hydronic). It uses much less electricity than many other heating systems and the water can be heated through traditional oil or gas boilers, or solar water heaters. Side benefit: they leave you with more floor space as the need for bulky radiators is eliminated.

♦ **Tubular skylights**—Tubular skylights are both an energy conservation strategy as well as a neat interior design concept. They are tube-shaped skylights that can redirect sunlight from the roof down through your home into just about any room and diffuse that light at ceiling level. In fact, it doesn't even have to be sunny out. It will capture ambient light on a cloudy day, too.

Trick of the Trade _____

Tubular skylights have an added health bonus. By bringing more light into a living space that otherwise wouldn't have it due to the location within your home, it can help combat depression in people who suffer from it.

- **Spray insulations**—The old-fashioned or traditional fiberglass insulation leaves gaps. It just can't seal every crack in your home. It can also sag inside walls after time. Spray insulation such as liquid polyurethane foam expands as it is sprayed into your walls and attic. It leaves no gaps and you will be about as close as you can get to being air-leak-free.

- **LED lighting**—Most of us have grown up using standard incandescent light bulbs. Consider using LED (light-emitting diode) or compact fluorescent bulbs. LED light bulbs last about 100 times longer than incandescent, and compact fluorescent use about 66 percent less energy. Both fit into standard sockets.

- **Window films**—Window films are something that you put on your windows to help insulate your home further and preserve heating and cooling costs. They also reduce sun glare as well as UV rays to protect your furniture and flooring. They also have improved resistance to shattering and hurricane-force winds.

Energy Star Appliances and Materials

Energy Star is a highly successful joint program between the U.S. EPA (Environmental Protection Agency) and the U.S. DOE (Department of Energy). The program recognizes and labels energy-efficient appliances and other materials with the Energy Star emblem right on the packaging. Millions of Americans have already saved billions of dollars in energy costs by choosing Energy Star products.

For more information on the Energy Star program, as well as information on how to make your home green, visit these websites:

- www.doe.gov

- www.epa.gov

- www.epa.gov/greenbuilding

The Least You Need to Know

♦ Overimproving by putting on an expensive addition or using super-expensive materials just before you sell may cause you to suffer a financial loss.

♦ Have a Realtor evaluate your renovation idea before beginning it to ensure that it will make you money on the sale. Make a list of every noncontractor expense such as materials, appliances, and fixtures.

♦ Some major cost-saving strategies include keeping the original footprint of the home, living in the home during the renovation to avoid paying rent, and "general contracting" or supervising and coordinating your own renovation.

♦ There are loads of ways to save money on energy costs, including geothermal heat, solar panels, tankless water heaters, and energy-efficient light bulbs.

♦ Planning saves money by helping to avoid delays and mistakes.

How to Find and Hire a Top-Notch Realtor

In This Chapter

- ◆ How using a Realtor impacts the sale
- ◆ Choosing the right Realtor and agency
- ◆ What a Realtor does
- ◆ Negotiating commission

If ever there was an industry where advice and performance varies from professional to professional, real estate is it. All Realtors are not created equal. Some of them work full-time and have made a career of real estate, while others work part-time or dabble in it. Experience doesn't necessarily equal talent, and a Realtor with only a few years in the business does not indicate a lack of talent.

If you are looking for a Realtor to represent you, it is crucial that you find a great one. Think of choosing a Realtor like a director casts a Broadway show. Once he finds the right players, the hardest part of the job is done. Once you find the right Realtor, a big part of your job is done. He will be the driving force in the sale of your home.

Your home is probably the biggest financial investment of your life, and you must protect it. The money that you make on the sale could be your retirement fund, a college education for one of your kids, or even the means for you to escape to Fiji. After putting your heart and soul into the property, making upgrades, and building equity, you want the person managing its sale to be top notch.

In this chapter, we discuss the steps to finding the right one for you.

Finding the Best Realtors

Working with a Realtor to sell your home is like being in a temporary marriage. You will speak with him almost daily and sometimes several times a day for an extended period. As in a marriage, the entire relationship is based on trust. It's about knowing that this person truly has your best interests at heart. He not only needs to be good at what he does, but you must feel a connection—an ability to communicate with each other effectively.

Seller Alert

The Realtor that you choose to hire will have a direct impact on your sale price. One Realtor will get you more money than another depending on how he positions the home price-wise, stages it, reaches out to buyers, and negotiates a deal.

You may already know who some of the more prominent Realtors are in the community. You've seen their ads in the local paper, seen their names on signs, and perhaps you've even wandered into some of their open houses. Someone who has been in business in one community for years will have a recognizable name. But having a prominent name does not necessarily make someone a good Realtor, or the right Realtor for you.

How to Begin

When you're starting the process, you may be tempted to just call the agent who sold you the house or the woman in your book club who happens to be a Realtor. Both of these Realtors may very well be fine choices. However, we strongly recommend (and by the way, most good Realtors encourage this) that you interview at least three of them, each one from a different agency.

Here are the steps to begin your search:

1. Target three different real estate agencies.

2. Contact the agencies where you do not already know a Realtor and speak to the broker or manager about recommending a good one for you.

3. Have a face-to-face meeting with the Realtor candidate.

What to Do If Your Friend or Relative Is a Realtor

This is an issue that comes up almost every day in real estate. Most Realtors are socially ingrained in the same community where they do business. Therefore, most people know at least one Realtor, or perhaps several. It's an awkward situation when you are not sure that your friend or relative is the best Realtor choice for you. You may worry that someone's feelings will be hurt.

But imagine if you needed open heart surgery and you had a brother-in-law who was a heart surgeon whom you were not sure you wanted to perform the operation. You probably would do what was necessary to make sure that you were in good hands, and you'd do so without guilt because your health is so important.

The point is that choosing a real estate agency and Realtor is a business decision—maybe one of the biggest of your life. You will be paying a lot of money to hire this person to do an important job. You need to feel that you are in the best hands possible.

Here are some things to consider when your friend or relative is a Realtor:

Concern: Your friend is a well-respected Realtor, but you're afraid the personal relationship will suffer if you mix business with friendship.

Solution: If he is experienced, then he has addressed this concern before. Bring it up. Give him a chance to explain how he will separate the friendship from the business. We make it clear to our own friends that, while their home is on the market, the communication—in both directions—will be open, honest, and professional. There needs to be a trust that they can express any business concerns without worrying about hurt feelings between friends.

Concern: Your friend is a new and inexperienced Realtor.

Solution: There are two ways to look at this issue. On the one hand, you might not want to automatically dismiss someone because of being new to the business. Some new agents can be the early superstars with plenty of smarts and energy. If they don't have an answer, they know where to get it. They are usually "hungry" for business and eager, and will often give you even more personal attention than experienced agents. Additionally, if they are affiliated with a good agency, they'll have a mentor (or several mentors) in place as support.

On the other hand, you may feel that your friend is just too new to the business, after all. If this is how you feel, he will hopefully understand. If he is truly a friend, we recommend that you tell him immediately before he finds out from another source that you are selling your home with another Realtor. Although you'd probably love to be able to support him at this early stage of his real estate career, the sale of your home is not something on which you are prepared to gamble. As always, honest and open communication is the way to go.

Concern: Your friend has been in the business a very long time, but he is not at the top of his game anymore.

Solution: "Not being at the top of his game" can mean a variety of things. Perhaps your friend has lost his enthusiasm for the business or cannot keep up with technology. Maybe he is working less and making different lifestyle choices. Whatever the reason, it's a sensitive situation and a tough decision for you to have to make. No one wants to hurt or disrespect a friend. Again, we recommend that you have a face-to-face meeting where you tell him that he is not the best fit for you. As cold and callous as you may fear this choice will be, remember that this is a business decision. Honest and direct communication is always the best way to go, especially when you're trying to preserve a friendship. That meeting may be uncomfortable for you but, we suspect, not nearly as uncomfortable as the one where you accidentally bump into him and learn that he already has heard that you have not hired him.

Targeting the Best Real Estate Companies

Every real estate agency has a certain number of talented agents. No single office will have all the good Realtors. Consider them all and then narrow it down to three. Evaluating an agency is different than evaluating a Realtor. It's important to ask questions. Don't take their advertising claims at face value.

Agencies That Claim to Be the Market Leader

The funny thing about real estate agencies is that they all claim to be the best. The reality is that they can't all be. If they claim to be the best or the market leader, you want to find out how they define "best" and "leader."

To illustrate our point, let's take two agencies that both claim to be the market leader based on "sales volume."

One medium-size agency in your community has agents who are all experienced and who do the highest volume of sales in town—on a per-agent basis. This office claims that they are the leader because their agents do the most business.

Now, let's take another agency which also claims to be the market leader for the same reason—highest volume of sales. But their numbers are based on the entire office as a whole.

To get this impressive statistic, they have hired a gigantic number of agents with mixed amounts of experience and many with very low business volume. In order to claim superiority over everyone else, they lump together the sales of twice the number of agents, even though they have the highest number of inexperienced agents of any agency in your community. Their claim to be number one is jaded at best, and misleading at worst.

We think that quality is better than quantity. We recommend going with the office where every single agent—without exception—is experienced, rather than the agency that is large for the sake of filling cubicles. Additionally, the caliber of work throughout the office will be more consistent.

Trick of the Trade

Real estate websites are ranked by number of hits as well as how often their company name is used as a search term. If the agency you are considering does not have these rankings to share with you, they may not be ranked very high, or even ranked at all. If they were, they'd have the statistics. These rankings also include real estate websites such as Realtor.com, Zillow, and Trulia, which are among the most popular.

Agencies with a Global Reach

As we discuss often in this book, one of the major factors in getting your house sold is "exposure." You want the entire buyer pool to know about your home. Having a highly active website is a very good thing, but it does not make a local real estate agency "global." Having real estate offices located across the country and around the world makes the agency national or global.

This matters because you never know where your buyer is coming from. Relocation for work or career is an exploding phenomenon. When buyers shop for a home, they will begin on the Internet. They will begin with agencies with which they are already familiar. A buyer in Tokyo has never heard of the local agency in your community or even in your state. Ask your Realtor candidate how many offices they have outside of your town and state, across the United States, and in foreign countries.

Interviewing Real Estate Agents

We strongly recommend that you interview more than one Realtor; in fact, three is best. What you're looking to evaluate is her style, track record, the quality of her listing presentation, marketing plan, the caliber of the agency she works for, and her response to your interview questions.

There are two meetings when interviewing a Realtor. The first one—a walk-through of your home—is brief, and the second one—a listing presentation at her office—is longer; they usually take place within a few days of one another.

Your Realtor's First Walk-Through

Very often, the first meeting happens when you have called the selected Realtors (or agencies) to say that you are thinking of selling and want to know how much money your home might fetch. You can usually expect the Realtor to immediately set up an appointment to do a *walk-through*.

def•i•ni•tion

A **walk-through** is when the Realtor comes to your home to visually inspect, take notes, and collect information about your property. He then takes that information and studies it to come up with a strategic list price or range.

We know that you're probably going to be anxious and excited to immediately find out the number at which your home should be priced. You may even be tempted to pressure the agent into giving it to you on the spot. But a Realtor should never give you a price at the moment he first sees your home, no matter how strong his gut feeling is.

Some Realtors will give you a number off the top of their heads in an effort to appear more knowledgeable and experienced. Real estate values are constantly shifting. The data can be read differently from day to day. The truth is that it's impossible, unless it's pure coincidence, to pick the right number without reviewing the up-to-the-minute data.

The Realtor's Listing Presentation

There are three parts of a listing presentation. We recommend that it take place at the office of the agency. If this company should end up representing you, you want to see the condition of the office and the people who work there. Also, there are so many distractions at home—children crying, phones ringing, dogs barking, etc. This is a crucial business meeting and you should be entirely focused.

The steps involved in a listing presentation include …

1. Agent gives you suggested list price or price range.

2. Agent presents a marketing plan.

3. Seller interviews agent regarding track record and credentials.

Suggested List Price

The Realtor, after reviewing all relevant data, will present a number at which he feels your home should be priced. You may disagree with that number. Healthy debate about such an important element as pricing may not be such a bad thing. You ultimately have the right to market your home at whatever list price you wish, but it is critical that you and the Realtor you hire are in agreement about the viability of that list price. After bringing three Realtors in, you will end up with three different opinions about suggested list price, and that's a good thing. It is yet another reason why it serves you to interview more than one Realtor. And, by the way, it doesn't cost you anything to do so, except your time.

 Seller Alert _____

Don't be seduced by receiving a high suggested list price from a Realtor candidate. The Realtor may be trying to flatter you in a misguided attempt to get your business. It's sometimes called "buying the listing." If it seems too good (or too inflated) to be true, it probably is.

The Marketing Plan

People often confuse a marketing plan with an advertising plan. A marketing plan is a strategy. It's the overall approach that will be taken in order to get your home sold. Advertising is only one part of a marketing plan. Advertising is exactly what it sounds like—taking out ads. Various other marketing strategies will be covered throughout this book.

In general, a real estate marketing plan should include …

◆ **A pricing strategy.** It's not just about the price at which your home will be introduced, but what approach you will take if it does not sell right away. Will you wait for your buyer passively or make aggressive reductions? For information on pricing strategies, see Chapter 9.

◆ **How your home will be presented and staged.** This is important, and not all Realtors present a plan for this. They should. We have devoted Chapter 6 to this topic.

◆ **When your home will go on the market.** Timing is key to maximize exposure and to get you top dollar. The season, the weekend within that season, and even the day of the week your home comes on the market are important. The Realtor should share with you what works best in your community.

◆ **How your home will be introduced to other Realtors.** There is a saying in real estate that you're not selling to buyers; you're selling to other Realtors. Imagine, if you will, that Pepsi or Coca-Cola are trying to introduce a new soft drink. They can't reach consumers without having a relationship with distributors. Distributors are connected to consumers and Realtors are connected to home buyers. Your Realtor should have a plan that will talk about reaching out to and communicating with other Realtors about your home.

◆ **How buyers will be reached.** Where will buyers see your listing? How will the Realtor give your home the exposure that it needs to reach the entire buyer pool? It should be clear how many and which Multiple Listing Services and websites the home will be accessible through. Further, there should be a reason or rationale given to you for using particular MLS's and websites. The Realtor should show you why and make you feel confident that it is an effective overall campaign.

◆ **How showings will be orchestrated.** Your Realtor will work with you to determine how, when, and with whom buyers will get into your home for showings. There are different approaches and points of view on this subject. We have devoted Chapter 8 to this subject.

◆ **The type of photo brochures or highlight sheets that will be created for buyers to take away.** Brochures are a terrific way for buyers, after they leave your home, to visually recall the best features. Buyers often see several homes in one afternoon. It is typical to have the fine details become blurry in their minds. When they get home, the brochure helps them to remember them. It is no longer prohibitively expensive to make professional glossy color brochures to market a home. Real estate has come a long way in this area, and you should expect beautiful brochures no matter how small or inexpensive your home.

◆ **How your home will be advertised.** There are wildly different opinions among real estate professionals about whether or not advertising and open houses help to sell your home. We address this in depth in Chapter 9.

Sellers usually want advertising and open houses, regardless. Your Realtor should be clear about where she will advertise, how often, and if you wish her to do a public open house.

◆ **How offers will be handled once they come in.** Buyers want and deserve to be responded to quickly, and treated fairly and with respect. What is your Realtor's style and policy on the handling of offers?

◆ **How will the Realtor manage the deal once your home goes under contract?** This is a major part of what you pay a commission for. All sorts of challenges, big and small, come up over the course of a deal. A good listing agent will not only make sure that all parties "hit their marks" on the way to closing and do what they are supposed to do, but will manage emotions that may run high. A good agent will continue to educate you and, in some cases, even the buyer and his Realtor, who may be less experienced. Ask questions about his negotiating skills and his strategies for keeping deals together. If he is talented, he'll know exactly what you mean and will be able to share stories or examples of how he does it.

From these elements, a good Realtor will pull together and present to you a strategic overall marketing plan to sell your home.

Questions to Ask the Realtor

Now that you know how to evaluate the caliber of a real estate agency, let's talk about how you'll evaluate the Realtor.

There is only one way to get the information you need, and that is to ask questions. But they need to be the right questions. Up until this point in the meeting, the Realtor has had the floor in making her presentation. Now it's your turn to conduct the meeting. Think of this portion as an important job "interview." You are about to pay this person a good deal of money, and this may be the moment when you get the best information to make your decision. She should be prepared to answer any of your questions with ease. If she cannot, perhaps you should move on to the next candidate.

Trick of the Trade

A sign of a really strong Realtor is someone who does not push too hard. The best ones have the confidence to share information with you, give you options, and let you make the best choices for you and your family. If you are feeling pressured about any part of the process, there is probably something wrong.

Here are some questions you should ask:

♦ How many years have you been in the business?

♦ Do you practice real estate full-time, or is it a part-time job?

♦ How many listings have you had in the last year?

♦ Do your listings typically sell above or below the asking price? What's your batting average on that?

♦ What is the average length of time (days on market or DOM) that your listings are on the market before they sell?

♦ Can you provide past clients for me to speak with?

♦ What will you do if I am not happy with you and want to be released from the listing agreement?

♦ What is your availability? How long will you typically take to respond to my e-mails and phone calls?

As the meeting is concluding, make a mental note of how well he listened to you. The best Realtors don't just talk, but rather ask questions and truly listen.

What a Realtor Does

We said earlier that not all Realtors are created equal. If you understand what it is that they should be doing for you, then it will be easier to spot a good one.

A listing Realtor has six broad duties, in the following order:

1. To educate you to the process and the state of the market

2. To price the property

3. To help present your home

4. To expose the property to the entire buyer pool

5. To manage the showings

6. To manage the deal all the way to closing after you have accepted an offer

Educating Sellers

It is so important that you begin the process of selling your home with a clear understanding of what is going to happen, but also of what is happening in the market, right now. A good Realtor can swiftly, efficiently, and clearly communicate all you need to know to make good educated choices.

Pricing Your Home Properly

Pricing a home well is a skill. It is not an easy skill to develop. It takes years of experience and requires three things we call *RIB*; these are summarized in the following list. We go through these in greater detail in Chapter 5.

- **R**elevant data: Comparable sales of homes in your community that have already sold, are currently still on the market, or have gone under contract but have not yet closed.

- **I**nsider access: You need special access to comparables that have gone under contract but have not yet sold. The sale price in these transactions is still unknown. When the sale prices are not available to the public, you need the assistance of someone who is "plugged in" or somehow connected to these transactions in order to get them. If you do not have access, your pricing process will be more challenging.

- **B**asic instinct: Instinct is critical when pricing a home with unusual features. Some characteristics add value, such as a special location or dramatic architecture. But how much value does the trait add? Other homes have unusual amenities such as an extra kitchen, recording studio, or koi pond. To some buyers, these have no value at all. Predicting the list price at which buyers will perceive value takes a good instinct.

Presenting Your Home Well

This is an area in which Realtors have varying opinions. We feel that *staging* is one of the most important elements in the sale, right up there with pricing and exposure. Some Realtors do not feel compelled to focus on it and may do nothing to help you stage your home. Maybe it's because they simply do not know how to stage a room. Other Realtors understand its importance but they may only guide you with a few tips here and there, pay for some fresh flowers, and give you the telephone number of a professional stager.

def•i•ni•tion

Staging is the process of transforming a home into peak selling condition through the strategic use of furniture placement, props, and colors to create visual appeal and a feeling of spaciousness. It allows buyers to take in the best features of a home, envision their belongings in it, and create a greater perception of value.

The Realtor who gets involved in guiding you (and sometimes physically helping you) to stage your home, as part of his commission and at no extra charge, is the most valuable. This kind of Realtor is also becoming more the norm as they become more and more competitive with one another.

Chapter 6 is devoted entirely to hundreds of tips and concepts on how to maximize the look of your home while it is on the market.

Exposing Your Property to the Marketplace

To know for sure that you will be getting top dollar for your home, it is essential that the property be exposed to the entire buyer pool. If only a fraction of the buyer pool is aware that your home is for sale, then you've stunted the natural competition for it. For specific guidance on exposure and reaching the whole buyer pool, see Chapter 9.

Managing Showings

Your listing agent should share with you the various approaches to conducting showings. In Chapter 8, we talk about them and other issues including your own Realtor's involvement, lockboxes, security, and contact information.

Managing the Deal When an Offer Comes In

This is a skill that is perhaps the most overlooked when sellers think about the commission they pay. When an offer comes in, the Realtor's job kicks into high gear. After all, what good is a great offer if it never makes it to the closing table? The best Realtors are those who are able to usher the deal through in spite of obstacles along the way.

The Commission

The most important thing to understand about commissions is that they are nego-tiable. They are not set in stone. In fact, the Realtor should voluntarily state that they are negotiable. There is usually a percentage or range that is typical in your commu-nity. If the local agencies charge anywhere between 5 percent and 7 percent, then it is up to you to negotiate a commission rate within that range at which you feel comfort-able.

How It Is Paid

In most states, it's the seller who pays the commission and it is then split between two companies: the seller's agency and the buyer's agency. The amount of commission you will pay will be a percentage of the ultimate sale price. You do not need to write a check up front. You will pay with proceeds from the sale at the closing table.

In some cases, your agency may take all of the commission. This happens in the case of *dual agency.*

The percentage will likely be in the single digits. Five to six percent of the total sale price is typical at many agencies across the United States. For example, if your home sells for $300,000 with a 5 percent commis-sion agreement, you will pay $15,000 to be split between two agencies.

def•i•ni•tion

If the agency that lists your home also happens to sell it, or bring in the buyer, then this is called **dual agency.** This means that the agency you have hired to repre-sent you is now representing two parties—both you and the buyer. Your agency keeps the entire commission. There is an ethical duty for the agency to represent you both equally, even though you (the seller) are paying the entire commission.

What Your Realtor Makes

There is a great myth about how much real estate agents earn on a transaction. In the case above, where you have paid $15,000 in commission, your Realtor's agency will probably keep 2.5 percent and give the other 2.5 percent to the agency representing the buyer. Out of that 2.5 percent—or $7,500, how much of that will the agent take home—after the broker takes his cut (often between 30 and 40 percent) and the agent pays her taxes and expenses?

*The Commission Split
Between Listing Agency and
Selling Agency.*

6%

3%
Seller's
Agency

3%
Buyer's
Agency

Remember, Realtors are independent contractors without benefits. Just about every dollar they spend is an out-of-pocket expense. Let's focus on the $7,500 going to the agency that has listed your home.

$7,500 (Total commission paid to listing agency)

− $2,625 (Realtor may give 30% or more to broker)

_____

= $4,875

− $1,463 (Federal taxes at 30%)

_____

= $3,412

− $244 (State taxes at 5%)

_____

= $3,168

− $1,500 (Expenses including brochures, photography, advertising, dues, MLS fees, desk fees, health care, automobile, and so on)

_____

= $1,668

As you can see, what your listing Realtor takes home is a fraction of what was paid out by you. Sometimes, Realtors will go months between transactions, so these dollars may have to stretch quite far.

The Listing Agreement

Any person whose name is on the deed must sign the *listing agreement* with the real estate agency. For example, one spouse cannot sign for the other if both legally own it. The contract is for a finite period of time. If, in that time, you find a buyer through your own resources, a commission is still paid to the agency. If the property does not sell in that time and the listing agreement expires, you are then free to go and hire another agency or sell it yourself.

def•i•ni•tion

A **listing agreement** is a legal contract between the seller and the real estate agency for the sole purpose of marketing and negotiating the sale of the property.

Types of Listing Agreements

The most popular type of agreement is called the exclusive right to sell. With this agreement, you give one agency the sole right to represent you regardless of which agency sells it. You pay the listing agency a commission. If another agency happens to sell it, it will share the commission. We recommend this type because, while only one agency lists your home, every agency works to sell it in an attempt to get a share of the commission. To see a sample listing agreement, visit www.TBA.com.

Other less common types of listing agreements include:

◆ **Exclusive agency.** This agreement means that you will allow only one agency to both list and sell it. The key thing here is that if you, the seller, find your own buyer, you do not have to pay a commission. In other words, you retain the right to sell it yourself. We do not recommend this type of agreement because it limits your exposure dramatically. You are depending on the hope that one of the Realtors in that office happens to have a buyer for you, or that you will find a buyer yourself and avoid commission.

◆ **Open listing.** These are not always in writing. You will pay a reduced fee to any Realtor who happens to bring you a buyer. The truth is that Realtors don't take these seriously because they want to focus on transactions that have a guaranteed payday.

◆ **Net listing.** These listings are illegal in some states. In this type of agreement, the property is listed at an agreed-upon net price. If it sells for more than that, the Realtor takes the balance as commission.

◆ **Flat-fee listing.** Where most commissions are paid at closing, in this case, the seller pays a flat fee up front. It does not matter if the property sells. Typically, they cover only certain services by the Realtor and you must negotiate them. If another agency sells it, you may have to pay additional money.

The Commission Section of the Listing Agreement

There is a space on the listing agreement where the Realtor will write in the percent commission to which you agreed. She will also stipulate the portion of the commission that will go to the Realtor who brings the buyer. Pay attention to this—it is referenced as the "offering commission split."

Some agencies charge sellers a higher commission than others. They will sometimes keep a larger portion of the commission for themselves rather than split it evenly with the buyer's Realtor. You may not agree with this policy. You may feel that the buyer's Realtor will be more incentivized by an even split and that she deserves as much as the listing Realtor for bringing the buyer in. Then again, the agent who listed your home has done more work to market your home and has likely gone out-of-pocket already on related expenses. Perhaps she does deserve a larger split. Decide what you think is fair and discuss it with your Realtor when signing the listing agreement.

The Term: When a Listing Agreement Begins and Ends

The term is the length of time that the agreement is in effect. Six months is typical from the time that it commences to the time that it expires (some states don't allow agreements longer than six months). You can also negotiate a shorter term. However, if you get the Realtor to agree to a shorter listing period, even if you sell your home relatively quickly, the listing will probably expire before you get to the closing table. In that case, you will need to fill out and sign a new agreement in order to extend the listing through the closing.

Other Sections of a Listing Agreement

Aside from the percent of commission and the term or length of the agreement, a listing agreement should also include the following:

◆ Date of the agreement.

◆ Termination date of the agreement.

- Parties (or persons) to the agreement.

- The right to sell (what kind of listing type, as described earlier, for example: exclusive right to sell).

- Listing price.

- Commission splits.

- Description of the property.

- Name of the listing service. (The service, or MLS, must be notified of the agreement within a certain time frame, usually 24–48 hours.)

- Possession date.

- Personal property included in the sale.

- Signatures of broker, agent, and seller.

- An anti-discrimination section.

Selling to Someone You Know Without Paying a Commission

If you have a friend, neighbor, or family member who has stated that they are interested in buying your home, then you must name them in the listing agreement as "exceptions." This means that, if one of them should buy the home while it is listed with your Realtor, you won't have to pay a commission to the Realtor.

Exceptions must be disclosed in writing at the outset, in the listing agreement, and on the MLS. This means that buyers will know, before they walk into your home, that you may sell the home to a friend and avoid paying commission. This can easily scare them away from entering into a contract with you. It generally hurts the seller to have a named exception on a publically listed home.

The thing about exceptions is that, if they are truly interested in buying your home, they buy it right away. On the other hand, it's possible that their interest is casual and they just want to be "kept in the loop." They may say to you, "Let us know if you get an offer and maybe we'll match it."

But the idea of holding the door open and naming them as an exception on your listing is damaging to the marketing of your home.

Seller Alert _____

If there is an "exception" to the listing, or a private party who may buy your home on the side without paying commission, you must disclose it in the listing itself, on the MLS, for everyone to see. The result is that buyers become very hesitant to fall in love with a home that they may lose at the last minute to one of your friends.

The risk is not worth the potential reward. We recommend that you go to the friend, neighbor, or family member and share with them the date that you are putting the home on the market. Give them a window in which to come forward with an offer. If they are truly interested, they will make one before it goes on the market. If they do not come forward, you have lost nothing, as they were unlikely to have ever come forward at all.

The Least You Need to Know

♦ Your choice of Realtor will have a big impact on how much money you net when the sale is complete.

♦ Assess a Realtor's track record thoroughly by finding out how many listings he's had in the last year, how long they were on the market, and how high they sold.

♦ Assess an agency by the amount of business that each agent does—not the entire office. Also look at where their offices are outside of the community, state, and country.

♦ A Realtor's duties include educating you as the seller, pricing your home, overseeing staging to ensure that the house shows well, exposing it to the entire buyer pool, managing showings, and managing the deal successfully all the way to the closing table.

♦ You can negotiate commission. It is not set in stone.

Chapter 4

To For-Sale-By-Owner ... or Not

In This Chapter

◆ The tasks and challenges of the FSBO seller

◆ How to price your own home

◆ How to describe your home and its best features

◆ How to reach buyers on your own

◆ How to show your own home

◆ Professional guidance

We understand the desire to avoid paying a commission when selling your home. Who wouldn't want to save money? When considering a private sale or a For-Sale-by-Owner (FSBO), the questions to ask are, "Are you sure that you will actually save money?" and "Will you reach the maximum number of buyers?"

Selling a home as a FSBO (pronounced *FIZ-bo*) is a difficult thing to do. If it were easy, everybody would do it. It's a venture that requires tremendous energy, loads of time, research, know-how, and patience. We guide you through the process. We also are honest about the fact that we think it's a safer bet, financially, to use a licensed Realtor. We believe that, even when you factor in a commission, a good Realtor should net you more money on the sale than if you sell it yourself. The reason is that the single greatest challenge for a FSBO seller is reaching the entire buyer pool.

It is not possible, at this point in time, for a seller to reach the same number and caliber of buyers that Realtors can. What this means is that, while you may have gotten your home sold on your own, you will never know for sure how much higher the sale price would have been had you exposed it to the highest number and most qualified buyers available.

In this chapter, we educate you about the process of selling your home by yourself and share tricks of the trade that help you to do the best job possible.

What Is a FSBO?

A FSBO is when a homeowner markets and sells his own home without the assistance of a licensed Realtor, usually in order to avoid paying a commission. He assumes all responsibilities himself, including pricing, marketing and advertising, staging, showings, open houses, negotiating, execution of contracts and other documentation, a final walk-through, and the closing process.

It's important to note that when you sell your home yourself, a buyer who is represented by a Realtor may want to see your home. You should make a decision early on in the process about whether or not to cooperate with a buyer's Realtor and pay a portion of the commission. Our opinion is that you should go ahead and pay a commission to a buyer's Realtor because, by not cooperating, you may never get that buyer to knock on your door.

Pricing Your Own Home

Pricing is the most important part of marketing any home. This is one of the main challenges facing you. You will not have access to some of the tools that a licensed Realtor will have. Nevertheless, it is still possible for you to come up with a reasonable list price without this kind of access.

In Chapter 5, we talk about using a *CMA*, or *competitive market analysis*, as the most common method of pricing a home. CMAs are made up of three types of comparables (or "comps" for short). No one single type is more important than another, and all three should be evaluated together to get a complete picture of the market and where your home should be positioned within it.

def•i•ni•tion

Usually performed by a licensed Realtor, a **competitive market analysis (CMA)** is a study of three kinds of "comparables" or "similar homes" in the area. They include homes that are currently on the market, homes that have recently sold, and homes that have just gone under contract.

Where to Get Information About Comps

Active comps are relatively easy to find because most of them are listed on online Multiple Listing Services (MLS's) (or real estate websites) accessible to everyone. They provide most of the information that you will need to compare value. One challenge is that, while some websites and online MLS's, such as www.realtor.com, provide the address of the properties, most of them still do not.

One way to find an address is to visit the websites of local real estate agencies. When you find homes that appear to be comparable to yours, you can call the agency and ask them to provide you with the addresses. Most of them will share that information over the phone.

"Under contract" comps are extremely difficult for nonprofessionals to access. Unless you have a relationship with the seller (or buyer) of a particular home, or if you hear a rumor about how much it went under contract for, it's next to impossible to learn the sale price. The sale price is a very valuable piece of information because it reflects the immediate pulse of the market.

On the other hand, comps of homes that have recently sold (or closed) can be found relatively easily through your local hall of records. Many local newspapers publish sale prices regularly as well.

There are also websites that provide all the prices for which homes have sold in your area. Among them are www.zillow.com, www.realestate.msn.com, and www.realestate.yahoo.com.

Using the Internet to Help You Price Your Home

Some websites may have a function by which you can price your home. They ask the user to complete an online valuation form—where you enter a few facts about your home and it spits out a suggested value.

Seller Alert _____

Pricing your home through a website is something that we do not advise. The idea that a computer model or software program can assign value to a home (or even a recommended list price) is absurd. Perhaps at some point in the future, the practice of real estate will change and allow computers to price homes. But that day is not yet here, as there are hundreds of factors (many of them subjective) to consider when coming up with a strategic list price.

Hiring an Appraiser to Help You Price Your Home

We speak throughout this book about the fact that it is impossible for a seller to establish value; it is the buyer who establishes value when he tells you what he is willing to pay.

While appraisals are typically done for banks and insurance companies when they are lending money or insuring a property, some sellers choose to have one performed in anticipation of selling the home and trying to come up with a reasonable list price.

Our issue with professional appraisals is that they only estimate value and sometimes rely heavily on sold comps that provide information that is too old to use exclusively. As we said earlier, there are three types of comps. To price your home properly, you must evaluate all three. However, it can be advantageous if you hire an appraiser who is very familiar with the neighborhood and who has done several recent appraisals in the area. We cover appraisals in more depth in Chapter 5.

Seller Alert _____

Be very careful about using your municipal tax-assessed value to price your home; they almost never reflect real value on the open market. For more information on tax-assessed value and appraised value, see Chapter 5.

Showing Your Own Home

Conducting showings of your home takes a lot of your time. If you're not sure how to conduct them properly, they can be awkward and actually counterproductive to your goal. They pose somewhat of a security risk, as well. And they can grate on your nerves after your home has been on the market for a few weeks or months.

We have devoted Chapter 8 to this subject, but that chapter is about conducting showings when your home is listed with a Realtor. In this chapter, however, we talk about how to handle them when you are going it alone.

Appointments and Preinformation

When someone calls you on the telephone to set up an appointment to see your home, ask him for the following contact information. If he is unwilling to give it to you, then do not show him the property. Nothing is more important than your safety, and any legitimate buyer should not have a problem giving you contact information:

- ◆ Name and home address
- ◆ E-mail address
- ◆ Telephone numbers (home, business, and cell)

Schedule the appointment for at least 24 hours from the time of the call in order to give yourself a chance to prepare for the showing and to verify his contact information. You might want to check the phonebook to see if the address matches the phone number. You can also call the person's place of business and confirm with the receptionist or operator that he is an employee.

Seller Alert

Try to keep your home in "showing" condition at all times. Not all buyers can wait 24 hours to set up an appointment. You may get last-minute calls from legitimate buyers who may be in your area for only one day, particularly if you live in a metropolitan locale or resort area. Some of these shoppers actually do buy.

Security

When a buyer has made an appointment and is about to come through your home without a licensed Realtor, ask a friend or family member to be in the home with you. If possible, don't show the property alone. In this day and age, you cannot be too careful.

If that is not possible, notify a neighbor that you will be showing the home and ask him to stay nearby until the buyer has left. When showing the basement or attic, let the buyer go up or down the stairs in front of you. In fact, try to remain on the stairs while the basement and attic are being viewed.

Other security tips include leaving the front and/or back doors ajar during the showing, hiding or putting away small valuables that can be easily picked up and pocketed, and carrying a cell phone or cordless phone in your hand while showing.

Seller Alert

We don't recommend ever letting potential buyers who knock on your door into your home. You have no idea who they are or where they came from. Speak to them at the door and politely ask if they will please call back on the telephone to schedule an appointment. This practice will also relieve you of being in the position of showing your home at awkward times, like when the baby is sleeping or when you are in the middle of a meal.

Any qualified buyer who is truly interested in your property will respect you, use good etiquette, and make an appropriate appointment that is convenient for you.

When a Realtor Knocks on Your Door

Sometimes a Realtor will knock on your door to ask if you will allow her to show the home to a buyer, but she will expect you to pay her a commission in exchange. As we discussed earlier in this chapter, you will have already made a decision as to whether or not you will cooperate with buyer's Realtors.

Assuming that you will cooperate, how do you handle the unexpected drop-in? Most Realtors will acknowledge that they are catching you off guard. However, they may only have noticed your lawn sign as they were driving by with their buyer already in the car. Perhaps the buyer is in town for just one day. It is still your prerogative to turn them away, but buyers who are working with Realtors are almost always qualified and ready to purchase. You may want to accommodate them.

We discuss how and why to negotiate with Realtors representing buyers later in this chapter.

Follow-Through with Buyers

After a buyer has come through your home but has not made an offer, it's always helpful to get feedback. Call the buyer and ask if he wouldn't mind sharing with you the reasons why he did not buy your home. Tell him that you are not trying to apply pressure, but rather, that you're just trying to educate yourself about how your home is being perceived in the marketplace.

How to Describe Your Home and Its Features

Writing a word description is one of the hardest parts of marketing a home properly. It's difficult and confusing to know what to include. It's not necessarily about using flowery words or simply cramming in as much information as possible. There is more nuance to it than that.

The confusion lies in understanding the goal of the words. Too many people think the purpose is to share every possible facet of the home that can fit in the allotted space on the listing or in the advertisement. But the true goal is to entice the buyer into making an appointment to see it. You may ask, "Won't more information entice them further?" Not necessarily.

When you disclose too much about a property, it creates more opportunities for the buyer to find something about the home that doesn't meet his needs. Offering room dimensions in a listing is one example. The buyer may tell himself that he must have a living room that is of a certain size. If, on the listing, you provide dimensions that are smaller than what he wanted, then he may not bother to make an appointment.

 Trick of the Trade _____

Study the home descriptions on real estate websites and MLS's to educate yourself about the style, form, and content in professional listings.

What he missed out on by not coming into your home was that the size of the room turned out to be unimportant. He might have overlooked the dimensions because he was attracted to the enormous kitchen instead.

Give the reader facts, but choose them carefully when you're putting them in writing.

The Big Three: Size, Condition, and Location

In describing size, buyers want to know how many bedrooms and baths your home has. There is no way to embellish those facts. If the overall square footage of your home is low, yet you have a nice floor plan, then you may want to focus on the layout. A sample sentence is, "The sunny and open main floor has wonderful circular flow for entertaining." When referring to size, avoid words like "charming" and "adorable," as they are often euphemisms for "small."

The way you talk about condition is important. Major upgrades should always be mentioned in a listing description. If you have a new kitchen or baths, then you should describe them as "updated" and perhaps even "state of the art," depending on how advanced the materials and appliances are. If your home is not renovated or updated, yet it is clean and well cared for, use words like "impeccably maintained" to describe the overall condition.

And, hopefully, you'll be able to say why the location is a good one. Is it near a park? Is it walking distance to a village with shops and restaurants? An important factor is your proximity to transportation, particularly if homeowners in the area commute to a nearby city for work.

The Architecture

Go out of your way to mention structural features such as high ceilings, original hardwood floors, built-in bookcases, leaded glass windows, crown, base, raised panel and dentil moldings, skylights, fireplaces, a breezeway between the kitchen and garage, covered or screened-in porches, decorative staircases, sunken living rooms, vaulted ceilings, bedrooms with private baths, kitchens large enough to dine in, and so on.

The Amenities

If you have a major amenity such as a pool, tennis court, outdoor hot tub, water treatments like a fountain or pond, playground, potting shed, oversized garage, or wine cellar, they're worth alerting buyers to in advance.

Where to Find Buyers

The goal of any seller is to get top dollar for the property. The only way to truly ensure getting top dollar is to expose the property to the entire buyer pool and then see what the market will bear. The following sections describe places where a FSBO seller can reach buyers and expose the property to as many of them as possible.

Online Multiple Listing Services

You can—and should—post your home with as many online MLS's as possible. Some of them are free and others require a fee. For a larger fee, they may even provide you with real estate forms and contracts to download and use in your process of selling.

What's important to note is that the MLS's available to you are not the same as the MLS's used by licensed Realtors. There are hundreds of Realtor MLS's across the nation (they cover regions) that only professionals have access to. They are complete listings of just about every single home on the market in that area.

MLS's available to the public are not complete. Buyers who are browsing public MLS's may not find your listing, although the more public MLS's on which you list your home, the greater chance you have of being found. For a resource list of public MLS's, see Appendix B.

Reach Out to Buyers' Real Estate Agents

Contacting Realtors may be one of the most powerful ways to reach buyers, but it will involve paying a partial or reduced commission. Buyers browse online for months when they are beginning their search. But when they are ready to actually buy, they choose and begin working with a Realtor. And why wouldn't they? It's free. In most states, the seller pays the commission, not the buyer.

There are some exceptions to this rule, as some buyers like to remain free agents, often approaching sellers directly. Still, they are in the vast minority. The most qualified and sought-after buyers are represented by Realtors. They have been screened, they have been preapproved for a loan, they understand value, and they have been educated about the market by a professional. They are, in a word, serious.

Trick of the Trade _____

You can reach out to local Realtors by calling them directly or circulating a flyer to their offices stating that your home is for sale and that you will pay a commission to an agent who brings you a buyer. Some Realtors will be responsive to you, not necessarily because they have a buyer for your home, but because they hope to ultimately represent you if you cannot sell your home yourself.

Canvass Neighbors

Canvassing neighborhoods works well sometimes in condominium and co-op complexes, where a next-door neighbor might want to purchase your unit and expand the square footage of her unit, or may have a relative or friend who has been interested in moving into the area. Go to the neighbors first. It cannot hurt to expand your message to the entire building or even the neighborhood. You never know!

Hold Public Open Houses

Public open houses have a questionable impact on selling your home, which we discuss in Chapter 9. But because a FSBO is at a disadvantage exposure-wise, and while individual private showings can be inconvenient and tiresome, a public open house is not a bad idea.

To maximize its power, advertise it in advance on regional websites, newspapers, and alongside open houses advertised by professional Realtors. You can also post flyers in your local supermarket, train and bus stations, YMCA, and churches, and advertise in local newsletters.

Trick of the Trade

On the day of the open house, post signs at the nearest major intersection. Attach balloons to the signs to catch the attention of drivers.

Put a Sign on the Property

A sign on a property casts the narrowest net in trying to reach buyers—but it cannot hurt, either. Perhaps you'll get lucky and that one ready-to-go buyer who happens to drive past your home will call to set up a showing.

The biggest mistake that FSBO sellers make with signs is that the phone number is not large enough or dark enough to see. Use a big fat black marker with permanent ink and make the telephone number large!

Seller Alert

Certain areas have local ordinances regarding the posting of signs on your property such as contractor's signs, political affiliation signs, and For-Sale-By-Owner signs. The ordinance may have a limit to the number of signs posted at one time as well as a rule about the minimum number of feet from the street where the sign can be staked. Check with your local authorities.

Professional Guidance on Managing a Deal

Real estate transactions are complicated. They involve so many different areas, from finance to law. When you are dealing with lenders and legal documents, it can be overwhelming. If you are neither a lawyer nor a banker and are not represented by a licensed Realtor, you should seek professional guidance. Mistakes made in a transaction run the gamut from delays of time that cause closing date problems to miscalculations that cost you money.

Because you are navigating this process alone, we strongly recommend that you consider hiring an attorney who specializes in real estate. There are many reasons:

◆ They represent your interests exclusively.

◆ They have information regarding new rules and laws pertaining to the transfer of ownership of real estate.

◆ There are many types of law that may come into play when you sell your home. Depending on your personal situation, they may include property law, estate law, matrimonial law, tax law, environmental law, lending laws, and civil law. If your attorney is not an expert in all of these areas, he can identify the issue and get you the proper advice and counsel.

◆ They are usually familiar with the area and the local ordinances, safety codes, tax codes, contractors, and departments of government.

An attorney will protect you and possibly even save you enough money to offset her fees. Some attorneys charge a flat fee, others an hourly fee, and still others charge a percentage of the sale price. Ask about the charges up front so that there are no surprises.

The Least You Need to Know

◆ A For-Sale-By-Owner seller assumes all responsibilities himself, including pricing, marketing and advertising, staging, showings, open houses, negotiating, execution of contracts and other documentation, final walk-through, and closing.

◆ A FSBO does not necessarily save you money by not paying a commission.

◆ There are three types of comparables to compare your home to: *active* or currently on the market, *under contract* or not yet closed, and *sold* or already closed transactions. Evaluate the sale prices of all three types—never just one.

◆ Using a private appraisal, the tax assessed value, or a website to price your home is not the best approach.

◆ When showing your own home to a stranger, security is the most important consideration. Do not show your home to a doorknocker unless she is with a Realtor.

◆ The two best strategies for a FSBO to reach buyers is to list the home with several online Multiple Listing Services and to reach out and cooperate with buyers' Realtors in the area—even if it means paying a small commission.

Chapter 5

How to Price Your Home Properly

In This Chapter

- ◆ The importance of good pricing
- ◆ Value versus price
- ◆ How to price
- ◆ Reductions: how and when to do them
- ◆ Gauging how overpriced your home is

Pricing your home correctly is the most important step in the process of selling. If you had to choose just one thing to do well, it's pricing. That's because a well-priced home will always sell—in any type of market.

There is a saying in real estate: in the absence of proper pricing, no amount of marketing or advertising will sell your home. You could have the most beautiful home in your community, have hundreds of buyers come through it, and advertise it all over the Internet and in magazines and newspapers … but if potential buyers do not perceive value at your asking price, they will not buy it.

This chapter takes you through the steps needed to price your home well. It also covers a key component of pricing—how the buyers perceive your asking price. The result is that you will sell your home for the highest amount of money and in the shortest period of time.

We share specific tools as well as some general concepts. We also talk about using hard data, getting access to hard-to-get information, and using your basic instinct (or your Realtor's). You should consider all three when trying to come up with the right asking price.

The Difference Between Price and Value

We're always surprised when we hear someone who has not sold their home say, "My home is worth about X amount of dollars." The truth is that there is no possible way to know what your home is worth until a buyer takes out his checkbook and tells you what he's willing to pay. At that moment, the value of your home is established. The market has spoken. In real estate, the buyer is the market. It is not the seller who establishes value. She establishes only the list price.

The Price

There are two types of "price." There is the asking price or *list price* that the seller sets along with a Realtor. Then there is the *sale price*, which is what your home will actually sell for. The sale price represents the value of the home or what your home was worth on the particular day that the offer was made.

def•i•ni•tion

The **list price** is the amount of money that the seller is asking for the home and hopes to receive from a buyer. The seller may ultimately sell it at that price, below it, or above it. The final, agreed-upon number is the **sale price**.

To understand how to set the list price of your home, you must first understand that a home is not a product like a pair of shoes in a department store. The shoes have a set value that has been established by the store. The store is saying, "This is our price, take it or leave it." If the shoes don't sell, so be it. They may eventually go on sale when the season is over, but, in essence, the seller (the store) has set the price and it is non-negotiable.

Now, to understand how the sale price of a home is arrived at, think of the real estate market as you would the stock or commodities markets. A pork belly is a commodity. If, on any given day of the week, pork belly trading slows up, then their price falls until buyers once again perceive value and trading resumes.

Like a commodity, a house will always sell, or "trade"—in any type of market—if the seller understands that the buyers determine the market value. If you think of a home as trading, rather than selling, then the analogy is complete.

Creating Value

When do buyers buy? They buy when they perceive value. In other words, they buy when they think they're getting a good deal at a fair price. When the market falls and home sales slow down, it is a common misconception that the buyers have gone away or that they have just disappeared. In reality, they are still in the market for a new home but they have simply stopped perceiving value. The minute that prices adjust to proper levels, buyers will instantly begin to make offers. When a sufficient reduction is made, the buyers are at the ready and the home sells immediately.

You can still sell your home even when the market appears to have stopped dead in its tracks. It's not because you're prepared to give it away. It's because you are the rare seller who understands how to price.

When you have created a perception of value through your price, your home will sell quickly and for more money than if you did not.

Again, we are not saying that you should give your home away, but rather that home buyers are avid comparison shoppers. They compare every detail of two similar homes priced in the same range. If a buyer is strongly considering two properties that are just about equal in most ways except in price, the odds are that an offer will be made on the lower-priced home.

 Trick of the Trade

There is a clear relationship between the number of days that a home has been on the market (DOM) and the price at which it sells. You are much more likely to get your asking or list price in the first few days or weeks. After your home has been sitting on the market for longer than what is normal for your area, the value goes lower and lower.

Setting Your List Price

There are three areas to tap into when you price your home. Ideally, all three should be used together to come up with the best number. None should be used alone. To help you to remember them, think of the RIB Rule:

◆ **R**elevant data

◆ **I**nsider access

◆ **B**asic instinct

Relevant Data

There is specific, relevant data that can be used to help establish a list price for your home. They are comparables, local market trends, appraisals, and tax assessments. Some types of data are more useful in pricing than others.

Comparables

This is the most popular tool used to price a home. *Competitive market analyses* (*CMA*), also referred to simply as the *comps*, are "comparable" listings of other homes which are similar to yours in style, condition, and location.

When reviewing any type of comps, there are key features to compare:

◆ List price

◆ Sale price (if it has closed)

◆ The date (the market conditions at the time)

◆ Length of time it took to sell (or days on market)

◆ Number of bedrooms

◆ Number of bathrooms

◆ Size of lot

◆ Property taxes

◆ Square footage (if provided)

◆ Overall condition

◆ Condition of kitchen and bathrooms

◆ Neighborhood

◆ Style

There are three types of comps, and we think it's important that you evaluate all three—never just one.

- **Active or currently on the market (your competition):** Listings of homes that are currently active or on the market. Active comps are helpful—these homes are what yours will be compared to. Pretend you're a buyer out shopping and ask yourself the hard question about how your home stacks up against the others on the market.

- **Under contract (the secret comps):** We call them this because, until these transactions close, the sale price is secret information and can only be obtained through private contacts or Realtors who keep themselves in the know. After they close, they become a matter of public record. But at the moment, the sale prices are unknown to most people.

  Under-contract comps are important because they reflect the current pulse of the marketplace. In other words, by finding out the agreed-upon sale price, you have a powerful indicator about what buyers are willing to pay for homes like yours, right now, in the current market climate. Buyer behavior patterns shift constantly, and tapping into these patterns is important but difficult to do.

- **Closed (factual data):** Because sold comp transactions are closed, the sale prices have become public record and are now factual data for you to use in comparing your home to others. The challenge with closed transactions is that they are, by definition, old information. The sale price offered by the buyers was established weeks, and more typically, months or years ago when the market was different. Try not to evaluate closed transactions from more than one year ago. It's still dated material, but if one of them happens to be your neighbor's home, and it's the only home on your street to sell in the last year, it will have some relevance to you.

Local Market Trends

When reviewing comps that have sold or have already closed, look at the sale prices compared to the list prices. You will notice a trend, and the trend will help you to price your home. All of the homes will have done one of the following:

- Sold below the list price
- Sold at or relatively near the asking price
- Sold above the asking price

Once you recognize the trend, you'll get a sense of how the buyer pool in your community is behaving, which will provide some guidance in terms of how aggressive you want to be with a list price If every single home is selling below the asking price, it will be much more difficult (but not impossible) to get a buyer to pay above the list price. Can you change that trend? Yes, but it will take the guidance of a very skilled Realtor. By having a thorough understanding of local market trends, you are more likely to position your home well pricewise, and to better anticipate the outcome of the sale.

Appraisals and Tax Assessments

Some sellers choose to use professional appraisers to help price their homes. While a Realtor will come up with a suggested list price, appraisers tell you what they think the value is. You already know how we feel about assigning an exact value to a home; it's nearly impossible to do. The value of a home shifts constantly, and its exact worth can only be determined on the day that a buyer makes an offer.

Appraisals are used most often for such things as getting home loans, obtaining property insurance, tax and estate planning, banking, and municipal tax assessments. The values that they come up with are relied upon and used for years by these institutions. They don't update them unless you are changing your level of insurance coverage, tax status, refinancing, or your town is going through a tax base revaluation (which is a relatively rare occurrence). Even if you've had one done recently, home values shift constantly.

Trick of the Trade _____

Even though a seller shouldn't use the tax-assessed value as a list price, it can be helpful as a starting point to assure you that your home is priced within a reasonable range as others of the same size and in the same neighborhood. For example, if all of the homes on the market priced at about $400,000 have property taxes of approximately $5,000, that information can give a reasonable range to consider before coming up with an exact list price.

Using your tax-assessed value is also a tricky thing; you should be careful if you use that number to price your home. It represents only what your municipality thought your home was worth on the particular day that it was assessed. That assessment may have happened years or even decades ago, yet your current property taxes are still based upon that value. The figure may have no connection to today's real home values. Our own town was reassessed a couple years ago. The value that was assigned to our homes is already nearly irrelevant. Some homes are now worth more than the assessed value, while others are now worth less. As more time passes, they will become completely irrelevant for pricing purposes.

Whether having a private paid appraisal done or having the town or city do it, they all try to establish your home's worth by walking, inspecting, measuring, and evaluating it. A tax revaluation covers every single home in the community. The reason is that, after time, the taxes from home to home get out of balance from one another as people make upgrades and the homes have turned over two or three times. To get them all back into balance with each other, a new reassessment (or revalue) is ordered for the entire community. The purpose is to be sure that each homeowner is paying his fair share of property taxes, not to state the homes' permanent value on the open market.

Seller Alert

A private appraisal costs you money, as it is a fee-for-service business. An appraisal done by your local municipality is usually free of charge, as is a CMA done by a licensed Realtor.

Following is a table illustrating types of appraisals, who orders them, and the value that they try to establish.

Types of Appraisals

Type	Value Sought	Ordered By
Private appraisal	Fair market value	Seller
Insurance appraisal	Insured value	Insurance company
Bank appraisal	Loan value	Bank or lender
Tax appraisal	Municipally assessed value	Office of the tax assessor, city, or town

Insider Access

Information is power. In residential real estate, some of the most relevant and powerful information that you'll need is also the most difficult to get. We're referring to the "secret comps" discussed earlier in this chapter. The sale prices for comps like these are not yet public information.

But they are valuable because they reveal what buyers are willing to pay for a home like yours right now, this month, and even this week. The only people who know how much that home down the street from you went under contract for are typically the buyer of the home, the seller of the home, the Realtor, the bank or lender, and the attorney (if there are any involved).

It is very helpful to find this information. If an exact number is not available, then an idea of how high a particular home recently went under contract for is usually sufficient. Many Realtors have it—at least those Realtors who are out there every day, working full-time in the trenches and communicating with colleagues. They don't share the information easily, nor should they, as sometimes it is considered a breach of ethics to reveal information about a pending transaction.

Basic Instinct

In the real estate business, there are certain Realtors who seem to have an uncanny sense of what buyers will pay for homes in certain price ranges. It's a skill. And it's a highly sought-after skill. Also, certain homes require a sharper instinct to price than others. They may be unusual or have special characteristics to them. Let's begin with the ability to interpret the buyer's perception of homes on the market.

Knowing What Buyers Will Pay

One of the ways that a Realtor acquires the skill to instinctively know what someone will pay for your home is by representing buyers in all price ranges. When Realtors work with buyers on a regular basis, they're plugged in right at the source. Showing the buyers homes, weekend after weekend, and putting in offers gives a Realtor a terrific sense of what they will pay in certain price bands. When that Realtor represents you and prices your home, it gives you an edge because the Realtor's instinct is based on what drives the entire market—the buyer's perception of value.

Trick of the Trade _____

Pretend that you are a buyer. Ask your Realtor to "show" you (physically take you inside) some of the homes that are currently on the market in your price range. Your Realtor may simply target some open houses for you to attend. This is an invaluable experience when pricing your own home.

Hard-to-Comp Homes

When a home is special or has uncommon traits, pricing it becomes even harder. Because the traits are unusual, it requires great instinct to know how much higher or lower the list price should be, or how the buyer pool will react.

Perhaps your home has one of these elements:

- ◆ Special location
- ◆ Dramatic architecture
- ◆ Unique amenities
- ◆ Largest home in town

Special Location

You know which neighborhoods are the better ones in your community. And within these neighborhoods, there may be pockets of sought-after real estate. Perhaps one particular street is magnificent, located on a park, or lined and canopied with giant oak trees. Maybe every house on the street has a sweeping view of the valley, mountain range, or a nearby city skyline. Or perhaps it is the first quiet and serene street that is still within walking distance to town.

It's not that you (or your Realtor) aren't aware that the location is special. Everybody in town knows it's a great street. It's just that it's so hard to quantify it in a list price. How much money should you add onto the list price because of the locale? To add to the difficulty, a home on that street may not have sold for two or three years, so there are no relevant comparables to help guide you. Clearly, it takes some instinct and experience to price a home like this.

Dramatic Architecture

Dramatic architecture is rare and can be valuable. But rare things are harder to appraise and extreme styles don't appeal to everyone. The pool of people in the market for them is smaller. If the style is different from that of the rest of the homes in the community, it can work for or against you.

Take, for example, an ultramodern contemporary amid a sea of center hall colonials. The buyers can appreciate the architecture, but it doesn't mean that they want it. They likely came to your community in the first place because they liked the colonials for which your town is known. On the other hand, a magnificent French Normandy in the same community might be extremely sought after for its originality.

We call these homes "love-'em-or-hate-'ems." Buyers walk in and either instantly dislike it or fall madly in love. The trick to pricing them is to have a gut feeling about whether their unusualness will be perceived as a commodity or not. A basic instinct can help you to predict.

Unique Amenities

If you live in Florida or southern California, a swimming pool is not a unique amenity. And its universal appeal in that region typically adds value. But in the Northeast, pools can actually take value away. A significant number of buyers don't want the headache of maintaining a pool that can be enjoyed only six months of the year. It needs to be opened and closed every year, it might require service several times a year, buyers may have young children whom they worry about, and they perceive it as an overall liability.

It's important to know whether your amenities are unique or universal upgrades. Here are some unique amenities we've seen that don't always add value to a home:

- Koi ponds

- Built-in outdoor Jacuzzi

- Wine cellar

- Riding ring

- Second kitchen ("summer kitchen")

- Putting green

- Boat dock

These amenities may appeal to some segment of the buyer pool, but many buyers won't see value in them. You may have enjoyed it immensely while you lived there, but the buyers don't want to pay a premium for an upgrade that they don't need, and that they may have to have dismantled or ripped out after they purchase.

Trick of the Trade _____

If your home has a unique amenity that may not appeal to the entire buyer pool, consider offering to have it converted back to a more universally usable space. Have the Realtor include the offer in the listing itself so that buyers will have a more open mind about the property before they even make an appointment to see it. Also consider marketing the property in specialty magazines about boating or horseback riding, where readers may be looking for specific amenities like a private dock or riding ring.

There are, however, upgrades that are almost universally appealing, like expensive countertops in a kitchen, central air-conditioning, a family room, or a master bathroom. These are easier to incorporate into the asking price than unique amenities that may be more valuable to one person than they are to another.

The Largest or Most Valuable Homes in the Community

To use a cosmic analogy, there is a part of the atmosphere—at the top of the world—where the sky ends and space begins. It's known as the stratosphere, and for most of us it represents uncharted territory. This is where the seller finds herself when her home is the largest or most valuable home in town. To put it simply, there is no local comp for her home. She's flying almost blind. Her home is at what is called "the top of the market"—the top price range or price band in the area.

When this home sells, it may become the most expensive property ever sold in your community. On that day, a brand-new top-of-the-market value has been set. It's extraordinary and interesting to witness. The buyer pool for such a home is much smaller than it is for other homes. And the buyers within this pool are going to be leery of paying the highest price that has ever been paid. You can bet that they are going to proceed with great caution. They will drive a hard bargain and negotiations could drag on. The buyer for this home will justifiably challenge the seller and the listing agent on the asking price. And he'll have the advantage because there is thin air up there at the top of the market—in any community. There usually aren't a whole lot of buyers lined up to buy the most expensive homes in town.

Reductions

You've priced your home and now it's not selling. Let's talk about reductions in price. What we love about reductions is that they give everybody a second chance, a fresh start. The only trick is to know when to do one and how much to come down in price.

How Overpriced Is Your Home?

As we discussed earlier, if your home is not selling, the reason is that it's overpriced. To use an analogy, it's like when people think it might be time to lose a few pounds. Down deep, they know they're overweight. The only question is how much do they need to lose? When your home has no offers on it, you probably recognize that you need to make a reduction, but how big a reduction do you need to make?

Any reductions should be meaningful in size. We know that "meaningful" is a relative term. The purpose of a reduction is to regain the attention of the buyers—and the Realtors who represent them. With a good reduction, you'll encourage the buyer pool to take another look at your home and hopefully, the new price will spur a sale.

There is, however, a way to figure out approximately how overpriced your home is and what size reduction to make. It is more art than science and it's a relative gauge, but we have found it to be helpful. It has to do with tracking showings.

Tracking Showings

The number of times that your home has been shown is an important gauge of whether it's overpriced, particularly when it is not selling. You will probably labor over the decision to reduce and by how much to reduce. Monitor the showings yourself or tell your Realtor that you would like a weekly report on the number.

Here's how to apply the number of showings to the size of a reduction:

- ◆ A lot of showings: If your house has had many showings, none of which result in an offer, then your home is probably only a little overpriced. Your list price did not prevent buyers from making an appointment to see it. If it were grossly over-priced, they would never have made the appointment at all. And yet, once they got inside your home, they didn't perceive quite enough value to buy it. A reduction is needed but not necessarily a huge one.

- ◆ Occasional showings: If your showings are dwindling, then your reduction should be significant to make an impact. What's happening when the showings are just beginning to dry up is that they actually do dry up! But you have warning—a chance to do something before your property gets completely stale. Decreased showings are a clear indicator of what is to come. It's a gift to have foresight. Seize the day and make a decent reduction so that you are not chasing the market downward. You'll spare yourself a lot of stress and heartache.

Seller Alert _____

Some people feel that a price reduction is not necessary when buyers are still making appointments to see a property. This is not true! If you were at the correct price, you would have an offer.

◆ Hardly any showings: If buyers are no longer coming through in any meaning-ful numbers, then your home is grossly overpriced. The reduction needs to be immediate and very large. If a large reduction is not made, the home will possibly sit permanently.

When to Do a Reduction

To figure out when to do a reduction, you first need to determine if your home has been sitting on the market longer than most homes in your community—particularly homes in the same price range. This measurement is the days on market (DOM), which we referred to earlier. Remember, pricing your home at the right number is a competitive process. Your home will not look good once it has been on the market a long time, especially if it's longer than your competition. The best scenario is to have your home sell ahead of the curve—that is, more quickly than your competition. You will get a higher price as well. (See Chapter 9 for more information.)

If the market is going down and you do not make reductions fast enough (or large enough) to get a buyer to make an offer, you can end up in the dangerous position of chasing the market. When this happens, it is hard to catch it. Being proactive and realistic is the key to making reductions that actually result in your home selling.

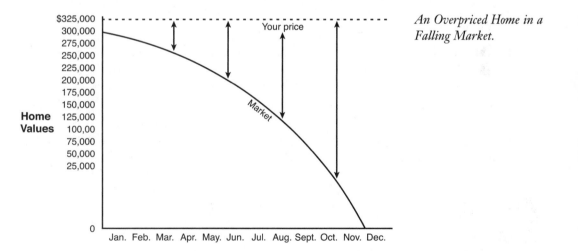

An Overpriced Home in a Falling Market.

As you can see, the gap between your list price and the direction the market is heading gets wider and wider every day.

As you can see below, even making multiple reductions too slowly can result in chasing—not catching up with—the market.

Making Reductions Too Slowly in a Falling Market.

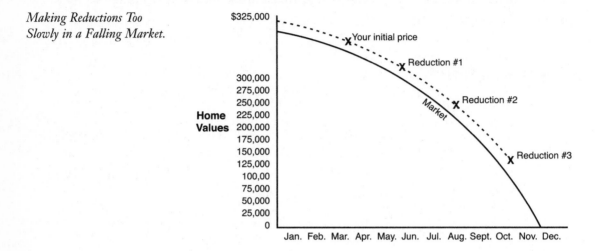

The emotional trap that sellers sometimes fall into is believing that the reductions will cause them to lose money. This is a myth. You cannot lose what you never had. Buyers did not perceive value at your original price. Soon thereafter, the market fell even more. The value of your home came down; that's true. But you did not give it away or lose money. The value is always changing and, in a falling market, it's better to sell it before the price goes down any further.

Trick of the Trade

The week you make the reduction, try to get it done by Wednesday or Thursday. That way, buyers making appointments for the weekend will hear about it and have time to include your home in their list of homes to see.

What's good, yet questionable, about numbers is that you can often manipulate them to make them work for you (or against you). The word "value" is a relative term, and finding the sweet spot when pricing is hard to do. The good news is that you get more than one chance to get it right. You can reintroduce your home to the marketplace with a new price and a new attitude if you track your showings, understand what kind of market you're selling in, and are proactive.

The Least You Need to Know

- ◆ Pricing is the single most important factor when selling your home.

- ◆ Don't fall into the trap of assuming that your list price is what your home is actually worth. Buyers establish the value when they tell you what they're willing to pay.

- ◆ To price your home, use relevant data, market trends, insider access, and your gut instinct.

- ◆ If your home is not selling, track the number of showings to figure out how big a price reduction you need to make.

- ◆ You can always correct the price!

Chapter 6

Staging Your Home to Get Top Dollar

In This Chapter

♦ The power of good staging and its effect on sale price

♦ Room-by-room staging tips and ideas

♦ Increasing curb appeal

♦ Creating outdoor rooms

When your home goes on the market, the most important factor, aside from the way you price it, is the way you stage it. The goal is not just to make it look better, but to make it look *bigger*, as well. Aside from price, buyers consider three things in a home: size, condition, and location. Staging affects two of these factors and will therefore have a huge impact on the sale price.

If the sale of your home were a Hollywood film production, the house would be the star. Like the star, it's the structure that buyers have come to see, not your personal belongings. Don't take it personally! Your décor might be lovely, and it's true that good décor helps sell a house. But what buyers need most is a clear and unobstructed view of floors, walls, ceilings, windows, and countertops. If they cannot envision their own things in your home, they won't buy it.

Staging is a process that transforms your home into peak selling condition. We're going to teach you how to stage it to get tens of thousands of dollars more on the sale than if you had not staged it at all.

In this chapter, we share over 100 staging ideas and concepts, including our "fast fixes." Don't panic—you don't have to adopt every single idea. The purpose is not to overwhelm you with checklists. What we're hoping is that, after reading these suggestions, you will look at your own home differently and be inspired. You'll have the confidence to make some of these improvements when you realize how easily the eye can be fooled through good staging.

The First Impression

Buyers make a major judgment about your home as soon as they open the front door. Make the most of that moment. When buyers single out your home and schedule a showing, they are already on your side. They're hoping to fall in love. When you have impressed them as they come through the door, it's amazing what they will overlook as they walk through the rest of the home.

Of course, the home, as a whole, needs to fulfill their needs. But, at this moment, they're thinking about the impression that their friends and family will get when they first walk inside. This is why homes with magnificent entry halls have an advantage over those that don't. In the absence of a dramatic entry, you want the first impression to be a strong one.

To catch a buyer's eye, try to create something visually attractive or welcoming. It could be something as simple as a small bud vase on a table with cut roses or tulips, or more dramatic props such as a piece of art, an area reception rug, topiaries, or a large floral arrangement.

Room-by-Room Staging

We are about to take you through each room in your home and share loads of staging ideas. We understand that sellers, for whatever reason, cannot implement all the ideas that we have to share. In this case, if you can do nothing else, the three most important staging goals are to declutter, let as much light into the house as possible, and make the home completely clean.

To stage the interior, most sellers need to begin by taking things *out* of the house—even pieces of furniture! Too many items in a space make it appear *smaller* than it really is. Having fewer pieces opens a room up.

We find that this is the hardest thing for a seller to do. Once items such as family photos, ottomans, unnecessary side tables, and even some rugs are removed, the house may appear to you to be empty, cold, or unlived in. What's important is to not confuse decorating for everyday living with staging to sell your house. They are very different! *Good staging* showcases the architecture, space, and amenities—the things that buyers are really interested in.

The Living Room

Living rooms are so important because they are usually the first room that a buyer sees and they are particularly susceptible to having too much furniture. A sofa and a loveseat together are often overkill and can really shrink a small- to medium-size living room. So is having one too many armchairs. Ottomans should almost always be removed, as they take up too much valuable floor space. End tables and floor lamps should be used sparingly. The good news is that the items you take away can possibly be repurposed for use in another room in the house.

Here are some of our favorite living room "fast fixes" that make a difference, cost little or nothing, and have a big impact on the home's look.

Trick of the Trade

Every home gets tiny paint nicks all over the trim from everyday wear and tear. Grab a Dixie cup with paint in it and walk around your house using a small brush to repair chips in moldings, stair risers, balustrades, doors, and windows.

- Mirror magic. It's very expensive to buy good-quality artwork. Instead, try using a large decorative mirror over the fireplace or above a couch. It's a terrific substitute and a much less expensive way to create a focal point in the room. The side benefit is that the reflection makes the room look bigger.

- Turn furniture on an angle. Most of us put pieces of furniture straight or flush to the wall. Try turning things on an angle to make the floor space around them seem larger. You'll open up the room in the process. (This works for beds, too.)

- No need to reupholster. Take an old, dated couch or armchair and place a neutral or solid slip cover over it. Add a splash of color with modern pillows or throws.

♦ Give the fireplace an instant face-lift: borrow or buy new fireplace tools to place beside it. This really raises the bar for the whole mantle area. For a clean look, place new firewood inside—or candles for a fake fireplace.

Trick of the Trade _____

Yard sales are fantastic places to pick up vintage brass or wrought-iron fireplace tools, decorative mirrors, vases, and planters—for just a few dollars.

♦ Give your rugs a haircut! If the fringe on the ends of your area rugs is irreparably dirty or frayed, have your local rug dealer remove and bind them. You'll instantly have a modern, updated rug. And by the way, bare floors are better than bad rugs. Use rugs only if they are currently in style, in very good condition, and sized proportionately to the room. Rip up and remove wall-to-wall carpeting if it is badly stained or has an odor to it from smoking or pets. Any kind of floor, even subflooring, is better than having a foul smell in the house.

♦ Keep their eyes up. If your home has high ceilings or beautiful moldings, put a tall vase, plant, or piece of art on top of a cabinet or armoire to draw the eye upward.

♦ You're selling a lifestyle. Display expensive-looking coffee table books or magazines about upscale living. A side benefit here is that this reading material will hide scratches on the table, as well.

Seller Alert _____

It's very important not to overdo it with family photos while your house is on the market. An entire wall of snapshots distracts from a room. Use them to your advantage. Stick to black-and-white photos and display just one or two select shots. For an upscale look, frame them in silver or solid black. These not only look great, but blend well with any décor.

The Dining Room

Formal dining rooms are used less and less for everyday meals. When buyers stand in yours, they are actually visualizing themselves at a special family event or holiday gathering. Therefore, the dining room table is important for staging because its size affects how the buyer perceives the scale of the whole room.

For example, bigger isn't always better. An overly large table can really shrink the room. If your table has too many leaves in it, remove one. Do the same with chairs.

Also remove wall clutter such as hanging dishes, too many framed photos, and other adornments. Don't forget to remove the nails and picture hangers and touch up the holes. We see leftover nails in walls all the time, and it's a very unfinished and shabby look.

Sideboards and china cabinets can work nicely in a dining room as long as they are not too big, either. You should be able to walk the perimeter of the dining room table without having to turn sideways. If it's cramped, extra furniture should be removed and stored. In fact, fine china is one of the items that we recommend prepacking (as discussed in Chapter 19) so you can kill two birds with one stone.

We think that dining rooms are actually one of the easiest rooms to stage quickly. Mainly, the buyer's focus is on the size of the room and the table.

- ◆ **Hide the flaws and dress it up.** Drape an old or scratched dining room table with a crisp white or cream-colored cloth and place a beautiful centerpiece of silk or fresh flowers in the center. A runner can work almost as well if the flaws happen to be in the middle of the table.

- ◆ **Centerpieces on a budget.** Dining room tables need a focal point. If fresh or silk flowers are out of the question, substitute with something equally impressive, such as an heirloom silver or china soup terrine or a large bowl of vibrantly colored seasonal fruits or vegetables, fall gourds and nuts, or even glass holiday balls or Easter eggs.

- ◆ **Brighten and expand with paint.** Paint can actually make a room look larger than it really is. If your dining room is small, stay away from dark hues, which will make it appear even smaller. And, like clothes and accessories, paint colors go in and out of style. Choose modern, soothing, and neutral colors, as they will appeal to a wide portion of the buyer pool. Remember that just because the paint isn't chipped or peeling doesn't mean that it's not dated and tired looking. Repainting is one of the most dramatic improvements you can make to affect sale price. If you're on a budget, save money and do it yourself. By the way, sometimes walls just need a good washing. You'd be surprised how many wall stains can be removed with soap and water.

The Kitchen

The kitchen is the most expensive room in a home. Upgrades made to it are worth tens of thousands of dollars and, in some luxury homes, they are worth hundreds of thousands. Staging the kitchen well is imperative for getting top dollar on the sale.

Whether you have a state-of-the-art masterpiece or a circa 1972 special, our advice is the same. Take things away! If your kitchen is renovated, clutter distracts from your expensive upgrades. If it's old, clutter makes it seem even older.

Start by removing everything from the countertops, even your toaster. This makes the counters look bigger and the whole kitchen look sleeker. (If you cannot live without a particular appliance while your house is on the market, tuck it away in a corner.)

What to remove and hide (or store away):

- All countertop appliances.

- All sink paraphernalia, including sponges, pot scrubbers, steel wool, dish towels, and dishwashing liquid.

- Everything from the outside of the refrigerator, including magnets, schedules, artwork, photographs, and calendars.

- Some chairs from kitchen table (if the area is at all crowded).

- Mismatched bowls and vases displayed on top of cabinets. These give a cluttered look. Collections work when the items fall within one theme (for example, wooden bowls or baskets) and are few in number.

Now that you have cleared off the countertops, it's time to stage them with props. To create an upscale look, try something fun, like filling an oversized apothecary jar with fruit of any kind, such as oranges, Bosch pears, or limes. Or try to pair colors that you wouldn't normally put together, such as lemons in a cobalt blue bowl. We also love the look of vine-ripe tomatoes on a rustic yellow platter. Accessorize the rest of the countertop with a couple of beautiful hardcover cookbooks.

Another simple and inexpensive trick is to use mineral water in colored-glass bottles. You can find these in most grocery stores. They come in green, cobalt blue, and even ruby red. Group them on the countertop or line them up above cabinets. If you happen to own one, another way to prop a countertop is to display one brand-new state-of-the-art appliance, such as a stainless-steel cake mixer or sleek espresso machine.

These suggestions have a powerful effect because they accomplish much more than making the room look larger and more attractive. They make the room look more expensive—and that's what it's all about in the kitchen!

◆ Cabinet face-lift. One of our favorite ways to make old cabinets look like a million bucks is to replace the hardware with modern, whimsical handles and pulls. You can find expensive-looking and unique pieces in most major chain stores now. They come in hundreds of styles in wrought-iron, animal shapes, and even jeweled. Have fun with it. Then repaint chipped or peeling cabinets, and you've made a real transformation!

◆ Countertop tip. A fantastic way to freshen granite or stone counters and make them gleam is to apply a high-gloss sealer just before you put the house on the market.

◆ Hit the floors. Any type of kitchen flooring can be truly made over. For a dull linoleum or wood floor, apply a couple of coats of high-gloss polyurethane finish to make it shine. For a ceramic-tile floor, use grout cleaner to make it look like new again. For the tiles themselves, use the high-gloss sealer that you used on your granite counters to give them new luster.

◆ Sink or swim. Sinks are often the focal point of the kitchen. Some of them, even in newer kitchens, can quickly look old and dreary. An instant face-lift is to install a new faucet, which gives the illusion of a new sink. To further brighten and lift your sink, we love to replace the old, dirty, or mismatched accessories with perhaps one brand-new tea towel and one matching hand lotion and liquid soap set.

◆ Pantry perfect. Clean and organize the pantry. Remove anything you can to make it appear more spacious. To a buyer, a crowded and disorganized pantry sends a message that there is insufficient space, or worse, that it's dirty.

Trick of the Trade

Glass-front cabinets are pretty as long as the contents are orderly and not overstuffed. Remove some of the dishes to make it look as though the cabinets are roomy and spacious. Keep the dish colors to one palette for a clean look. Too many styles and colors look messy.

The Bathroom

As with the kitchen, updated bathrooms bring you big money when selling. Even if your bathroom is not renovated, there are things you can do to fool the eye and give a feeling of freshness.

For starters, cleanliness is more important in the bathroom than in almost any room in the house. Remove your toothbrushes, old soaps, toiletries, and any extraneous personal items. Sanitize everything and, if there is a window, let the light in. Fresh flowers in a little bud vase is a nice touch.

The bathroom may be where you'll have the most fun staging. It's not expensive, it's fast, and the tiniest little touch can make all the difference.

- ◆ Money is tight? Go white! One of the best and cheapest ways to make an old, tired bathroom look crisp and fresh (no matter what color it is) is to use stark white towels, a white shower curtain, and a white window valance. This brightens and gives a feeling of cleanliness.

- ◆ Eau de Money. Toiletries can be terrific props, but they must be new or like new, and should look expensive. Replace your everyday lotions, soap, and shampoos with upscale ones and tell the family "hands off!" to keep them looking new.

- ◆ Floor fix-up. If the floor is old, lay a stark white bath rug to cover up and deflect attention from it. It's also a nice anchor for the white towels, shower curtain, and window valance.

- ◆ Epoxy paint. This amazing product covers up a multitude of sins in your bathtub, including rust, chips, and discolorations. Apply it and save yourself from having to buy a new tub. Use with caution and in a well-ventilated bathroom.

- ◆ Reglazing. For a much more finished porcelain look than you'd get with epoxy paint, re-glazing wall tiles, tubs, and sinks is one of the most powerful things you can do for a bathroom without completely renovating it. The process is magical and will make these items sparkle.

- ◆ Grouting and recaulking. Taking the time to bleach and clean the grout between shower wall tiles and to recaulk the perimeter of the bathtub makes it look very clean. Conversely, a dirty bathtub sends buyers running for the door.

Seller Alert

We cannot stress enough that reglazing is not a do-it-yourself job! It involves the use of acids, urethanes, and full-face respirators. Let a professional do it for you.

◆ Replace fixtures. Toss out that rusty old faucet and gummy showerhead. New fixtures affect sale price because they give the illusion of having made upgrades. Replacing them doesn't break the bank, either. Note: we recommend using a licensed plumber to avoid chipping or damaging the fixtures, particularly with vintage sinks and tubs.

The Bedroom

In most bedrooms, the first place that your eye goes is to the bed. It sets the tone for the whole room. In fact, the bed is so important that it would be okay if it were the only piece of furniture in the room—provided that it's well styled.

This might seem obvious, but bed linens should always be clean, crisp, and wrinkle-free because they send a message about pride of ownership and the quality of the house. In particular, master bedrooms should be luxurious; children's rooms and nurseries are cute and fun; and guest rooms can be whimsical.

Of all the bedrooms, the master is the crowning glory and should be styled accordingly. Almost every house has a designated master bedroom. It's the first thing buyers look for in the sleeping area. If all the rooms are about the same size, then it falls to you to designate a master. Quite simply, you do this with the bed.

To turn the bed into one fit for a king, begin with a bed skirt. It is the foundation of the bed and is essential for a finished look. For the bedspread or duvet, go for quality and serene colors. When in doubt, white always works. Fold back layers to reveal pretty linens. Finally, to achieve and finish the look, you should have (or create the illusion of having) a headboard. If you don't have a headboard, use lots of pillows at the top. Use the wall to lean them on; pile high and forward on the bed.

 Trick of the Trade _____

Here's an insider's headboard trick. If you don't have enough pillows to create height and fullness, you can fake it with a bolster pillow. To make one, place two or three large bath or beach towels on top of one anther. Roll into a cylinder and tie on each end. Place it in back of your good pillows and no one will be the wiser.

As we mentioned, the master bedroom serves a particular purpose and should be styled to reflect the buyer's expectations for elegance and serenity. Children's rooms, nurseries, and guest bedrooms have a different set of guidelines, however. You can be much more creative and have fun with cute or whimsical props as long as the room is neat, clean, and, most importantly, uncluttered.

Here are some "fast fixes" for bedroom props that can make a big difference in each bedroom.

Master bedroom and guest rooms:

- Fresh or silk flowers in a neutral color

- Heirloom sterling or silver plate brush and comb

- Reading chair and lamp (if there is space)

- Mirrors to enlarge the room, reflect the bed, anchor a dresser

Children's rooms and nurseries:

- One of your child's drawings, framed (it's an instant and inexpensive piece of art)

- Large decorative baskets repurposed as toy containers

- Your three favorite stuffed animals (plush and in good shape), placed strategically around the room; lose the plastic multicolored toys

- Rocking chair; every good nursery needs one

Trick of the Trade _____

If you have a nice-looking throw blanket (nothing old, please!) in a rich material that is in the same color scheme as the rest of the room, use it at the foot of the bed or drape it casually on a nearby reading chair .

Closets

Remove and store away at least one third of the clothes and shoes in your closets and organize the remaining items in a military fashion and by color. This makes the closets look bigger. It's a pain in the neck, we grant you! But you're moving soon and will have to begin packing clothes anyway. Organized closets show an attention to detail that carries, in the buyer's mind, throughout the house.

Windows and the Importance of Light

This may surprise you, but window treatments and drapes are not a requirement for staging your home. In fact, we often recommend scrapping them altogether, particularly when the windows are beautiful or new. We have had them taken down in cases where they were blocking light or taking the focus away from the architecture. We find that sellers are sometimes concerned that the buyers will think the room is cold or less attractive without any window treatments. Remember, the house is the star; windows are the spotlight on the star. Letting the natural light into your home while it is on the market is critical. Light can create more beauty in a room than any staging idea. Let it in!

If you do use drapes, curtains, or shades, don't let them upstage your windows. If you decide to use them, make sure that they are open when the home is being shown. Next, make sure that they are not cutting into the window frame too much or blocking light even when they are open. Simplicity in style and patterns is the way to go. Hues should be soothing and understated, not busy and loud or overdone. Panels in neutral tones are very effective. Sheers can be lovely, too, if they are modern. A simple white eyelet valance can be perfect in a bathroom or kitchen. They also make gorgeous shades these days that look expensive and let light filter through them. Shades soften the edges but still allow buyers to see the moldings.

 Trick of the Trade _____

Views matter. In fact, the view from every single window in the house should be evaluated. If you're looking out of a second- or third-floor window and see a couple of missing roof shingles, replace them. If the house next door is really close to your dining room window, lower the blinds on that particular window while the house is being shown to buyers. If you can see a rusted old shed from the children's bedroom, move the shed or paint it.

If you have any money to spend, we strongly suggest that you invest in a professional to wash your windows. It's hard to make windows completely streak-free, especially when the sun is shining through them. Professionally cleaned windows are super powerful when a home is on the market. They make old windows look newer, they bring the sunlight in, and they even make a room look bigger. Conversely, a room with cloudy or dirty windows, and without enough light, looks depressing and smaller than it really is.

Basements, Attics, and Garages

If you can, buy plenty of large plastic bins and store as many items in them as possible in the basement, attic, or garage. Line up the bins in neat rows. Buyers need to be able to see the floor, walls, and four corners of the space in order to visualize how they will use it. If these areas are filled with disorganized debris, potential buyers get over-whelmed and simply *cannot* visualize the use of the space.

Seller Alert _____

Grab your flashlight and walk your attic, basement, and garage. Dispose of cob-webs, dead insects, little pieces of glass, and ant or mouse traps. Enough said?

The Exterior and Curb Appeal

Most people think of staging as something you do only to the inside of a home. Actually, staging begins on the outside—with what is known as *curb appeal.*

def•i•ni•tion _____

Curb appeal is a real estate term that has become very popular. It's all about how your home looks from the street, or curb.

Buyers will make an instant judgment about your home the minute they pull up to the curb. Think of selling your house like you're interviewing for an important job. The minute you walk into the boss's office, he has already made some judgment about whether he's going to hire you. It is made before you speak or even shake his hand and it's based strictly on the way you look. It's the same for a house and a potential buyer looking at it from the street.

Shaping Up the Lawn and Garden

Decluttering is not just for the interior of your home. Like the inside, the outside of the structure should be the star when looking at the home from the curb. If your lawn has objects on it that are not necessarily found in nature, re-think them! They can seriously distract the buyer from a clear and positive vision of your home.

The following are some ideas to improve your curb appeal:

◆ Move or put away extraneous items that are visible from the street, such as water hoses, lawn art, garbage cans, children's outdoor toys, and bicycles.

- Dispose of the cracked or unused planters strewn about. Remove leaves and debris from around shrubs; trim and edge the beds.

- Lay fresh mulch around shrubs, trees, and plant beds.

Trick of the Trade _____

Like porridge that is too hot or too cold, you want to use the shade of mulch that is just right for your house. Red mulch can clash with brick or red-toned homes. You may find that black mulch is too dark and intense. Light-brown mulch may not be quite vibrant enough. Dark chocolate brown is our favorite because it is rich in color and suits most houses. Look for brands that claim to not fade quickly.

- If the lawn's faded, sparse, or dead, allow two to three weeks for new grass seed to grow before putting the house on the market.

- If the driveway is faded, our favorite fix is a sealant made to coat blacktop surfaces. You can apply it with a long-handled paint roller; also available is a combination squeegee/broom made specifically for this purpose.

- Paint, clean, and adjust shutters and gutters so they hang straight.

If you suspect that your curb appeal needs more charm (or lacks it altogether), these are some of our favorite "fast fixes," which will enhance your home's charm from the street:

Seller Alert _____

Don't cut it too close on the mulch. New mulch will have a pungent odor for a few days and may also attract bees. Try to mulch at least three or four days before showtime.

- Install flower boxes on second-floor windows with colorful flowers and/or hanging ivy. (On the right house, this is an amazing transformation in itself.)

- Create a circle of large rocks around the perimeter of a prominent tree about 3 feet out from the trunk and fill in with mulch. This really helps define the property and draws attention to a pretty tree.

- Affix a wall adornment to the exterior in order to compensate for a lack of architectural charm. Two examples are a wrought-iron swirl or an eagle in flight. These work well on garages, as well.

- Add a weather vane to the roof (this works only on certain kinds of colonials).

◆ Consider new shutters and mailbox to sharpen the overall look. You'd be surprised how a tired mailbox can drag your curb appeal down.

◆ Polish brass door knockers and doorbells. If you've got brass, make the most of it!

Decks, Porches, and Patios

Decks, porches, and patios add tremendous value to your home and create a great space in which to entertain or escape to with the Sunday papers. They are especially powerful when interior living space is small, or if you live in a warm climate where these spaces are used year-round. When staged well, and visible from the indoors, they can make a home seem as though it has more square footage than it really has. A small living room or kitchen will appear bigger if the eye is guided to the outdoor space. To do this, place an object of color and beauty outside that will draw attention from the inside. It could be a statue or an urn filled with vibrant annuals, a water treatment, birdbath, or lovely piece of outdoor furniture.

Trick of the Trade _____

Make your patio pop! Fresh new cushions on the chairs and chaise lounges do wonders for brightening the overall look of a patio. If you can't buy new ones, give your old ones a good washing.

Decks, porches, and patios should be staged as outdoor rooms. To do this, give them a beginning, middle, and an end. Rooms have borders. They have walls, a floor, and a ceiling. Outdoor spaces can have them, too.

Let's begin with open porches and patios:

◆ **Walls:** Place large and colorful planters in the corners of the patio. Flower boxes or benches also work well. These are your walls and give a sense of parameter.

◆ **Floors:** Most deck or patio floors will be made of wood, concrete, pavers, or bluestone. If they're not in good condition, paint, stain, repair, or refinish them. The patio and deck are structural elements in a home. If they have been neglected, buyers perceive them as expensive repairs.

◆ **Ceiling:** Unless you have an umbrella, gazebo, arbor, or awning in new condition, the sky is the best ceiling you can have. If these items are faded, rusted, torn, or dated, it's better not to use them.

◆ **Furniture:** Clean, hose down, or paint the furniture. It should be arranged in the same fashion as a living room or family room—that is, to encourage conversation or to accommodate a group gathering. But again, don't make the mistake of having too much furniture. It'll make the patio seem small.

Here are tips for enclosed porches:

◆ **Walls:** Enclosed porches already have walls and ceilings. If it's screened in, make sure the screens are in great shape. If they are ripped, sagging, or faded, and you cannot afford to replace them, it is sometimes better to take them down altogether to create an open-air porch. But open-air porches need borders, too. As with patios, use large planters, benches, or chairs.

◆ **Floors:** If you have bluestone, ceramic tile, or good hardwood floors, don't cover them up. These are high-end materials and translate to more money on the sale … if they show well. Like decks, if the floor materials do not show well, it's worth it to repair, paint, or stain them. Another reason not to cover porch floors is because they can be a red flag to buyers. When they cannot see what's underneath, they tend to assume that you're hiding a damaged or cheap floor.

◆ **Ceilings:** If, and only if, you have a large porch with reasonably high ceilings, do not hang things from it. Stick to a nice light fixture and a fresh coat of paint. Hanging items from a ceiling lower than 8 feet is encroaching and claustrophobic.

◆ **Furniture:** Because furniture on a covered porch is not exposed to the elements, you can scavenge pieces from all over your house. Don't skip the basement and attic! Some examples are rocking chairs, area rugs, and end tables. If the porch is big enough, create more than one seating area to make the space more usable and inviting. Wicker, wood, or wrought-iron are usually the best styles to work with. If you have electricity on the porch, adding a lamp and side table is another great way to give the illusion of a usable and cozy outdoor room.

Trick of the Trade _____

Go with great greenery! We cannot emphasize enough the power of lush green plants or flowers. In any space, greenery gives a feeling of life and positive energy. Plants for patios are even easier as they require less maintenance, if you live in a region that gets rain.

For some reason, porches are an area of the home where people tend to go crazy with decorating. Too many knickknacks, fishing nets, and signs pointing to the beach are a no-no! Let your porch shine through. As with kitchens, less is always more.

If you have a good-size porch with high ceilings, here are some fast-fix ideas that we love. Following are items to hang from a porch ceiling:

- Planters with cascading ivy or flowers

- Hurricane lanterns

- Small chandeliers or chandelier candles

- Bamboo, cane, or tropical-style fans

- Wind chimes

- Bird cage

Vacant Homes

Empty homes reveal every little flaw. They can also look cold. A few strategically placed pieces of furniture can mask cracks in the walls, uneven paint jobs, and stains on the floor. Even newly constructed or flawlessly renovated homes show better with a few select props in them.

Very often, it's just one piece that makes the difference in an unfurnished room. A tasteful area rug can make an empty room look homey. A bare corner can be warmed up with a large floor plant. The size and scale of an empty family room can be better understood with an armchair or sofa in it. These props give the buyer a suggestion of what it will look like with their own belongings, without having to fully furnish.

Professional Stagers for Hire

There are a lot of professional stagers out there, and they charge anywhere from a couple of hundred to thousands of dollars.

After reading this chapter, we hope you have learned that you do not need to spend that kind of money to stage your home well. You can do a beautiful job yourself if you employ the ideas we have shared with you. That said, if money is not a consideration and you would like someone else to do the work for you, there are professionals out there.

To find them, you can use the Internet (use the search term "real estate stagers" or "home stagers," along with the name of your town and state) and you'll get a list of contacts. There are national associations for home stagers, as well. You can also ask local Realtors, who are used to referring stagers to their clients.

 Seller Alert

Be sure to ask professional stagers to define what and how much they will do in each room. Ask for before-and-after photos of their work and check their track record through testimonials from past clients.

The Least You Need to Know

- Don't confuse decorating for everyday living with staging to sell your house.

- Less is more. Most homes have too much furniture, too many knickknacks, and too much clutter. Remember that the house is the star. You want the structure and architectural beauty to come through.

- Let there be light; don't block it. Pull shades up and drapes back. Being able to see the outdoors from the inside makes a home appear larger and happier.

- Attics, garages, and basements need to be clean and organized. You're moving soon anyway. Stack it, store it, or get rid of it.

- Make your home seem larger by creating outdoor rooms. Stage them as usable spaces for solitude as well as entertaining.

- Curb appeal is very important. Brush up the landscaping and consider adding a window flower box or new shutters.

Part 2

It's Showtime: When Your Home Is on the Market

Part 1 of this book covers everything that you need to do before you put your home on the market; Part 2 shows you how to actually do it. You have come a long way to get to this point when you are ready to introduce your house to the market. This part addresses all the things that you must do and what you can expect to happen while your house is "out there."

Our goal is not only to make sure that your home sells in any market and at any time, but to make sure that you get top dollar, too. When your home comes on the market, you create an entire package that directly affects how much money you will make when it sells. This package includes how well you describe it and photograph it for the MLS's, how well it's physically presented, how well you manage showings (targeting the right buyers), and what you can do to enhance the value of your home.

Putting Your Home on the Market

In This Chapter

- ◆ How to write a description of your home
- ◆ How to photograph your home
- ◆ Brochures and handouts for buyers
- ◆ The two kinds of open houses
- ◆ Advertisements

The act of putting your home on the market involves a series of steps. To begin with, your Realtor, with your input, will write a description of your home for the MLS and possibly for ads, will have your home photographed, and will probably create brochures or flyers. A lawn sign will go up. There also may be disclosure forms to fill out for buyers. And the guidelines for showings and open houses must be established.

Some sellers make the assumption that their Realtor will take charge and do everything, sort of like going to see the doctor. This is a mistake. Any physician will tell you that his most successful outcomes are among those patients who were most actively involved and invested in their own care. Get involved and become a team with your Realtor. We have seen firsthand that sellers who are truly invested in the process of selling their home actually get more money in the sale. Those who are not get less.

The steps in this chapter are simple, but they are not easy. They are simple in that they appear to be a checklist or a to-do list. However, they can be done poorly and incorrectly. If mistakes are made at this stage, it can affect your ability to sell the home. Buyers, and even Realtors, are reviewing dozens and sometimes hundreds of listings. If they are not enticed, they will pass right over yours if it's poorly photographed or inadequately described.

How to Describe Your Home

The way that you describe your home in writing is of the utmost importance. The description will have a powerful influence over whether or not a buyer wants to make an appointment to see the house. The written description is one of the first things that buyers look at on a new listing.

The first five things buyers look at on a listing are the following:

◆ Price

◆ Address

◆ Exterior photograph

◆ Written description

◆ Interior photographs

Writing is not easy. When you, or your Realtor, struggle to find the right words to put in the listing or advertisement, begin by evaluating the big three: size, condition, and location. Which one is your home's strongest selling point? You may have all three—a really big home in spectacular condition and in a much sought-after neighborhood. If so, say that right away, in the first sentence, and you'll have their attention. Get to the other features and details in the second, third, and fourth sentences.

However, many sellers have only one or two of these selling points. You might have a home in a great location and in wonderful condition, but it's not large. That's still good. In fact, it's excellent. As Realtors, we place a huge premium on location because it's the one thing that a homeowner cannot change. You can improve the condition and enlarge the home with additions. However, the address is the address. You've heard the phrase, "When it comes to real estate, it's all about location, location, location." It's true.

Seller Alert

Buyers don't always view properties for the purpose of making an appointment, but rather to justify to themselves why they don't really need to. They are busy and they don't want to go see yet another home that's not for them. If there is a specific trait of your home that is not what they want, they may dismiss the idea of seeing it at all for that reason alone. Make the writing powerful enough to entice them but keep it general. Use writing to pique their interest, drive them to schedule a showing, and let them take in the details (and fall in love with it) in person.

Location

In describing the location, if it's a good one, simply tell the reader why it's good. If it is within walking distance to something locally important, such as a shopping village, major transportation, a park, or the beach, say that. If there is a view of a lake, mountain, or city skyline, say that, too. Buyers will not always take, at face value, a statement such as, "Great home in great location." You need to spell it out for them. If you live near a major town or city to which many homeowners commute for work and your home is close to transportation, it will be worth a great deal of money and should be emphasized.

Size

If your home is small, then less is more when writing your description: say as little as possible about it. In some parts of the country, it is common practice for Realtors to provide, in a listing, the total square footage of the home, as well as the dimensions of each room. In other areas, it is not provided. Giving a buyer an exact number of square feet before she has actually seen the home might be a deterrent to scheduling a showing. She might feel that she needs 3,000 square feet and won't consider your home with only 2,700. However, if she had visited your home, she might not care about the missing 300 square feet when she sees your magnificent deck overlooking the valley. Unless your home is quite large or you have rooms with large dimensions, think twice about including the specific size, unless it's routine and expected by buyers in your region.

There are, however, ways to describe a small home in a flattering manner. Focus on attributes other than size in the listing. A sample sentence is: "The main floor plan has wonderful circular flow for entertaining." Be careful how you use words such as "charming," which are often code for "small" or "tiny."

Condition

Condition is our favorite element of a home to write about because most sellers have at least one area that is new, has been upgraded, or is in very good shape. There's much to say about condition, and you have more latitude in this area than you do with size and location. You can almost always find something nice to say and you can be very creative.

If you have made major upgrades such as a new kitchen or renovated baths, it should always be mentioned in a listing description. These are among some of the most expensive upgrades that a homeowner can make. You might even be able to use phrases like "state of the art," depending on how advanced the materials and appliances are.

 Seller Alert

> Be careful when describing the age or condition of appliances or systems in your home. If you label something as "brand new," make sure that it's accurate. The buyer will often ask the seller to provide the warranty. When the warranty is produced, the buyer may learn that it has expired and in fact the appliance is not brand new. This can cause problems with the deal because the buyer feels that he was misled. This also happens with other big-ticket items such as the roofs, furnaces, and central air-conditioning systems.

If you have absolutely nothing in your home that is new, renovated, or updated, there are still many ways to describe it so that it sounds attractive and valuable. Assuming that it is clean and tidy, use words such as "impeccably maintained" or "open and sunny floor plan." Go out of your way to mention structural features such as high ceilings; expensive crown, base, raised panel, and dentil moldings; coffered ceilings; original hardwood floors; built-in bookcases; leaded-glass windows; skylights; a fireplace; a breezeway between the kitchen and garage; covered or screened-in porches; decorative staircases; a sunken living room; and more.

These are valuable to buyers in a different way than renovated kitchens and baths are. Anybody can install a new state-of-the-art kitchen, but it's hard and expensive to re-create original architectural elements from the early 1900s. Your home might be old, but to some buyers it can be a better purchase than an updated home without valuable architectural elements.

Photographing Your Home

A picture is worth a thousand words, so you want to get it right. Photography is perhaps the most mismanaged part of the administrative process of putting a home on the market. Bad photographs of homes are all over the Internet. It's a shame to have a home handicapped on the Internet with pictures that don't show or even take away from its true beauty. Bad photographs prevent buyers from coming to see your home, and you cannot afford to lose even one buyer, because she might be the one who purchases it.

You and your Realtor have three options: to hire a professional real estate photographer to take pictures of your home, have the Realtor take them, or take them yourself. We use only professional real estate photographers. We hire them and pay them ourselves. They are not nearly as expensive as you might think, and Realtors know where to find talented and affordable ones. If this is not an option, we share some great tricks of the trade to taking your own good photographs.

The Purpose and Importance of Good Photographs

Like writing, taking good photos is very hard. Most people think of themselves as pretty good photographers. Manufacturers have made digital cameras so easy to use that even small children take pictures now. When it comes to your family vacation, you're probably going to take some terrific shots. When it comes to packaging and selling your home, don't count on it. There are much higher standards in photographing your home as opposed to your family vacation.

The main purpose of real estate photographs is to entice buyers *just enough* to schedule a private showing. The goal is simply for them to want to see more. The goal is not to provide a photo album of every room in the house. Too many sellers, and even Realtors, feel that a listing should be crammed with as many photos as possible. There's nothing wrong with a lot of pictures; the buyers love them. However, use photos only if they are "good" photos. If they are not, provide just three or four great ones—the buyers will want to see more and will schedule a showing.

On the other hand, if you have 10 poorly shot photographs, the buyer may not make the appointment. First, he has seen almost the entire home online. There is less of a need to go see it in person. Second, if the photos were not flattering, he won't like it enough to come see it anyway. Either way, you've lost the buyer without ever having met him, all because of the way the home was photographed.

Begin with these two steps:

1. **Select the features to be photographed:** You've already taken some time with the word description to decide what the best and most appealing features are in your home. Determine which among them will make the best photographs; not all of them will. For example, updated bathrooms are a great feature to describe with words but are often a bad idea to shoot because they don't photograph all that well—even the really big ones. Additionally, there is usually a limit to how many photographs you can use in the MLS, and there are other bigger and/or main rooms that buyers want to see.

2. **Preangle:** Don't pick up the camera just yet. Move all around each room that you plan to shoot. Look, with the naked eye, for the best angles. If your living room is rectangular, for example, you want to shoot it in a way that emphasizes the length or the longest dimension. You don't need a camera to figure this out. Do this even if you are hiring a professional real estate photographer. She may shoot more than one angle in order to provide you with more choices and leave the selection process up to you and your Realtor. It will be much easier on you if you take the time to plan and compose your shots in advance.

Biggest Photography Mistakes and How to Avoid Them

Mistakes are very easy to make. That's why there are so many bad photographs online. Here are some of the most common mistakes—and ways to avoid them.

◆ **The angle is too narrow.** In this type of photo, all you see in the frame is a corner or a piece of a room. It is impossible to get an idea of the size of the room or what it's used for. When you preangle the photographs, as described previously, choose what you want to have inside the frame from all four sides—the right, left, top, and bottom. For example, if you and your Realtor have concluded that the two best features in your living room are the fireplace and the French doors, then from what angle can you be sure to capture them both?

◆ **The angle is unflattering.** This is when the room, or the exterior of the home, is photographed in a way that makes it look very small, cluttered, or distorted. Sometimes the exterior photo makes the home appear to be right on top of a neighbor's, or the kitchen is shot with a low hanging hood in the way, a staircase is distorted and looks way too skinny, or the dining room chandelier blocks the view into the entry hall. The solution, again, is as we mentioned previously: choose and preplan your angles.

Seller Alert _____

Take care to check your camera settings before you begin. You'd be surprised how easy it is to find that you did not have the lens set on "wide angle" or that you mistakenly left it in zoom mode, both of which make it impossible to capture a large portion of the room.

◆ **The frame is filled with furniture.** This is so common. There are thousands of photos out there of couches with captions that read "Living Room" or of beds with a caption that reads "Master Bedroom." Remember, it's the structure and the architecture that are the stars of the show, not your furniture.

◆ **The photo is too dark.** This is also common. It is hard to light a large area evenly. Most digital flashes light only to about 8 to 10 feet. If you are shooting a big room, part of it may be dark and part of it light. Try turning the flash off altogether, turning on every light in the room, raising the shades, and pulling back the drapes. An outdoor photo of a home might turn out too dark when it is taken "into" the sun. The sun should always be behind you and the photo taken at a time of day when the sun's bathing the front of the home in light. Likewise, when shooting interiors, try to shoot the rooms at different times of day to find the most light. When you do, shoot with the source of the light behind you.

Trick of the Trade _____

Your computer may come with a photography software program already installed in it. When you view photographs, it provides simple ways to make them better by enhancing the color, light, and contrast. Often, it's done with one keystroke on an icon that might be labeled "enhancements" or "sharpen." These improvements can make a big difference. There will also be other, more sophisticated ways to manipulate the photos for the more advanced user. If you play around with it, you can teach yourself pretty easily.

Brochures and Handouts

There are several choices available to you for creating attractive and informative materials that buyers can pick up while they are inside your home, and take with them when they leave. They are usually provided by and paid for by your Realtor and have different names including listing sheets, feature sheets, highlight sheets, home brochures, property flyers, and property profiles. Each presents written and photographic descriptions of your home and its various rooms and features. They also sometimes include information about your community.

Types of handouts include:

◆ **Multipage or folding brochure:** This is the most expensive type of handout to produce because of its sheer size, number of photos, and paper quality, or paper stock. The paper usually has a glossy finish and is much heavier than regular paper. They are often four pages long and usually done with a full-color (also known as four-color) printing process that allows a very wide range of color in the photos. The Realtor's agency logo, name, photo, and contact information will also appear on either the front or back of the brochure.

◆ **One-page flyer:** This type of flyer is often just a smaller version of the multipage brochure. It can be one-sided or two-sided. We recommend using both sides. It is very difficult to provide more than one or two photographs when using a one-sided flyer.

◆ **The MLS listing sheet:** This is a simple printout of your listing from the Realtor's regional Multiple Listing Service (MLS). A buyer will already have received this from his own Realtor days earlier, but he may have forgotten to bring it with him to your home. It's nice for him to have it in hand while walking through so he can reference facts like total number of rooms, the property taxes, condo maintenance fees, and so on.

◆ **Upgrades or features sheet:** We strongly urge you to create one of these if you have made steady improvements to your home over time. Many of them cannot readily be seen by the buyer. It will drive home the message about how much money you have spent and point out the areas of architectural value. Present this list, or sheet, and it will enhance the perception of value when you need it most, when the buyer is in your home. There is rarely enough room on an MLS listing sheet to highlight every single special amenity such as custom cabinetry; upgraded kitchen appliances; architectural features like original fireplaces, moldings, and leaded-glass bookcases; and systems such as radiant heat, multizone central air, new furnace, updated electric, hardwired sound and security systems, and more.

◆ **Community services information:** Information about your community—such as schools, day care, public swimming pools, tennis courts, festivals and fairs, transportation, hospitals, and anything else that makes it attractive to newcomers—is a very good idea to display. Best of all, flyers and brochures describing them are often free and can be picked up from the school district board of education, town or city hall, and train or bus stations. Some towns create community resource booklets with contact information for everything from the fire department to the local veterinarian's office. As we've said before, you cannot rely on the buyer's Realtor to have given the buyer as much information as you'd like about your home or your community.

Lawn Signs

About the same time that your home goes into the MLS, the Realtor will have a for-sale sign installed on your front lawn. There are a couple of things to keep in mind about signs. Some of them have a large post that requires digging a significant-size hole in your front lawn. This is not an issue while your home is on the market. But when it sells and the sign comes out, you could have a large dead patch in your lawn. Some agencies use very similar signs but they have a narrow spike at the bottom where the sign goes into the earth. No damage is done to your lawn. If the agency you are working with does not have these kinds of signs, then plan to reseed or resod. Ask the agency, in advance, to pay for that when the sign comes out.

Seller Alert

Sometimes sellers forget to remind their children that the home is going on the market on a certain day. When they come home from school and see the sign, they can be taken by surprise and get emotional. Take care to give them a gentle reminder on the day it will go up—and make sure your Realtor reminds you, as well.

Seller's Disclosures

A seller's disclosure form is required in some states and optional in others. It is a standard multipage form that the seller fills out when the home goes on the market, and is made available to buyers who express an interest in the property. It covers just about everything relating to your home including its age; structural issues; systems like plumbing and electric, the foundation, roof, attic, and basement; significant renovations; pests and environmental concerns like leaks and water damage, and the presence of lead, radon, asbestos, and mold; and the presence of underground storage tanks like oil and septic. The seller reveals everything she knows about these issues in writing and signs the form.

Even in states where the seller's disclosure form is not required, but only optional, we recommend that you provide one. You will be much better off if you disclose defects or problems right up front. In most cases, an inspection will reveal them to the buyer anyway and he then might question your reasons for withholding the information.

Secondly, when a buyer has all the facts before he makes an offer, then his price will reflect his awareness of the problems. Therefore, the deal is less likely to fall apart because the buyer went into it with his eyes open.

Choosing the Date to Introduce Your Home

Let's begin with the month you choose to bring your home on the market. Ask your Realtor when the peak selling season is in your area. For much of the United States, it takes place between January and June and is commonly referred to as "the spring market." Don't get us wrong—homes sell every day of the year, even on holidays. But if you are thinking of selling, choose a month that coincides with the most activity. For example, in the Northeast, particularly in and around New York City, there are hundreds of thousands of Wall Street employees who received bonuses right after New Year's. This adds to the flurry of business done between late January and June. Additionally, it's a region with seasons. Sellers often like to market their homes when their lawns are green and their gardens are in full bloom.

After you choose the month, you'll pinpoint the week and day. The week will depend partly on coordinating your schedule with your Realtor's, but also on planning around holiday weekends, of which there may be many. Again, we have sold homes on holidays before but there is no need to aim for one when marketing your home. If there is a chance that buyers will be out of town for a holiday weekend, why risk it?

The day that you introduce it should be dictated by what the common practice is in your area. Some communities have an unwritten agreement among Realtors that all new homes for sale are introduced on Wednesdays. In our community, it is Friday. Go with the flow and follow the Realtor's lead because more of her colleagues will see it. If there is no standard day, then we recommend choosing one that is not too close to the weekend—no later than Wednesday—so that Realtors have a chance to preview it for their buyers before the first weekend that it is on the market.

Entering Your Home on the Multiple Listing Service

Your home is officially "on the market" when you have signed a listing agreement and have it entered onto the Realtor's MLS. At that moment, all of the Realtors in the region will see it and notify clients who may have an interest.

But we do not recommend allowing showings to take place immediately. We recommend delaying the beginning of showings for a few days, for two reasons. The first is so that the best buyers will have a chance to hear about it from their Realtors and schedule an appointment for when it does become available for showings. Secondly, the delay builds a buzz of excitement about your home among the buyer pool. This can be a very effective tactic.

In Chapter 9, we use the analogy of a new film release. Movie studios tease audiences with coming attractions and clips. They understand that the film will have its highest box office receipts in the first weekend, so they maximize that by creating advance buzz. The same theory applies to a new home on the market. It works.

Seller Alert

Ask your Realtor about the rules and regulations of his local MLS, as some of them require that a home be available for showings as soon as it is entered on the MLS.

The Realtor Open House

In many areas, a Realtor open house is held on the first day that a home comes on the market—before buyers have seen it. The purpose is to allow the Realtors to preview it and establish if it's right for any of their clients. If it is, then they want to become familiar with all its features to be prepared when they show it that weekend.

Realtor open houses are a seller's best friend. Have one. The Realtors who come to see it are there because they are working with (and directly represent) ready, willing, and able buyers. This one event is often what puts the wheels in motion for a home sale. As they walk through, they are thinking about which clients might have an interest in it. There might be hundreds of homes on the market in your area. To get Realtors physically inside your home, and actively preview it, is the first step in actually getting it sold.

Realtor open houses usually last a couple of hours, take place on a weekday, and are not open to the public. Your listing Realtor will host it. As the other Realtors come through, they seize the opportunity to ask the listing Realtor questions about the home. After the Realtor's open house has concluded, showings to buyers may begin immediately.

Running Ads

As we'll say over and over in this book, advertising will not sell your home because it's designed to attract buyers who are not yet ready to buy. The ones who are ready to buy don't shop the ads because they already know about your home. The listing was sent to them directly from their Realtor, days or weeks ago. But buyers who are still window-shopping and researching do shop the ads because they are not yet working with a Realtor. Newspapers, open houses, and the Internet are the only ways in which they can begin the education process—emphasis on the word "begin." Of course, there is the occasional exception to the rule, but it is rare.

The Real Reason Agencies Run Ads

The reason that real estate agencies run advertisements is to make the phone ring at the agency. They need to have a steady stream of new business. And they will get it. But people who call in on ads are just beginning their home search and still in the research or information-gathering stage. Someone at the agency answers the phone and makes a connection with the caller. The caller will likely begin working with that Realtor, or another one somewhere else, and start his education in home buying. He is on his way to home ownership but he is not buying your particular home.

Many sellers still want the ads, just in case. And Realtors are happy to oblige because the ads raise their profile in the community; it's sort of a brand-awareness campaign. So let's assume that you will run an ad because you've established that it is in your Realtor's budget anyway, and it certainly can't hurt.

An Advertising Plan

The first step in any advertising effort is to determine how much money is in the budget. Next, how will it be spent? If you read and followed the steps in Chapter 3, you will already have had a conversation with your Realtor about how much money there is for ads, and how often and where they will be placed.

If you do have an advertising budget, and plan to run ads, the first round should be run the week that your home comes on the market.

Ads typically include the following:

- A photograph of the front exterior of the home

- The price

- The town or city

- A brief description of the property

- Contact information for the Realtor or agency

- A time and date for a public open house, if there is one

- Federal fair housing logos, which are required by law

Trick of the Trade

Your home may be advertised quite a bit over time. Space ads out and coordinate them with strategic price reductions. Your goal is to try to recreate demand with a new price, which thereby infuses new energy for your listing. When advertising real estate, the most effective approach is to advertise only when you have something new to say. Otherwise you're just reminding the buyer pool that your home is not selling and reinforcing a perception that it's stale and something is wrong with it.

The Public Open House

We feel the same way about *public open houses* that we do about advertising—that they do not sell your home. This is because they do not attract real buyers. Real buyers will see the home privately with a licensed Realtor. They have no need to see it among throngs of people when they have a representative who can give them access to a full, guided, and private tour.

Further evidence that people who attend public open houses are not real buyers is that they almost never want to speak to the listing Realtor. Attendees often barely acknowledge the Realtor and would prefer not to even make eye contact with her, if possible. They want to see the home and be left alone. The reason for this is very simple: they have no intention of buying the home. If they did, they'd be seeing it privately. In Chapter 9, we discuss in detail all the different types of buyers and how understanding them is the key to marketing your home.

So who does attend public open houses besides buyers who are not quite yet ready to buy? The two other types of people include:

def•i•ni•tion _____

A **public open house** is typically hosted by the listing Realtor in a two- or three-hour window of time when anyone can come through and view the home. They are advertised in advance on the Internet and in newspapers.

- **Nosy neighbors.** We use the word "nosy" in the kindest possible way. Some of your neighbors just want a good peek at your home. Others may be thinking of selling their own homes and want to compare yours to theirs.

- **People seeking entertainment.** Some people attend public open houses for fun. They enjoy looking at homes and appreciate architecture and interior decorating, so it's a great day of entertainment for them.

The Least You Need to Know

- When writing a word description of your home, begin with the big three: size, condition, and location.

- The purpose of photographing your home is not to provide a photo album of every single room, but rather to provide a few carefully selected and outstanding shots in order to entice buyers to schedule private showings.

- Brochures and handouts for buyers are a great way to communicate every upgrade and feature of the home.

- Your home is officially "on the market" when it has been entered into the MLS and you are allowing buyers to come through.

- Having an open house for Realtors only is one of the most powerful things you can do when introducing your home to the marketplace.

- On the other hand, having an open house for the public will not do much to help sell your home because it will not attract real buyers.

Chapter 8

How Your Home Gets Shown

In This Chapter

- ◆ How buyers will get inside your home
- ◆ What to do right before a showing
- ◆ Emphasizing the features during a showing
- ◆ The do's and don'ts of showings

Everything you have done up to this point has been in the pursuit of one goal—to get showings. Your home won't sell without them. You have prepared your home by staging it and making repairs. You have exposed it to as wide a buyer audience as possible. Now is the moment of truth. If you have done everything well, the buyers will come. They will stand in your home and they will fall in love, or they won't. However, do not make the mistake of thinking that your job is finished.

Buyers can be very fickle. At the point that your home is shown, buyers have not yet committed to it in any way. In fact, they have virtually nothing invested in you or the property. If there are problems related to showings and the home is not easily accessible, it can frustrate buyers and you can lose them before they even walk through your front door.

It's very important to understand the process of showings and how to manage and control them to maximize the buyer's experience. The vibe that you create, and the experience that the buyer has, will have a direct impact on the decision to buy it—or not. This decision if often made in the midst of a showing.

In this chapter, we discuss the different ways that buyers have access to your home and how you can make the most of the showings.

Showing Guidelines

This chapter focuses on the most common methods of showing. The golden rule—above all else—is to make the scheduling of appointments, and access to your home, as easy as possible. This isn't quite as simple as it sounds, however. If you don't have clear instructions and guidelines, there will be miscommunication and problems for the buyers. When they confront challenges and obstacles with regard to viewing your home, they can get turned off. Some buyers are more flexible and easygoing than others, but you don't want to take the chance that any buyer would let the inconvenience deter him from considering your property.

The following are some examples of problems related to showings:

- Limited showing hours that prevent buyers from getting in when they need to or when it's convenient for them.

- Difficulty obtaining a key or physical access to the home.

- Confusion about whom to call to schedule appointments.

- Leaving an unleashed dog in the home during a showing.

- Locks that are extremely difficult or impossible to operate.

- Inability to see certain locked rooms, storage areas, or garages.

- When the seller is home during the showing and/or attempts to conduct the showing.

Scheduling Appointments

The process begins with a telephone call from the buyer's Realtor requesting an appointment for a showing. It is up to you and your Realtor to decide up front who the contact person will be. You usually have two choices—your listing Realtor or yourself.

When your Realtor fields all the calls, she must then take the step of calling you for every appointment to see if the time slot is convenient for you. The upside of this arrangement is that you only have to speak to one person—your Realtor. The downside is that it creates an extra and unnecessary step, which causes delays for everyone.

If you are the contact person, there is no middle man. Realtors will have access to your name and telephone number and call you directly. It's faster and more efficient. You are the homeowner and no one knows better than you what the most convenient time is to show the home.

You and your Realtor will establish the hours during which buyers can see your home. We recommend allowing showings seven days a week, including evenings, because the goal is to make your home accessible to all the buyers and their schedules. When a Realtor asks to show your home, say yes, whenever possible. You will benefit from creating easy access. If the time does not work for you, reschedule a better time right there on the phone. Don't let the Realtor hang up without making the appointment—he may not call back.

In the first few days that your home is on the market, particularly that very first weekend, we encourage you to try to be out of the home entirely for most of the day(s). Showings can be very plentiful, creating a "revolving door" feel at the home. And that's a good thing! Many of our sellers go out of town for the first weekend. This way they do not have to worry about keeping the home clean and beds made, and being out before the first showing of the day. If this is an option for you, take it. It's a great excuse to get away for a minibreak—especially after all your hard work and preparation.

How Buyers Get Inside Your Home

There are several different ways that buyers will gain entry to your home, and it varies depending on how real estate is practiced in your area.

After the appointment has been set up, the next matter is how they will get inside. There may be a *lockbox* installed on your front door, or perhaps the buyer's Realtor will need to pick up the key from your listing Realtor's office. In some cases, the listing Realtor shows the property.

Let's consider each way.

def•i•ni•tion

A **lockbox** is a small, heavy box with a handle on it that can be attached onto to your front door handle, gate, or railing. The key to your home is locked inside.

Lockboxes

Some lockboxes have a simple combination to open the box and retrieve the key. This type can be purchased in most hardware stores.

Other lockboxes are more sophisticated and used only by licensed Realtors. They have a computer chip inside that is triggered by a small keypad, about the size of a cell phone. Realtors punch their individual code into the keypad. The lockbox then opens and the key to your home pops out. After the Realtor has taken a buyer through the home, the key is returned to the lockbox.

The lockbox opens only for licensed Realtors. The computer chip inside records the serial number of the Realtor who entered and the time of entry. The serial codes are registered with the local real estate board or state real estate commission. If anything is amiss in your home, the Realtor's name, the date, and time of showing has been recorded and is easily tracked. The lockboxes are also preprogrammed not to open at all before a certain time, perhaps 9 A.M., or after 7 or 8 P.M.

Lockboxes are very convenient for Realtors. They can show your home without your being present, yet they are safe and easy to use.

Picking Up the Key

In some areas, the common practice is to force the buyer's Realtors to pick up keys at the listing office of every single home that they plan to view that day. This is inconvenient and very time consuming, for both the buyer and the Realtor. However, if it is unavoidable, try to make it a little easier. Help the Realtors by letting them leave the key with you when they are done to save them a return trip, or be there to let them into your home yourself.

Seller Alert _____

Always have backup keys. Keys can get lost, or broken off in the lock. When so many different people are opening an unfamiliar lock, it can be forced or jammed. This happens typically with finicky or hard-to-open locks. To avoid this, have the lock serviced or use a little WD-40 to loosen it up. Also, place a small piece of masking tape across the additional locks on the outside of the door so that there is no chance of a Realtor forcing the key into the wrong keyhole.

Listing Realtor Hosts and Supervises Showings

Having the listing agent supervise showings for buyers and their Realtors is usually done for luxury properties. To be honest, it is more of a "service" that high-end listing Realtors provide to create an image of exclusivity. It's slightly silly because it means that there are two Realtors showing the home at once, which is, of course, unnecessary no matter how big or expensive the home is. And again, the buyers feel awkward because they are not free to express themselves or fully explore the home on their own. Additionally, if your listing Realtor is asked to be present for all showings, it will eat up hours and hours of his time, keeping him away from more important work associated with marketing your home.

If You Must Be Home During Showings

When a homeowner is present for a showing, it can make the buyers very uncomfortable. When you are introduced to them, the buyers' focus immediately shifts away from the home and over to you. Now the buyer is concerned about being polite and making a good impression, should they want to purchase the home.

After the introductions are made, and you remain in the home, the buyers will be aware of your presence throughout the showing. They will be robbed of their freedom to openly discuss the pros and cons of the home with their Realtor and with each other. They will also worry that, if you overhear them, your feelings may be hurt.

A big mistake that some sellers make during a showing is to actually follow the buyer and his Realtor around, pointing out features. We understand that sellers can get caught up in their enthusiasm for the various features of their homes. However, it's difficult to read whether the buyer appreciates the information that you are sharing or is distracted from exploring the home on his own terms. In the worst case, the buyer feels pressure, even though that is not the message that you meant to send.

If you have no choice but to be home during a showing, let the buyers know that they have free rein in the home and that you will remain in one room and out of their way. If the buyer has a direct question for you, answer it and then excuse yourself. If you are concerned that they will not notice the features that you would like them to, read on. We will cover emphasizing the best features of your home during showings later in this chapter.

Seller Alert _____

If you have a sick child at home for the day, or you yourself are feeling under the weather, call your listing Realtor and suspend showings for 24 hours. When buyers learn that showings are suspended due to illness, they actually appreciate the warning and would rather view your home under better circumstances.

What to Do Right Before a Showing

When buyers walk into your home, most of their senses will be on alert, particularly sight, sound, and smell. In the last moments just before you leave, and the buyer is about to arrive, there are some easy steps that will help to maximize the showing experience. There are also some things to avoid when a buyer is about to walk through your home.

Things to Do When a Buyer Is on the Way

The following are easy and highly effective last-minute strategies for readying your home just before each showing takes place:

- Turn on every light in the home. Don't forget the recessed lights underneath kitchen cabinets, stovetop hoods, shower stalls, and closets. It's important to show where you have spent money to highlight all the nooks and crannies as well as having every room lit to present its full potential.

- Turn on some relaxing background music. Buyers are under a certain amount of stress when shopping for something as expensive as a home. Background music can be very soothing and add a touch of elegance. You don't need a hardwired sound system to bring music into the showing experience. A radio works well, and some homeowners even tune their flat-screen TVs to a nice music channel.

- Open every curtain and shade. We've talked a lot about light flooding into a home and how it brightens and expands the whole structure. Windows also have the benefit of bringing the outdoors inside. The overall feeling of your home will be lighter and happier with the shades up and curtains drawn back.

- Display brochures and listing sheets. Choose an impossible-to-miss location within your home to present information about your home and community. The dining room table is a popular spot.

◆ Light a fire in the fireplace. Do this if your fireplace is attractive and in good working order—and if it's not too hot out! It can instantly draw the focus to one of the best features in your home while creating a warm and cozy atmosphere. Additionally, a popular question that buyers ask is whether a fireplace is wood-burning or gas, so this step will answer it immediately.

◆ Remove pets. Even if your pet is friendly, many people are afraid of dogs. There are also a lot of people who are allergic to or are not fans of cats. If you cannot remove pets, try to put them in a cordoned-off area and leave a note stating that the animal is friendly. Include the pet's name on the note for a nice touch. Don't forget to clean pet hair off furniture before showings. It's unsightly and can contribute to an allergic person's reaction upon entering your home.

Seller Alert _____

Be careful when considering certain strategies like having a fire going in the fireplace or placing lit candles for the purpose of creating a cozy atmosphere. They can pose a significant fire hazard even if you'll only be out of the home for a brief period of time while the showing is taking place.

◆ Address the temperature in your home. Your goal is to create an atmosphere in which the buyer can best experience your home. Like the background music that soothes, it is imperative that the buyers are comfortable as they walk through. This is particularly important for sellers who go away for the weekend, leaving windows closed and the air conditioning off, or the heat turned down too low. A hot, stuffy house is claustrophobic. A cold one makes them long for the moment when they can return to their car.

◆ Empty the garbage receptacle. Just because the garbage can is under the sink and behind a cabinet door does not mean that odors from it cannot be detected. Also, buyers often look under the kitchen sink and in cabinets—particularly in the kitchen. Remove bathroom garbage as well.

◆ Put out a dish of candy or fruit. This is optional but can be quite nice. Leave a little note that says "Help yourself." Otherwise, most buyers will not presume to eat it.

Trick of the Trade _____

If you have young children and a house full of toys, keep a couple of empty plastic laundry baskets on hand. When a Realtor doesn't give you enough time to tidy up, toss the toys into the laundry baskets and put them in the car trunk and go for a drive. You could use this tip for items other than toys, as well.

Things Not to Do When a Buyer Is on the Way

You might be surprised how little things can have a negative impact on the showing of your home. Consider the following when your home is in the showing stage:

♦ Don't leave appliances such as washer, dryer, or dishwasher on. From the perspective of sound, a running appliance can be very distracting as the buyer views the kitchen or laundry room. Worse, if it's loud, you'll only be drawing attention to a noisy or old appliance.

♦ Don't smoke indoors. If you're a smoker, remove all ashtrays and dispose of any evidence. Better yet, while your home is on the market, try to smoke only outdoors. The presence of stale cigarette or cigar smoke can be a deal killer as soon as your front door is opened. Many people can detect an odor even if your last smoke was weeks ago. Consult a cleaning service for rugs and upholstered furniture. If that is not an option, get a rug and upholstery deodorizer and use it before you put your home on the market so that the scent of the product isn't overwhelming, either. Open windows and ventilate as much as possible.

♦ Don't leave important documents and mail around. You don't need buyers knowing your personal business. Sometimes a buyer cannot avoid seeing what's on a piece of paper lying on a desktop or counter. We have seen all sorts of documents left out in plain view—bank statements, lab test results, love letters, wills, and even documents relating to flaws in the home. Protect your privacy and the potential deal you are about to enter into.

♦ Avoid lingering cooking smells or intentional scents. You may love curry, fish, garlic, roasted meats, baked cookies, and breads. However, one man's cuisine is another man's nausea. You never know what's going to turn a buyer off. To be safe, open windows after cooking each meal and air the place out. The same applies for trying to create an appealing smell with scented candles and potpourri. Like perfume, scent is a very personal thing, so the odds that a buyer will not enjoy your chosen scent are high.

♦ Don't have dirty litter boxes and grimy pet food dishes. This can be very unappetizing to look at, not to mention the odor. When you live with it every day, it's not very noticeable. However, it will be to a buyer or anyone else entering your home for the first time.

♦ Put away small valuable items. Theft is the rare exception and not the rule during private showings, but don't tempt fate by leaving small valuable items such as jewelry around that can easily be picked up.

◆ Don't leave beds unmade. What you're aiming for—all over your home—is a message of pride of ownership. An unmade bed is more than just sloppy. It sends the wrong message—one of apathy and of a home that is possibly in disrepair or been neglected. And it completely undoes whatever staging you've done in the bedroom because the rumpled covers are all the buyer will really see.

◆ Don't leave dirty dishes in the sink. Buyers will look at the dishes and not the sink. It's unattractive and may have an odor. Don't forget to churn the food inside the garbage disposal as well.

Seller Alert

One of the big things that sellers forget is the lawn. If you are going to be away for a week or more while your home is on the market, don't forget to have someone mow and water it in your absence.

How to Control Showings Without Being There

Some Realtors are very proactive and detailed when showing a home to a buyer. They choose the order in which rooms will be shown, control the pace at which they move through the home, and decide which features will be discussed in detail. But other Realtors can be quite passive—hanging back and letting the buyers explore the home on their own. Neither way is wrong; it depends on the buyer's needs and the Realtor's style.

Either way, there are many things about your home—big and small—that you don't want a buyer to miss. As we've said, it's a bad idea to be home during a showing in order to point them out. And yet, you cannot rely on the Realtors to do it for you. So how can you—the seller—control and direct the showing when you are not there?

One way, which we discussed in Chapter 7, is to provide highlight and feature sheets somewhere in the home for buyers to pick up and take away. This is very effective. But there is much more that you can do to have some control over the showing experience and to ensure that the buyer doesn't miss something important.

Let's look at some tips for controlling showings.

Demonstrate the Potential of Your Home Through Blueprints

Some sellers display architect's blueprints (which they have paid for) for additions or renovations that they never got around to making. This is a brilliant thing to do. We have seen many buyers purchase a home that they otherwise would not have—had they not seen the home's potential through the blueprints.

Reveal Hidden Hardwood Floors

Hardwood floors covered with wall-to-wall carpeting are another big feature that could easily be missed during a showing. Sure, you could rely on the Realtor to communicate it to the buyer—or you could leave a note somewhere in the home stating that there are hardwood floors underneath.

We advise our sellers to find an inconspicuous location where a portion of the carpeting can be pulled back by the buyers for a peek at the wood beneath. Buyers are encouraged to do so with a simple sign or note. The buyers can be also be directed to closets where, very often, wall-to-wall carpeting does not extend.

Direct the Eye Toward Hidden Appliances and Fixtures

You'd be surprised to know how often wonderful appliances and fixtures get skipped over in a showing. It's not that it was done on purpose, but rather that the Realtor didn't know it was there and the buyer may have been too timid to open drawers and doors herself. Sometimes, even a powder room can be missed! Among the most common oversights are freezer drawers, warming ovens, convection ovens, trash compactors, sump pumps, interior cabinet shelving that is on casters, lazy Susans, recessed cabinet lighting, recessed spice racks, luxury showerheads and steam features, windows that tilt in for cleaning, cedar-lined closets, hidden storage areas, and much more. Put a note directly on or near the appliance or fixture so that it cannot possibly be missed by the casual observer.

Point Out Captive Attics

Because a *captive attic* is usually accessible only through a bedroom, it can easily be missed in a showing. Its door is usually mistaken for a closet.

def•i•ni•tion _____

A **captive attic** is an attic that is not accessible from the second floor hallway or landing. It is only accessible through a bedroom or large walk-in closet.

Your goal is to point it out as well as its valuable features. To lead the buyer, post a visually appealing note that says "Attic accessible through this room." If it is an unfinished attic but has been Sheetrocked or has rough plumbing for a bathroom, emphasize that in the note, too. Finishing an attic is very expensive so you should spell out for the buyer—with a note—how much you have already accomplished.

Show Off Your Pool, Garden, and Landscaping with Photos

If you're selling your home in the winter or when the foliage is gone, brag to the buyers about your beautiful plantings by displaying seasonal photographs of them in full bloom. Write captions so they can visualize where the plants exist on the property. If you have a swimming pool, show it in its summer splendor complete with lawn chairs, cushions, and umbrellas.

Point Out Neighborhood Amenities

If there is a great playground, tennis court, swimming pool, or sports field, alert the buyers with a note describing it—especially if it is very close by. If it is really close, it may help the buyer overlook a small yard.

Multiple Showings at the Same Time

Sellers sometimes express concern about the issue of multiple showings in their home that are happening at the same time. They often worry that the buyers will be put off if they don't have the home completely to themselves. Obviously, the ideal situation is for a buyer to have the property to himself while walking through it. But it's not always possible—particularly on the first weekend that your home has been on the market. There may be great excitement about it and there are only two days in a weekend. If 15 sets of buyers all wish to see it on Saturday afternoon, the chances are that they will cross paths.

Conducting Multiple Showings

Realtors know how to show a home when another set of buyers is on the premises. It's not that difficult. If another buyer is in one section of the home, the Realtor simply leads her own buyers to another section of the home. If one of these buyers is truly interested, he will often come back for a second and third showing anyway.

Go ahead and allow more than one buyer to tour your home at the same time. When a buyer has a window in which to see your home and she is denied access because another buyer has already booked the time slot, then she may never reschedule. The risk to you is of losing a potential buyer. That is a risk you cannot afford. You will be taking on the stress and confusion of trying to keep all showings separate and private and, in the process, get hurt by limiting the number of buyers coming through.

Multiple Showings as a Positive

We believe that multiple showings at the same time help to heighten the energy and excitement around your home. When buyers see one another viewing the same home, they can't help but feel competitive. Competition is always good for you. Whether they'd admit it or not, buyers need validation from other buyers that their choice is a good one. Having several of them in your home at once gives them that validation, and a sense of urgency.

Rallying the Neighbors

It's helpful to involve your neighbors when your home is on the market and being shown. Buyers will often engage neighbors in conversation about a variety of topics, including the safety of the street, the school system, and even their opinion of your home. Most neighbors will cooperate as they have a vested interest in your home selling well. Speak to them before you put your home on the market. It's also nice to have another set (or several sets) of eyes on your property when so many people are coming and going. It adds an extra element of security. Give them your cellphone number so that you can be reached in a hurry if there is a need.

Tracking Showings

Keeping track of the Realtors who have shown your home is a smart thing to do. If your home is not selling, your Realtor may want to contact each Realtor who has shown it in order to get feedback on what their clients thought. This can be valuable information for repositioning (price-wise) and/or correcting any problem areas in your home.

If Realtors will be scheduling showings directly through you, keep a list of their names and agencies on a pad near the phone so that you can give it to your listing Realtor. Realtors usually leave a business card behind after a showing, but sometimes they forget. This is why you should keep your own record.

The Least You Need to Know

◆ A lockbox with a key inside provides an easy and safe way for Realtors to show your home.

- Before a showing, turn on every light, open drapes, turn on some relaxing background music, adjust temperature, empty trash receptacles, and remove pets.

- Beware of odors from recent meals, put away important documents and small valuables, and do not leave appliances like a washer, dryer, or dishwasher on.

- Never stick around when your home is being shown unless it's absolutely unavoidable.

- Having more than one buyer viewing your home at the same time is not just okay; it can be a positive.

- Tracking showings and getting feedback can help pinpoint why your home is not selling.

Chapter 9

How to Sell Your Home in Any Type of Market

In This Chapter

- ◆ The four steps that will sell your home every time
- ◆ The three cycles of buyers
- ◆ The power of the Internet and MLS's
- ◆ The myths about advertising and public open houses

Your home will sell in any type of market—even in a rapidly falling one where home sales appear to have stopped altogether. It will sell in any city or town in the world, with the exception of locations where a natural or environmental disaster has occurred.

We understand that the prospect of selling your home in a market where prices have fallen dramatically can be very frightening. The newscasters and other media may report daily on a crisis in the real estate market. You'll hear statistics about falling values, foreclosures, and sellers who owe more on their homes than they are worth. It's true that many homeowners will lose money when they sell and may even face the possibility of personal bankruptcy. Perhaps they put too little money down when they bought, received bad advice from a lender about affordable monthly payments, borrowed too much money against the property during the course of ownership, or made overly expensive renovations or upgrades.

However, the majority of homeowners do not owe more on their homes than they are worth. The goal of this chapter is to show that not only can a buyer be found in any economic climate, but you can make more money than other sellers in your neighborhood with similar homes.

Why Some Homes Sell and Others Do Not

Even when it appears that the buyers have disappeared, certain homes in any area will always sell no matter what is happening in the real estate market. Why? The simple answer is that those homes were properly priced and marketed. This chapter is going to show you specifically how to do that for your own home. There is an enormous misconception out there that buyers simply stop shopping in a falling market. This is not true. There are always buyers in search of a home. Life goes on; housing needs are always changing. People have growing families, get relocated, get divorced, and retire.

In a rapidly falling market, it may feel as though buyers have stopped buying because it takes time for most Realtors and sellers to catch up to changing home values and make appropriate price reductions to reflect the declining market. Once they do, a home will sell. You may be thinking that anyone can sell their home if they give it away for a bargain basement price, but you will not give your home away if you use the strategies discussed in this chapter. On the contrary, you will not only attract a buyer and sell your home, you will actually *outperform the market*.

def•i•ni•tion

To **outperform the market,** or beat the market, is to sell your home for more money compared to similar homes in the neighborhood.

What Sells Your Home Every Time

Let's look at a fictitious but typical example of Anytown, USA. Perhaps there are 140 properties on the market. In the last three months, only eight of them have sold. What did those homeowners do differently that separated them from the pack? Why did they attract buyers and receive offers while your home sits on the market with no offers—not even a lowball offer? And more importantly, do you want your home to be one of those eight?

Following are four steps that will sell your home anywhere, anytime, and in any type of market. To remember the steps, think of the word "SALE."

◆ **Stage your home**

◆ **Aggressively price**

◆ **Lead the deal**

◆ **Expose your home**

Stage Your Home

Staging is essential when selling. There is no question that you can drive the sale price up by presenting your home in a way that appeals to the majority of buyers. Through staging, you can get thousands, and often tens of thousands, more than what you'd get without staging. If you do not take the time to address staging, you can actually undersell your home or experience what's called "leaving money on the table." This is when your home sells for less than it is worth because of a poor perception of value.

You might wonder why a homeowner would not bother to stage when it has such a big impact on the sale price. There are a number of reasons. The seller's Realtor might not know how to stage or appreciate its importance. The seller might think that it costs a lot of money or that the home doesn't really need it. But every home needs some degree of staging, even professionally decorated homes. Interior decorating for everyday living is not the same thing as staging a home in order to sell it.

With some relatively easy and inexpensive steps, you can strategically manipulate the value (sale price) of your home. Best of all, it's not hard! If you have read Chapter 6, you know how easily the features can be highlighted and how the eye can be redirected away from weak spots by rearranging furniture, removing certain pieces, painting, letting light in, and creating outdoor rooms.

Aggressively Price

Of the four steps, pricing is the most important. It is so powerful that it is the one step that can get a home sold on its own—without proper exposure or staging. As we said in Chapter 4, in the absence of proper pricing, no amount of advertising, marketing, or staging will sell your home.

What we are focusing on here is not just listing your home at a *reasonable price*, but listing it at an *aggressive price*.

Why Aggressive Pricing Works

An aggressive list price draws buyers to your property, often in swarms, and away from others. It results in a high number of showings in the first days or weeks on the market which, as we all know, is when the highest sale prices occur.

The main reason that sellers get higher sale prices in the first days and weeks of being on the market is that the most desirable type of buyers view the home in this time period. There are three different types of buyers, and they come in "cycles"; therefore, we call them "The Three Cycles of Buyers" (discussed later in this chapter). Understanding and targeting them is the key to selling your home for top dollar.

You may have heard of the term *target marketing*. It is based on the belief that, in order to market something effectively, the sellers must first understand the buyers, their behaviors, and which among them are most likely to buy. Corporations spend billions of dollars in market research trying to understand what motivates a consumer to buy.

def•i•ni•tion

Aggressive pricing is when a home is priced to create a perception of value. It makes your home appear to be a better value than your competition—other similar homes on the market. A **reasonable price** is merely one that is not perceived to be irrational.

Target marketing is a term that businesses use when they identify or "target" a certain segment of the market (consumers) that they believe is most likely to buy their product or use their service. Once these consumers are identified, their behaviors and spending habits are studied. The goal is to set the group apart from all others and save time and money by reaching out to those consumers directly and efficiently.

The Three Cycles of Buyers

There are three types of home buyers. They each have certain traits which affect their ability and readiness to buy. They include:

- Cycle-one buyers: the hunters
- Cycle-two buyers: the chameleons
- Cycle-three buyers: the tire kickers

Cycle-One Buyers: The Hunters

Cycle-one buyers represent the brass ring for sellers because they are always poised to make an offer. They are clearly "in pursuit," very proactive, and focused. They will come through your home when it first comes on the market—typically within the first few hours or days—maybe even a week or two. They see it early because they are very tuned in to the housing inventory and found—or more likely, their Realtor sent them—your listing the day that it came on the market.

Cycle-one buyers are experienced, highly motivated, nearly fearless, and have a strong sense of urgency. If they like your home and it is priced well, they will make an offer quickly.

A cycle-one buyer is easy to spot for the following reasons:

◆ He has been searching for a significant amount of time.

◆ He has decided on the community or neighborhood he wants to live in.

◆ He is educated to the market conditions and the buying process through the aid of a licensed Realtor.

◆ He is fully preapproved for a loan.

◆ He knows exactly how much he can spend.

◆ He will make a fair offer based on experience.

◆ He will do his part to make it to the closing table.

◆ He remains confident in the choices he's made.

He is a great buyer because he has seen enough houses, perhaps dozens and dozens, and understands the value of homes in your area, as well as the style and type that are right for him. He has been thoroughly screened by a bank or lender and is in a strong position to buy. And he knows exactly where his financial *comfort zone* is.

def•i•ni•tion

A buyer is in her **comfort zone** when she has distinguished between what she is *able* to spend and what she *should* spend on a home. Many buyers are approved to borrow more money than they really should. Just because she can afford the monthly payments today doesn't mean that she always will. People's lives change. Income can fluctuate from year to year. Homeowners should have a monthly payment that is very conservative and easily met, even in rough times. This is how so many homeowners end up in foreclosure—by being miseducated as to what their comfort zone actually is.

This buyer is very motivated—partly through experience, and partly because he is growing weary of shopping. Buyers get tired. It's an exhausting and taxing process to find a home. For many weeks or months, he has been fighting the fear that the right home may never appear. When it finally does, he is no longer afraid. He is rejuvenated and excited. He is focused and wants to move forward. He will make an offer and it is usually realistic. He will have an inspection performed and negotiate in good faith. Overall, he will do what's necessary to keep the deal together.

You can target cycle-one buyers through aggressive pricing. If you don't, these buyers may still walk through your home, but they won't buy it because they didn't perceive value. They will move on to the next new listing until they find and buy a home that is priced well.

Cycle-Two Buyers: The Chameleons

Cycle-two buyers are the second group that comes through your home, typically when your home has been on the market for about two to six months. They are far less attractive for a seller and we call them "chameleons" because they are not always easy to spot. This buyer did not see your home in the first few days or weeks because she has been looking casually, is not yet highly motivated, and is still in the early part of a home search.

She may think of and present herself as being "in the market" for a new home. However, when you pull back the layers of skin, you see that, in reality, she is still only window-shopping. The cycle-two buyer is often unprepared to make a serious offer. But that doesn't always stop her from making one anyway—often making the ride to closing a very bumpy one. She will negotiate in an overly aggressive or unrealistic manner, drawing lines in the sand while subconsciously willing the deal to fall through. In a word, she is a risk and that risk is to *you* because she was not fully educated and experienced at the time she made the offer. Many cycle-two buyers have not seen enough homes, or been in the market long enough, to make educated decisions.

A cycle-two buyer is sometimes hard to read for the following reasons:

♦ She will drift in and out of public open houses and browse homes on the Internet for months before approaching or committing to a bank or lender for a loan.

♦ She is still unsure of exactly how much money she can or should spend.

♦ She has learned a lot but is still slightly confused by the process of home buying and what she really needs in a home.

♦ She is nervous and skittish, prone to changing her mind without warning or explanation.

◆ Because of her lack of confidence and experience in the market, she is not fully committed to some of the decisions she makes.

Cycle-Three Buyers: The Tire Kickers

Cycle-three buyers are the least likely to make an offer on your home. They come in after it's been on the market for six months or longer, sometimes even a whole year after it was introduced. They are at the earliest period of home buying and are still in an information-gathering stage. That's why they are so late to the party at your home. They are educating themselves by looking at every home in their price range. They remind us of the buyer who is in the market for a new automobile and goes into the dealership and browses the various cars for sale. "Tire kickers" is an old-fashioned term for unmotivated buyers. They do research to gain knowledge, perspective, and experience so they can morph into cycle-two and eventually cycle-one buyers.

If your home does not sell for over six months, you will be in the business of scheduling showings for cycle-three buyers. You don't have to worry that they will make an offer and then back out of the deal. They are not likely to make one in the first place.

The greater danger is of having your home used by Realtors as a teaching tool for these buyers. It has grown very stale by now and Realtors may only be showing it to help sell another home in your neighborhood that is newer to market and better priced than yours.

The cycle-three buyer is easy to read for the following reasons:

◆ She will fully admit that she is not ready to make any big decisions yet.

◆ She is trying to assess the market, how it works in your area, how much "home" she can buy or how far her money will go, which homes are selling and which ones are not.

◆ She is considering several communities at once and has not yet committed to one.

◆ She just began working with a Realtor and is still in the getting-to-know-you stage.

◆ She is still comparison shopping banks and other lenders.

◆ She is in no rush and has no sense of urgency.

◆ She is prepared for a long search and has plenty of energy to conduct it.

The cycle-three buyer is well aware of who she is and how much further she must go before she buys a home. It is you who must recognize that this is the kind of buyer who will most likely be in your home after it has been on the market for several months—and making no offers.

Lead the Deal

After you get a contract on the sale of your home, it's up to you and your Realtor to take a leadership role in managing the deal all the way to the closing table. This is not the time to sit back and be passive, expecting the buyer and his Realtor to hit all their marks and get through each stage of the transaction. There are many ways for this deal to fall apart on the road to closing. Your Realtor may be more experienced than the buyer's Realtor. Your buyer may need help and direction. We have seen hundreds of deals that were kept together only because the seller and seller's Realtor were pro-active, cooperative, and involved.

The following explains how to lead and manage the deal:

◆ **Pay attention to the time line.** There are stages to a deal, actual dates when the buyer (and his Realtor, attorney, and lender) must perform certain duties and fulfill obligations such as forwarding deposits, conducting the inspection, and scheduling an appraisal. Remind the buyer, and give advance warning, that these deadlines are coming up. Be sure that he is on his schedule and provide access to your home as needed.

◆ **Offer, share, and control the flow of information.** After the home inspection is done, there may be a need for contractor estimates to establish how much a repair might cost. If you have estimates yourself or the names of reputable contractors, share this. It will save time and probably money. Have your Realtor present when the appraiser comes to your home. Give the appraiser hand-picked comparables to show that your home is worth what the buyer paid, and perhaps more. The buyer will be strongly influenced by his own Realtor. Sometimes, your Realtor can influence and educate the buyer's Realtor on issues with which she has had more experience.

◆ **Manage emotions.** A real estate deal can sometimes be volatile with the buyer and seller ending up at odds with one another. When emotions are running high, negotiations can become even more challenging. The best strategy for managing emotions is to always try to keep your eye on the big picture: the successful sale of your home. Getting caught up in disagreements about whether or not the dishwasher repair costs $100 or $150, or whether the freezer in the basement was actually included in the sale is not worth the risk of having the deal fall apart. The financial (and emotional) cost to you, if you have to put your home back on the market, can be really high. Sometimes, it's better to give in and keep the sale intact. Communicate and negotiate with flexibility and fairness.

♦ **Anticipate certain problem areas.** This is where you'll really need the advice and counsel of your Realtor, who has the experience to see around corners and know where the potholes are on the road to closing. For example, if you have an underground oil tank, make sure that there is insurance in place on the tank before you put it on the market. In many cases, this can take weeks and can seriously delay the closing. Or perhaps you are divorced and your ex-spouse's name is still on the deed and is legally still considered an owner. It will take time to reach your ex and have the name legally removed in order to close.

Expose Your Home to the Whole Buyer Pool

If your home is sufficiently exposed (marketed) to all of the buyers looking for a home in your price range and community, the real estate market will speak and ultimately tell you what your home is worth. But the exact worth will fluctuate month to month, week to week, and even day to day, depending on the market conditions and if the entire buyer pool was made aware of your home. A seller whose home was not sufficiently exposed to all potential buyers may have gotten a lower price than a home that was properly exposed.

There are several steps that you must take to achieve maximum exposure. They include how buyers will hear about your home, when it becomes available to be shown, the window of time in which they can see it, and how soon you will consider offers.

The Power of the Internet

Today, there is no single greater vehicle to expose a home for sale than the Internet. It can reach billions of people in seconds. But just because it *can* doesn't mean that it *will*. The Internet is a crowded place. Reaching the right buyer on the Internet is one of the top goals of just about any business in the world. It can be done—in one of two ways.

The first way is if money is no object and you can place your message anywhere and everywhere on the Internet. That's not realistic, of course. The second way is by strategically targeting buyers within the Internet. We talked about target marketing earlier in this chapter—by using price to capture cycle-one buyers. You can also use the Internet to target and capture cycle-one buyers through their representatives, their Realtors.

Multiple Listing Services and Reaching Cycle-One Buyers

By now, you are familiar with Multiple Listing Services (MLS's). There are hundreds of MLS's available directly to buyers. Some of the more well known are referenced in the back of this book. But the listing information is not always complete, and many of the buyers browsing these MLS's are cycle-two and cycle-three buyers. It's not that you can't sell your home to one of these buyers; you can. But if you want to sell your home, get top dollar, and make it to closing, you need to reach the best buyers, which are cycle-one buyers.

Cycle-one buyers will get your listing e-mailed directly to them without having to surf the Internet to find it. It will be forwarded to them by their Realtors, who reviewed it on a comprehensive, private, and regional MLS, accessible only to licensed professionals. The MLS's used by Realtors are their most powerful professional tool. Without it, they cannot do their jobs. Realtors are using their MLS daily and often hourly. They are communicating all day with cycle-one buyers. They have the buyers' home and cellphone numbers, and they are beeping, e-mailing, and texting them on a constant basis.

Most other businesses spend a great deal of money trying to target their buyers. For all the billions of dollars spent on research, at the end of the day, it's still almost impossible to accurately measure whether they actually reached them. However, in the field of real estate, the best buyers can easily be found because they are communicated with, educated, and represented by Realtors.

Delayed Showings

When you put your home on the MLS, announcing that it is for sale, it is sometimes a good idea to delay showings for a few days. This gives buyers time to plan when they can come see it within the first few days that it is on the market. If you give the buyer pool little or no warning, you can miss or lose some of the best buyers due to sheer scheduling conflicts.

In addition, this tactic often helps to create buzz among the buyers; it helps build excitement. Think of a new film. The movie studio releases clips and previews before it opens in theaters. By the time the movie comes out, audiences have been waiting to see it. This is why movie studios place so much emphasis on the first weekend's box-office receipts. They know that the most money a film will make is usually in its first weekend. A very similar analogy can be applied to homes. As you know by now, homes sell for the highest prices in the first few days or weeks on the market.

If you've ever sold a home before, you may recall cars driving slowly down the street with the passengers craning their necks to get a closer look. There is a certain level of energy around a home that is about to come on the market.

Seller Alert _____

In some areas, it is a violation to purposely delay showings after the listing has been entered into an MLS. Check with your Realtor about MLS rules and regulations.

Open Houses for Realtors Only

Figuratively speaking, you are selling your home to Realtors, not to buyers. Cycle-one buyers will have your home screened by Realtors first. It is imperative that the Realtors are very familiar with it and its features. Having an open house exclusively for them is a terrific way to do this. Even better, serve food; that will keep them in the home for a longer period of time, which leads to conversation about the selling points. Many Realtors will conduct these open houses, with refreshments, at their own expense.

Don't Listen to Offers in the First Couple of Days

It amazes us when we hear stories about how a seller was so happy because he received and accepted an offer one hour after his home went on the market. It's true that homes sell at the highest numbers when they first come on the market—but only after it has been exposed to the entire buyer pool! It is not physically possible to get all of the interested parties through your home in an hour or day, or even two days. Give them a fighting chance!

Create a window where all the legitimate cycle-one buyers, who have done basic due diligence in finding your home, have a chance to actually see it. If you receive an offer one hour or one day after it's been on the market, you will never know if you under-sold your home. If you put it on the market on a Thursday and sold it on a Friday, you will never know what a buyer might have offered on Saturday or Sunday. This is why aggressive buyers make offers contingent upon your immediately putting a halt to showings. They know they're getting a deal. Your home had a very strong perception of value. That's why the buyer has such a sense of urgency.

Instead, allow showings to take place for at least three days or perhaps even four or five. If there is an interested party on day two who wants to present her offer, let her know that you would be happy to hear it but that you cannot respond until after the other buyers with appointments have concluded their showings.

She may feel that you will "shop" her offer or use it to find another buyer who will beat it. If she feels this way, ask her to hold it and then present it on the designated day. If she is a real buyer, she will wait. Tell any other buyers who are interested in the first few days that you will hear offers on day three, day four, or day five (at a certain time). This way, the playing field is level for everyone involved, and you will know that the property was sufficiently exposed to all the cycle-one buyers and you did not undersell the value of your home.

Advertising and Public Open Houses

Most sellers want or expect their home to be advertised and to have their Realtor conduct a public open house, but relying on these two approaches to get your home sold is a mistake. The reason is that they attract cycle-two and -three buyers. Buyers who respond to ads are usually "free agents" who are not yet working with Realtors. And, if they are not yet working with a Realtor, they are typically just beginning their home search and are not truly prepared to buy.

Good, qualified buyers working with Realtors don't need to search advertisements to find homes in your area. Every home is presented to them personally by their Realtor—usually before the ad even runs.

He alerts the buyer immediately to every new home on the market in his price range. If it appears to fit his needs, he will request a *private showing*, and usually quite quickly. This is the key: cycle-one buyers see a home as soon as it comes on the market, usually within the first week or so, and in a private showing.

def•i•ni•tion

A **private showing** is when a buyer simply schedules an appointment to see a home when other buyers are not necessarily there, as opposed to seeing a home among dozens of people at an open house.

So why do Realtors advertise and conduct public open houses if they don't work? For one thing, sellers have come to expect them as part of the package that a Realtor provides. Realtors are happy to conduct them because they bring in new clients. If most of the buyers who walk into an open house are not represented by a Realtor, then they will need one eventually. When the Realtor strikes up a conversation, makes a connection, and gives them her business card, she may work with them one day soon.

Additionally, advertising accomplishes something called *branding*, or creating an ongoing awareness of the Realtor in the community. When readers repeatedly see the name of the Realtor or agency in print, they may recall it when the time comes for them to buy and sell.

It's not that the Realtors are dishonest about the benefits of advertising and public open houses. It's just that it is a mutually beneficial practice between sellers and Realtors. Both parties seem to get something out of it. But the goal is to sell your home and you just can't rely on these two approaches to do it.

def•i•ni•tion

Branding is the process of trying to create a favorable and recognizable identity for a product or service.

What to Do When Your Home's Been on the Market Too Long

When your home has been sitting on the market for several months or more, it can be very depressing. Don't despair. You are not powerless. Now is the time to re-create demand.

You can still capture the cycle-one buyers after your home has been on the market for a long time and has grown stale. The way to do this is to recreate demand.

Supply and demand is a phrase that people tend to throw around. They usually refer to it when things are not selling. They say, "Oh, well, there is too much supply … not enough buyers. They can't give the stuff away." They assume that the demand somehow went away. It did not. It's a myth that demand goes away. The demand (or a buyer's willingness to pay that price) is temporarily on hold. Demand becomes active again at the very moment that the price has been properly adjusted.

When homes stop selling, it's not because there is no demand. It's because, over time, the prices became high enough to temporarily slow down selling. The minute that prices adjust lower to reflect appropriate values, the items will sell. It works every

def•i•ni•tion

Supply and demand is an economic principle about the relationship between how much consumers want a "thing" versus how much of the "thing" is available. Often referred to as the "law of supply and demand," it is really about pricing and the need to keep balance between the two.

single day for commodities like pork bellies and orange juice, and it works for homes. As soon as a seller makes an appropriate price reduction, the buyers instantly reappear to make offers.

If your home has been on the market for months, you are showing it to cycle-two and cycle-three buyers. It's time to get the cycle-one buyers back. The way to do that is to make your home seem new to the market again by adjusting the price. It's not enough to simply make a price reduction. It must be an appropriate price reduction. It must accurately reflect the current climate or market conditions. As we said earlier, a home always has value—unless there has been a natural or environmental disaster. The trick is to find the value. After it's found, the home will sell—always.

Sometimes a seller (or his Realtor) feels that the home has been on the market so long, and has become so stale, that an entirely new approach is called for. This may be the time to consider temporarily withdrawing the property and reintroducing it a few weeks later with some strategic changes. A price change is a given, but perhaps there are some tactical changes that can be made in terms of staging or upgrades. Be careful about spending a great deal of money at this point unless you and your Realtor are sure that it will have an impact.

The Least You Need to Know

- ◆ Your home will always sell if you stage, aggressively price, lead the deal, and expose it to the entire buyer pool.

- ◆ There are three types of buyers: cycle one, cycle two, and cycle three. The best are cycle-one buyers because they are poised and ready to buy.

- ◆ The single most powerful way to expose a home, and reach the best buyers, is through the regional Multiple Listing Service used by and accessible only to professional Realtors.

- ◆ It can be foolish to accept an offer on your home in the first few hours or couple of days.

- ◆ It's never too late to re-create demand for a home that is not selling. The law of supply and demand is really about adjusting the price to keep demand up.

Chapter 10

How Buyers Behave When Home Prices Are Down

In This Chapter

- ◆ Predicting buyer behavior
- ◆ The buyer's most common trait
- ◆ The buyer's biggest fear
- ◆ How to handle lowball offers
- ◆ The "what's wrong with it?" perception

Buyer behavior patterns are predictable. They behave one way when prices are up (which we discuss in the next chapter) and another way when prices are down. Psychology is a major factor in selling real estate. When you truly understand how a falling market affects a buyer's actions—how he thinks and what motivates him—it's amazing how much more effective you will be, and as a result, how much money you can make on the sale. On the other hand, if you do not understand buyers, it can cost you tens or even hundreds of thousands of dollars. We discuss buyer behavior patterns in detail in this chapter. Use the knowledge you gain here to your advantage—you will come out way ahead financially.

If you understand the mindset of the buyers, you will target and attract the best and most qualified among them. When you attract them to your home—getting them to physically walk through it—the odds of getting an offer go up. Once you have an offer (even a lowball offer), we will show you how to be a more strategic negotiator. And when you finally accept an offer, you will be able to anticipate and defuse problems, which will result in a smoother, cleaner transaction.

Predicting Buyer Behavior in a Down Market

Let's begin with what buyers believe in a down market:

- They shouldn't have to pay full price for a home.

- There will always be another home to see, as there is plenty of "inventory" to choose from.

- If they don't make an offer today, your home will probably still be available in a few weeks.

- They can drag out negotiations until they wear you down and you agree to their price.

The irony of this mindset is that it prevents many buyers from buying at a good time because in a falling market, most homeowners are open to negotiating. As a seller, however, don't make the mistake of believing that if you negotiate, you are making a bad deal or "underselling" your home. When done right, you can successfully negotiate with a cycle-one buyer and still outperform the local real estate market.

The Buyer's Most Common Trait: A Low Sense of Urgency

Many buyers shopping in a falling market are somewhat tortured by the idea that, while they need or want to buy now, they may be looking at the wrong time. They wonder about waiting and finding something cheaper. They have no urgency, experiencing a form of "analysis paralysis"—emotionally bouncing back and forth between their desire to buy and their fear of it. It affects the way they shop and, if they make an offer, it continues to affect them while negotiating.

Your goal is to target the one segment of the buyer pool that is not plagued with a low sense of urgency. That group is the cycle-one buyer group, or the "hunters," as we discussed in detail in Chapter 9. These buyers have a very highly developed sense of urgency. They are people who need to buy and have been shopping for quite some time. Cycle-one buyers have seen many homes before walking into yours. They understand value, know what they like, know what they can reasonably afford, and are growing weary of searching. Cycle-one buyers are poised and ready to make an offer the moment they find the right home—in any type of market.

The Buyer's Biggest Fear: Paying Too Much

The universal fear among most buyers in a down market is that they will overpay. If they make an offer and it gets accepted, they immediately fret, believing they probably could have negotiated a better deal. Their thinking is that, if the seller was so willing to accept the offer, they must have overpaid. Many buyers confess to waking up in the middle of the night and asking, "What have I done?"

The best way to reassure a buyer that he's not paying too much for your home is to *validate* his choice to buy it. While most buyers would not admit it, they all need validation. Psychologically, it confirms their desire, helps to escalate the sense of urgency, and removes the fear of overpaying.

Give buyers validation with the following methods:

- Price it aggressively (with a strong perception of value) so that it appears more worthy of a buyer's attention than other homes on the market.

def•i•ni•tion

To **validate** is to confirm, establish, or support the worthiness of something.

- Prove its value by providing comparisons to other homes.

- Don't insist on showing the property to only one buyer at a time. Allow more than one party in the home to make the level of interest in the property transparent and visible.

- Work with cycle-one buyers right away (the very first parties who will come in) who have the experience and ability to negotiate fair market value.

Trick of the Trade

Sometimes it helps a little for sellers to write and display a note for buyers about why they have loved living in their home. It can refer to the features and upgrades, or even the quality of the neighborhood and the people who live in it. It may not have a big impact on whether or not a buyer makes an offer, but it can't hurt and some buyers love it.

Why a Buyer Won't Make an Offer When Your Home Is Overpriced

The number-one question from sellers whose homes are overpriced and not selling is, "Why won't anyone make an offer?" It's not that the seller expects full price. He is aware that his home is priced too high but he is ready to negotiate. He is wondering why no one comes forward with any offer, even a lowball offer.

The reason a buyer will not make an offer, even when she knows that you are ready to negotiate, is because of the overall perception of the home. It goes back to validation. "There must be something wrong with it if no one else wants it; therefore, I don't want it either." The buyer knows that she can negotiate down, yet she still doesn't want to. She doesn't want it at any price because no one else does.

Many people refer to a home that's been on the market a long time as having grown "stale." We actually think the situation is more serious than that. The home actually becomes stigmatized; it is labeled by the real estate community and buyers as a property that is somehow flawed. It doesn't matter how beautiful or well maintained the home is. This negative perception is powerful and can attach itself to any home that sits for an extended period of time without offers.

Fighting the "What's Wrong with It?" Perception

When a buyer sees a home that nobody else wants, he cannot help but ask, "What's wrong with it?" It's only natural. The buyer's Realtor will have a hard time convincing him that the only thing wrong with the property is that it is priced too high. The buyer still doesn't want to make an offer. The negative perception is just too strong. Again, the irony is that a home with no offers is actually a golden opportunity where the buyer can negotiate one on one with the seller, and without competition from other buyers.

Fighting the "what's wrong with it?" stigma is also a hard thing for a seller to do because it means that she has to recognize and acknowledge the fact that her home is worth substantially less than she thought it was. This is a jagged pill to swallow and she really only has two options to reverse the perception.

- ◆ **Make a substantial price reduction:** You immediately recapture the buyers' attention when you make a serious reduction in price. It might as well be a brand-new listing. Suddenly, the buyers ask their Realtors to take them back to your home for another look. It's extraordinary when just last week they wouldn't even make you a lowball offer, yet this week they are seriously reconsidering it because it now has a perception of value.

◆ **Temporarily withdraw property and reintroduce it:** Sometimes a property has grown so stale and is so stigmatized that it can benefit from being withdrawn from the market altogether and then reintroduced a short time later. When it is reintroduced, it should be at a new list price and with some additional improvements made. Again, like advertising, always have something new to say when you are marketing a home. Wait at least a couple of weeks to reintroduce it to the market. The buyers may well remember your home from before but it will now have a greater perception of value at the new price and with the new changes.

Lowball Offers

There are buyers out there who will see it as an opportunity when your home is priced too high and will submit a lowball offer. They see value in your home, but only if they can get it for a great price—a "steal." This type of buyer figures that he has nothing to lose by making the offer in the remote chance that you will accept it.

Trying to Define a Lowball Offer

Every seller will have a different definition or perception of what a lowball offer is. Some think that a few thousand dollars under the list price is "lowballing" it. Others think that it's an offer that is at least 10 percent below the list price. It also depends on what the trend is in your community or region. In some locations, the average home may sell for about 95 percent of the asking price, while another area may have their homes sell at about 90 percent of the asking price. If a buyer offers you 80 percent of asking, it would be fair to categorize that offer as lowball based on local trends. While it is very difficult to define, one thing is for sure: the person who has labeled it as a lowball offer thinks that it is far below the actual value.

Responding to Lowball Offers

Lowball offers can be perceived as a great insult. Some sellers reject them out of hand or do not respond to them at all. We recommend that you respond to them, always. The main reason is that you never know how far the buyer will come up in dollars unless you engage her in a negotiation.

Seller Alert

When you feel insulted by an initial offer from a buyer, remind yourself over and over that it's not personal—it's business! The buyer isn't trying to anger you. He's just trying to get a good deal for himself. But be smarter than he is. Stay above the fray. Respond to him without emotion and see how far "up" you can get him.

It's true that some buyers who make lowball offers cannot be negotiated with and adopt a take-it-or-leave-it approach. They can be very cocky and unattractive to do business with. If you (and your Realtor) are sure that her offer is completely unrealistic and that you can do better, then you are right to reject her.

But no matter how infuriating this person's initial approach may be, don't close the door until you have at least made a verbal counteroffer. If she does not respond, then you have lost nothing. If she does respond with a realistic number, then you may be about to negotiate a real sale.

How to Negotiate a Lowball Offer

After responding to the initial lowball offer, the goal now is to keep the negotiation alive. Never lose sight of the cost of a failed negotiation. If you fail, you have not only lost a potential buyer but your home may not sell for several more months, costing you thousands or tens of thousands of dollars more. Talk over your approach with your Realtor, who has undoubtedly been involved in many negotiations.

Negotiating is easy for some people, but others seem to shoot themselves in the foot the very minute that negotiations begin. The latter is usually a person who becomes a victim of his own emotions. The perceived insult of the lowball offer makes him angry and causes a knee-jerk reaction where he either refuses to negotiate at all or begins the negotiation on the wrong foot. This kind of negotiator thinks it's a sign of weakness if he doesn't express outrage over the dollar figure. However, he is actually in a much stronger position if he avoids emotion and keeps the dialogue going and the buyer at the negotiating table.

It's sort of a game, really—but with very high stakes. It involves some good old-fashioned psychology, some number crunching, and an ability to keep your eye on the goal posts—of getting a signed contract. This last skill may be the most important when negotiating real estate.

Seller Alert _____

After receiving an offer, you will be the one to set the pace and speed of the negotiation. If you take three days to respond to the offer, the buyer will probably also take three days to respond to you. If you want a speedy negotiation, respond to all offers and counteroffers within 24 hours. Tell the buyer that you expect the same.

The offer. Let's say that your home is listed for $400,000 and has been on the market for a long time without any offers. A buyer comes along and has no intention of paying your list price. He makes an offer for $355,000 (secretly knowing that he might go up as high as $375,000). That's more than 10 percent below the list price and it may immediately sour you on this buyer. While your home may be worth more than that, you are probably aware that it's not worth $400,000 if it's had no offers over a long period. So where is the value? What do you do?

The counteroffer. Respond with a counteroffer that is at least meaningful—perhaps $10,000, depending on what is going on with similar homes on the market in your area. If you respond swiftly (usually within 24 hours), then you have sent a message to this buyer that, while you have no intention of giving your home away at a bargain basement price, you are realistic and open to negotiating. Now both parties have an elevated heartbeat. There is a chance that, if this negotiation stays alive, there could be a deal.

If you had responded with a tiny counteroffer, at perhaps $398,000, the buyer would have probably walked away, thinking that you are in denial about the market conditions, unrealistic, and not open to negotiating in a meaningful way.

The second counteroffer. Here is the turning point in the negotiation—the second meaningful counteroffer. If the buyer walks away without countering back, there's not much you can do about it. It was over quickly; you found out that he wasn't serious, and you didn't expend much energy. No harm; no foul. However, if he stays and gives you a counteroffer, you have got him. There absolutely should be a deal at this point. He's invested in the dialogue and he has tipped his hand to show that he will come up quite a bit because if he weren't, he would have walked away by now.

If he comes up $10,000 more, to $365,000 and then stops, you may think that if you take it, you have lost $35,000 on the value of your home. But you have not. Even at this point in the negotiation, you may have already outperformed the market! At $365,000, you're now within 9 percent of your original list price. If the market in your area has fallen 12 percent, you are ahead of the curve. You will sell your property for approximately 3 percent more than other similar homes on the market.

This is the moment we referred to previously, the moment where you have kept your eye on the goal posts. Many sellers will, instead, focus on that $35,000 and miss the point that they actually outperformed the market.

If this negotiation was one of the truly great ones, the counteroffers would have continued up to an agreed sale price of $375,000—the amount that the buyer was always prepared to pay. It's a great negotiation because both sides won. The buyer felt from the beginning that $375,000 was a fair price and the seller got a sale price that is within 7 percent of his original list price. Even better, he outperformed the market by 5 percent. Not bad for a deal that began as an "insult."

The Myth That Buyers Have Gone Away

One of the worst mistakes that you can make when your home has no offers is to miscalculate the demand among buyers, and instead believe the idea that "nobody's buying right now." It may be a fact that the market has slowed down, but it's not because the demand isn't there; it's always there. Cycle-one buyers will buy in any type of market.

Cycle-One Buyers Never Go Away

When prices are down and homes aren't selling, everyone is asking, "Where are the buyers?" Believe it or not, they are still there. Not only have they not gone away, but they are poised and ready to make offers. When you wonder what a buyer is doing in a down market, think of a lion sitting under a tree on the plains of Africa. He may appear to be resting, bored, or disinterested, but he's not at all. The minute that prey comes into his field of vision, he will launch into action in a split second to pursue his goal.

Just when you think that buyers are not paying attention, they are actually at their most aggressive. They have so much experience shopping for a home that they are now nearly fearless and will pounce the minute they find a home that is priced properly and has a perception of value.

The Buyer's Best Talent

Cycle-one buyers' best talent is that they are trained to spot value. In fact, they are better at it than you are. For months now, they have physically walked through dozens of homes in your community. They have the most experience in local real estate values (and each specific home) than anybody, with the exception of the Realtors themselves.

What we mean by "spotting value" in a down market is that, amid a sea of overpriced properties that aren't selling, cycle-one buyers can find the diamond in the rough. Cycle-one buyers are smart. No matter how bad the real estate market gets, they will find, recognize, and buy that one home that a seller has priced properly and that has been given a perception of value.

The Least You Need to Know

- Buyer behavior patterns are predictable in any type of market. Their biggest fear, in a falling market, is of overpaying.

- When home prices are coming down, buyers lose their sense of urgency. You must create urgency around your home with aggressive pricing, staging, and exposure.

- When your home is not selling, you may have to fight the "what's wrong with it?" perception.

- Most buyers subconsciously need validation from other buyers when interested in a property.

- A seller should respond to all offers—even lowball offers. Fight the urge to feel insulted. You never know if the buyer will come up to a reasonable price.

- The best talent that cycle-one buyers have is the ability to understand home values in your area. They know them better than anyone, except the Realtors.

Chapter 11

How Buyers Behave When Home Prices Are Up

In This Chapter

- ◆ Buyers' most common trait
- ◆ Buyers' biggest fear
- ◆ Driving your sale price up
- ◆ Handling bidding wars
- ◆ Buyer's remorse

Prices will come up again. Never before have they gone down and stayed down. Like the stock market, prices go down for a period of time and then rebound to higher levels than ever before. History tells us that, even when there has been a crash in the markets, they will recover. When they do recover, buyer behavior patterns will change dramatically. The power base in real estate will shift away from buyers and back toward the sellers.

When this happens, you may assume that it will be easy to sell your home and that you will do quite well. But even in a climate where most homes are selling at full price or higher, some homeowners can still undersell their properties. If you do not understand buyer behavior patterns when selling in this kind of market, and how to leverage the momentum, you could leave a significant amount of money on the table. It is our goal to make sure that you get every dollar possible out of the market in which you are selling. To us, leaving even one dollar on the table is unacceptable. The financial windfall from selling your home in this market may be the biggest of your life. It is crucial that you take full advantage of it. What a fantastic opportunity for you. We want to make sure that you get the most out of it.

In this chapter, we discuss the behavior, attitudes, and specific scenarios that motivate buyers to pay top dollar.

Buyers' Most Common Trait: A Strong Sense of Urgency

When home prices are going up, buyers have a sense of urgency that is based on the valid fear that, if they don't pay a seller's list price (or higher) now, they will pay more money down the road when prices have risen even more. And they are less afraid of overpaying, or paying a "premium," because they have confidence that the real estate market is strong and may get even better. Further, buyers believe that the home they buy will only be worth more as time passes, particularly if they plan to live there for a long time.

Sometimes (but not always), when home prices are up, the entire economy is also doing well. The stock market index may be climbing, salaries are high, and jobs are plentiful. This perception—and overall confidence—can drive home prices even higher. Even when the real estate market is up and the rest of the economy is down, it reinforces the flight from the "risky" stock market and into real estate. It becomes the place to put your money.

Because buyers are more actively buying, there are fewer homes to choose from and there is a growing perception that supply is running short. Homes sell more rapidly and everyone is busy and making money, including the mortgage brokers, banks and credit unions, builders, Realtors, appraisers, attorneys, title insurance companies, inspectors, and general contractors. Buyers perceive real estate in this kind of market as an attractive investment.

When everyone is running in one direction, it's hard to run in the other. The buyers feel validated by the herd that is galloping toward home ownership. The overall sense of urgency among the buyer pool drives prices upward, and sellers reap the benefit if they leverage it properly.

Buyers' Greatest Fear: Missing the Market

As we've said, the buyers' strong sense of urgency is rooted in a fear of missing the market. If they don't buy now, they think that they will pay more later and the type of home that they ultimately buy is smaller than the one they can currently afford.

How Buyers Miss the Market When Prices Are Rising

A buyer can miss the market when home prices and/or interest rates have gone up enough over the course of her search to affect her spending power. To understand this concept, think of the monthly payment that she can afford when she began her search. The monthly payment drives everything when applying for a mortgage. If her lender tells her that she can afford to pay $2,500 a month on a mortgage payment, and not one penny more, then that's it. That's her monthly budget and she must find a home that will cost her no more than that.

When she first began her search, let's say that she could afford a $400,000 home with taxes of $375 per month. If she is still shopping four months later and the cost of buying has gone up, she can no longer afford the same size home that she could just a few months ago. Her job is still secure and her salary is the same, yet it can be said that she "missed the market."

As a seller, it is important to understand that this is the main motivating force for buyers and what creates a sense of urgency to buy sooner than later. Let us offer an example of this and then discuss how to leverage this scenario into more money for your home.

The Incredible Shrinking Home

When home prices are rising as a buyer is searching, the size of the home that he can afford can actually grow smaller. His dollars are literally shrinking. Let's say that he began his home search in the month of January. At that time, he could afford a $400,000 home. He is able to borrow $320,000 and make a down payment of $80,000. But over the next four months, prices rose at a rate of 1 percent per month. Interest rates also rose—by a half a *point*—from 7 to 7.5 percent. Now, a $400,000 home is worth $416,242. He still has the same $80,000 for his down payment and the

def•i•ni•tion _____

A **point** is equal to 1 percent of the amount of money that you are borrowing. On a $100,000 loan, a point is equal to $1,000. A half a point is $500.

taxes are still $375 per month. Yet, his monthly payment will increase a few hundred dollars, which may now put homes that he could once afford out of his reach.

How Monthly Payments Change When Home Prices Are Rising

	January (7% interest rates)	May (7.5% interest rates)
Home Value	$400,000	$416,000
Loan Amount	$320,000	$336,000
Loan Payment	$2,503	$2,724

Difference: $221 per month or $79,560 over the course of a 30-year loan

You can see why this buyer would be highly motivated to purchase a home before prices rise any further.

Driving Your Sale Price Up

Now it's time to talk about how you can use this climate to your advantage and have it translate into a higher sale price on your own home. If you leverage it properly, not only are you more likely to get full list price but it's possible that a buyer will give you even more than your list price. When this happens, it can be said that they've "paid a premium." It may be difficult to imagine this at a time when home prices are down and everything is selling under the list price (if it sells at all), but buyers will pay a premium if the right variables come into play.

When Buyers Don't Mind Paying a Premium

When buyers find the home that is perfect for them, they will walk through fire to get it in any kind of market, but particularly when the market is hot and moving fast. A new home can be an emotional purchase. Buyers have a vision of the place they want to live in and raise their families or retire to and grow old in. When they find it, they will fiercely pursue it. If buyers are worried that one of their competitors will buy it out from under them, they will move into a state of mind where they are prepared to do whatever it takes to get it—even paying above the list price.

A buyer will pay a premium for your home when …

- ◆ He has fallen in love with it.

- ◆ He is competing for it against other buyers.

- ◆ He believes that it is far better to pay a little more today than to pay a lot more a few weeks or months from now.

As a seller, if you have done all the things that we have suggested you do so far—that is, to stage, aggressively price, and expose your home to the entire buyer pool—you should have buyers swarming your home on the first weekend. There may even be simultaneous showings, creating a sort of "revolving-door" atmosphere. This happens because the cycle-one buyers, who are anxious to buy, come in right away. The stage has now been set for a possible *bidding war*.

def•i•ni•tion

A **bidding war** is when several buyers make offers, or bids, on the same property, creating a competitive climate and usually driving the sale price up.

How to Inspire a Bidding War on Your Home

A bidding war can be created when your home is priced attractively (or aggressively) compared to similar homes in the area. Your home must have a better "perception of value" and therefore look like a good deal next to others on the market. This scenario or mentality of a bidding war is similar to that of an auction, where the opening price is low enough to draw more bidders into the competition. Think of eBay, which is essentially an online auction house. The approach is called "reducing the barriers to entry," which means you have actually expanded your buyer pool and attracted more of them with your low asking price. As the buyers become aware of the fact that there are several interested parties, human nature then takes over and suddenly all the players are caught up in the need to win. When they observe that others want the home as much as they do, their choice is validated and a "sense of urgency" is created around the sale of the property. The energy and competition among the buyers drives them to spend more money than they had originally planned to—hence your sale price is driven up.

Seller Alert

Neither you nor your Realtor can "guarantee" that a bidding war will take place no matter how low you set the price. Pricing is a subjective process and, if it's done for the express purpose of inspiring a bidding war, it is a dangerous gamble. There is always a small chance that it will not work.

How to Nurture and Handle Bidding Wars

If it appears that more than one buyer has an interest in your home, you may get multiple offers or have a bidding war. It is absolutely critical, at this point, to nurture the process and handle the buyers properly. If you mismanage it, you can lose some or all of them. If you do manage it correctly, you can reap thousands, or tens of thousands, of dollars more in the offers.

Here are the steps to take toward creating and managing a bidding war:

1. **Do not sign a contract the minute your home comes on the market.** Let all of the cycle-one buyers have a chance, or a big enough window of time, in which to see your home. This goes back to the importance of "exposure." If one buyer makes you an offer as soon as your home comes on the market, she clearly sees a perception of value and has a tremendous sense of urgency. In fact, she will often submit the offer and tell you that she'd like an answer as quickly as possible and that she'd like you to discontinue showings once the contract is signed. She may even ask you to cancel the upcoming open house. She doesn't want any other buyers to see it, and for very good reason. She's getting a deal, and she knows it. It should reveal something to you about how much your home might really be worth if someone wants it badly enough to buy it within hours of it coming on the market. If you accept an offer on the first day of showing, before all of the cycle-one buyers have seen it, you will never know how much you would have been offered on day two, three, four, or five. It could have been substantially more money. In the end, you may have sold your home, but you also may have left a lot of money on the table in the process.

   Instead, tell that one buyer that you are very anxious to receive it but that you will not actually be opening and reviewing offers before a certain day or, after the other buyers have had their initial chance—in that first week—to see the home, too. If she still insists on submitting it, you have the option of taking the offer and holding on to it until the designated day. However, we advise our own buyers never to submit their offers until right before the established deadline. This way, it eliminates the concern that the seller will open the offer early and reveal the number to other buyers.

   If she is a cycle-one buyer and she truly loves your home, she will wait and play by your rules. Don't be fooled when she says the offer is only good for 24 hours or she will walk away. She may, in fact, walk away. But, if she does, you can be sure that she was not a cycle-one buyer, or that she didn't really love your home. In either case, you have lost nothing.

Seller Alert

In many states, a Realtor has an ethical obligation to present any and all offers to the seller within 24 hours of receiving them—unless you, the seller, dictate otherwise. You have the right to delay the moment when you open and review offers. But you may need to give your own Realtor written permission to communicate this to other Realtors and their buyers.

2. **As soon as you have been alerted that one or more offers will be coming in, communicate this to all interested parties.** After you learn of an offer(s), create a buzz in the real estate community that will hopefully encourage even more offers. Have your Realtor communicate this information to all the Realtors representing other interested buyers. You don't necessarily want to scare them away. But you do want to gently communicate that there will be a certain level of competition around the sale of your home. This knowledge gives your home a greater perception of value—and the buyers a greater sense of urgency. This is precisely what fosters competition and what drives your sale price up.

3. **Set and communicate a date and time when you will review all offers.** This is not a mere step in the process. This is actually an extremely important strategy whereby the buyers are asked to wait a short period before submitting their offers. In this time period, they often decide to offer more money than they had planned to a day or two earlier. To begin with, the waiting period gives them some time to breathe and prepare. It provides them the much-needed time to reflect on potentially the biggest purchase of their lives. As they do that, their desire for the home often grows. But, most importantly, the threat of competition grows, too, as more buyers will have the time to enter the bidding process. The fear of losing the home to someone else now becomes very real. The buyers move from a state of mind of simply wanting your home to absolutely having to have it. They are now psychologically prepared to do whatever it takes to get it, which often means paying a premium.

Seller Alert

You may worry about losing a potential buyer if you ask him to wait a day or two to review his offer in order to be fair to all interested parties and review them at once, side by side. Don't worry. Let's analyze this buyer. If he is shopping for a new home in what is clearly a "seller's market" and walks away from something as important as his new home over a minor administrative delay, he was not a cycle-one buyer or, down deep, he did not really want the property. Either way, he is certainly someone with whom completing a transaction and making it to the closing table would be a major challenge.

4. **Establish and communicate the same rules and guidelines for all interested buyers.** There is one thing that will make a qualified cycle-one buyer, who happens to love your home, walk away from his offer. That is when he feels that he is being treated unfairly or misled, on any level. He may desperately want your home, but he is no pushover. And if you lose him, it may be that he was the right buyer with the best offer.

Blurry, inconsistent, or bad communication can make a buyer suspicious. When the buyer feels this way, he begins to mistrust the whole process, particularly if he believes that you are treating one buyer more favorably than another. For example, never negotiate with one buyer in a vacuum, giving him privileged information that the other buyers do not have. Never reveal what one buyer's offer is to another buyer. This is called *shopping an offer* and is perceived by buyers as one of the highest ethical crimes a seller can commit. The buyer's goodwill and motivation will disappear in a flash if he learns, or even suspects, that something unfair is taking place behind the scenes. While cycle-one buyers will pay a premium for your home, they will only do so if they feel that all buyers have the same information and are playing by the same rules.

Make it clear how the offers are to be physically presented, and how and when you will respond to them. For example, are they to be presented in person by the buyer's Realtor, or will they be forwarded in sealed envelopes? Will you accept one of them on the spot or will you respond with a counteroffer?

Receiving and Reviewing Multiple Offers

There are several approaches to receiving offers as well as to how they are reviewed. Among Realtors, there are different schools of thought about which ones are the best. We believe that there is no one single best way. The one that you use will depend on the type of market in which you are selling, what the common practice is in your area, how your Realtor advises you, and what you personally are comfortable with. Here are some choices.

Highest and Best, or the One-Step Bidding Process

After you decide the date and time that offers are due, you must also decide if you will accept and sign one of them on the spot, or give the buyers a counteroffer. If you do accept and sign one of them on the spot, that means that you have created a one-step process. This is when buyers submit their "highest and best," or an offer with their highest price and best terms. The buyers will have just one opportunity to get the home over their competition by submitting the absolute most that they are willing to pay, along with the best terms that they can provide. We discuss the various terms in an offer in Chapter 15.

Each buyer must reflect on and decide how strong her offer is without having any idea what the other buyers offer. She decides how much the home is worth to her and goes straight to that number. One buyer may offer $2,000 above the list price of $425,000 and feel that it's a very good offer. But the other four buyers may offer $9,000, $11,000, $13,000, and $20,000 above list price. Obviously, the home was worth a lot more to her competition. The other buyers paid a larger premium than she did. Again, cycle-one buyers don't mind paying a premium when they love a home and they know that other buyers want it, too. Let's look at the size of the premium that was paid in this example. The real value of the home was at one number, while it sold at another.

The Real Value of a Home Sold in Multiple Bids

List Price	$425,000
Offer from Buyer #1	$427,000 ($2,000 above list price)
Offer from Buyer #2	$434,000 ($9,000 above list price)
Offer from Buyer #3	$436,000 ($11,000 above list price)
Offer from Buyer #4	$438,000 ($13,000 above list price)
Offer from Buyer #5	$445,000 ($20,000 above list price)
List Price	$425,000
Final Sale Price	$445,000
Approximate Real Value	Mid-$430,000s

In a bidding war, a home usually sells for a premium, or above the real value. Depending on how many bids there are, the real value is usually where the majority of the buyers clustered. If a home is worth what a buyer is willing to pay for it, and the majority of the buyers participating in the bid submitted offers between $434,000 and $438,000, then that is where the approximate real value is. But the home still sold for $445,000. It can be said that the buyer paid a premium of approximately $10,000.

Beware of the Escalation Clause

Once in a while, a buyer who loves your home thinks he can get around the process of competing and attempts to get your attention through a back door. The way he does this is by sending a message to you that, when the bidding war is over, call him and he will beat the winning offer.

def•i•ni•tion

An **escalation clause** is a term in a purchase offer where the buyer tries to avoid participating in a bidding war by offering a certain amount of money over the highest bid received.

Be careful of this buyer. This is someone who either has not been properly educated to the process by his Realtor, or he simply thinks that the rules don't apply to him. Whichever description applies, he is a bad risk to do business with. One of the reasons that we are against *escalation clauses*, in theory, is that the buyer has created a scenario in which the final sale price will be imposed upon him by others. The price could end up being much higher than he anticipated and catapult him outside of his financial comfort zone. Additionally, because he did not choose the number, he may not believe the home is worth that amount. Therefore, his commitment to the deal may not be strong enough to stay with it.

Another reason that we are against escalation clauses is that they go directly against the seller's golden rule for bidding wars, which is to create clear and fair guidelines that apply equally to everyone. If you have five offers and you allow one of them to include an escalation clause, then the playing field is not level. Further, if you do attempt to level it—by allowing all five offers to include the clause—then it is impossible to determine a winner. Either way, we do not recommend the use of escalation clauses in a multiple bid situation.

The Two-Step Bidding Process

The two-step process is really just a drawn-out one-step process. You and your Realtor will still impose a deadline by which the first round of offers must be submitted. The difference is that you will not sign one of them on the spot. Instead, you will respond to all of the offers with a blanket counteroffer, or simply provide a second round for all to improve their offers, through price, terms, or both. When the second-round bids are submitted, only then are they considered to be their highest and best.

The attitude that buyers often adopt with a two-step process is that they don't take the first round seriously because they know that they will have another round to submit their final offer. This is why some Realtors find that the first go-around in a two-step process is a waste of time. They also sometimes worry about tipping their hand too early by giving their real highest and best when they aren't required to until the second round. That goes back to their fear that you will secretly shop their offer, or that it will somehow leak to other buyers and put them at a disadvantage.

On the other hand, there are many Realtors who actually prefer the two-step process because it gives the illusion that the buyers will have more time to think and mentally prepare. You should make the decision with your Realtor and base it on the method that the buyers are most familiar with in your area.

Presenting Offers in Person vs. Sealed Bids

The buyers have no control over how bids will be submitted, received, and reviewed. As the seller, you do. In fact, the choice is entirely yours. The Realtors representing the buyers will usually prefer to present the offer in person to you. You may enjoy this approach as you can sometimes learn more about the buyer through direct one-on-one conversation. The Realtor may not be able to tell the buyer's whole story in a cover letter. And you may have some questions you'd like to ask in person.

The downside is that, when there are several offers, it can be time consuming to sit through half a dozen or more mini presentations. Remember, when the presentations are done, you still need to review each offer with your Realtor and then contact each buyer with a response. For these reasons, many sellers are advised to request sealed bids, which are simply confidential written offers sealed inside an envelope. They remain unopened until you sit down to evaluate all of them, together, at the same time.

The cover letter becomes much more important in a sealed bid because it's all the seller has to get an overall description and profile of the buyer. The contract itself is a dry and businesslike document that tells little about who this person is other than her offering price, terms, and financial ability.

Choosing the Best and Handling the Rest

Resist the urge to judge offers with an eye only to the sale price. The best offer in a multiple bid is not always the one with the highest dollar amount. In fact, we have represented many buyers who won a home with only the second or third highest dollar amount. That's because they worked hard on making their terms as attractive to the seller as possible. If the seller had a special situation that required a flexible closing date, the buyer gave it to him. If his financing package was better presented than a higher bid, the seller preferred to do business with our buyer rather than with a riskier offer.

Look at and consider the whole package. Your Realtor may even write down the strongest and weakest selling points of every offer on one piece of paper. This makes it easier to evaluate them side by side. An offer should be strong across the board. After all, what good is a high sale price if the deal falls apart before closing due to a condition of, or a contingency in, the contract?

The Importance of Backup Offers

When notifying the buyers who lost out in your bidding war, be sure that your Realtor calls each of them promptly with the bad news, thanks them, and asks if they would like to remain as backup offers should anything go wrong with the winning bid. This is crucial. If your second and third offers were strong, and something does go wrong with the deal that you accepted, you should go straight back to them rather than going through the effort, and taking the financial risk, of putting your home back on the market.

If you are forced to market your home a second time, the buyer pool will wonder what happened to the first deal, and ask their Realtors, "What's wrong with it?" Your property will be somewhat tainted. You may get other offers, but the sale price, this time, may be much lower.

Seller Alert

If the first two offers were close, you can use this to your benefit to make the deal more secure. Make sure that the buyers who won the bidding war know that the second-place offer was similar to theirs. This validates their decision to buy it and the number they chose, and it reinforces that they didn't overpay. Because the margin between the two offers was so small, it makes their victory sweeter, overall.

Buyer's Remorse

Once in a while, a buyer gets caught up in the excitement of making an offer on a home that she thinks she loves and that she believes she can afford. Once the excitement of having an accepted offer wears off, she comes back down to earth and the reality of her commitment sets in. She may convince himself that she's made a mistake, driving her to back out of the deal.

Buyer's remorse is a characteristic of cycle-two buyers. They have not had enough experience in the home search process yet to have total clarity about value. Therefore, they do not have enough confidence, either, in the decisions they make. As a seller, doing business with them is somewhat risky. Cycle-one buyers are far less prone to buyer's remorse because—as we've said before—they are experienced home shoppers, they understand value, they are ready to buy, and when they do, they are nearly fearless. This is why it is so important to recognize what type of buyer has brought you an offer.

The Least You Need to Know

◆ When home prices are rising, buyers have a strong sense of urgency to buy a home. They fear they will miss the market and worry that if they don't buy now, they'll pay even more later.

◆ Buyers will pay a premium when they fall in love with a home and when other buyers want it, too. The way to drive your sale price up is by creating a competition among buyers.

◆ A one-step bidding process is when you receive offers all at the same time, review them, and sign one on the spot. A two-step process usually involves a blanket counteroffer or simply another chance to improve the initial offer.

◆ You can choose to receive offers through in-person, face-to-face presentations made by the Realtors representing the buyers or by asking for the offers to be delivered in sealed envelopes.

◆ The escalation clause comes from a buyer who wants your home but doesn't want to participate in a bidding war to get it.

◆ Buyer's remorse usually happens mostly to cycle-two buyers.

Chapter 12

Relocations and Estate Sales

In This Chapter

- ◆ Employee relocation packages
- ◆ Selling with a relocation clause
- ◆ Estate sales
- ◆ Executors and power of attorney

Sometimes there are unusual circumstances surrounding the sale of a home. Two of them are relocating for a new job and selling the home of a recently deceased loved one. If you are relocating for professional reasons to another part of the country or the world, your new employer may be picking up the tab. That's a good thing. However, as the saying goes, there is no such thing as a free lunch. If the company is paying, it may impose some limitations to how you market your home. These limitations are important, as they can affect how much money you will make on the sale.

If you are overseeing the sale of the home of a loved one who has recently passed away, this is also quite challenging, but in a different way. It's an emotionally charged time to begin with. On top of that, you are being called upon to perform a business transaction while trying to manage your feelings of personal loss, and those of your family.

In this chapter, we analyze the challenges of both types of real estate sales. We discuss your options in a relocation sale and provide information and strategies for coping with an estate sale. If you adopt some good approaches to these scenarios, you will save money and time and limit the stress on your family.

Selling When an Employer Relocates You

Relocations for new jobs are big business. U.S. companies alone spend $32 billion annually on domestic corporate relocation, according to Worldwide ERC (www.erc. org), an association for employee-transfer professionals. This doesn't even include international moves. When you relocate, most employers pay at least some of your expenses. And there are some companies that will pay all of them. But it is up to you to negotiate a deal, better known as a *relocation package*, with your employer.

def•i•ni•tion

A **relocation package** is a bundle of services and benefits that a business provides for an employee who is moving or transferring in order to work for the company.

On average, you will have only about 15 days to respond to a company's offer to relocate you for a job, and 31 days to move to the new location, as estimated by Worldwide ERC. That doesn't give you a whole lot of time to think about the opportunity itself, let alone to work out an acceptable agreement about how much of the relocation costs and logistics the corporation will help you with.

And the logistics may be grueling. You need to simultaneously sell the home in which you are currently living, while searching for a home to purchase in the new location. This will require trips to familiarize yourself (and your family) with the community and the housing inventory. You will need to research schools and enroll the children. There is time and expense associated with any relocation.

The good news is that you are lucky to have an employer to negotiate with. Many Americans don't have a relocation company to lean on when they move to a new city for a job. You are already in a good position. You can make it even better by negotiating a strong package for yourself. You can do this by understanding the various services out there. After all, how would you know what to ask for if you don't know that they exist?

Employee Relocation Packages

Some companies manage employee relocations through their own human resources departments, while others outsource it by hiring a separate company that specializes in this area. Hiring an outside firm benefits the company because it allows it to focus on day-to-day business and not be distracted by running the side business of providing real estate services to its employees. They hire an outside firm because they're better at it.

But another reason that impacts you is that your new employer doesn't want to negotiate directly with you. They want to preserve the relationship. By outsourcing this business, the relocation firm becomes the "bad guy." The outside firm adopts the responsibility of keeping costs down and controlling the process, so they have the ability to be a little tougher.

 Seller Alert _____

Before you decide how aggressive a negotiator you want to be, it is critical that you make a value judgment, along with your family, about the overall appeal of the move. You may not get the ideal relocation package. But the benefits of the new job and lifestyle may outweigh the short-term expense of the move. On the other hand, if you are a highly sought-after professional with unusual skills and you know that the company needs you more than you need the company, then negotiate aggressively. You have only one chance to speak up about your needs. Establish what your package will be before you accept the position.

Relocation Package

There are different types of relocation packages that are bundled as specific services. Each corporation bundles them together differently. Some have preset tiered packages based on job levels, whereas other companies have customized packages that address an employee's individual needs.

Some of the most common expenses and services associated with relocation packages are moving expenses, finding a Realtor and real estate commissions, advice and assistance with financing on the new home, closing costs on both the sale and the purchase, inspection charges, etc. Some transferees get an allowance for miscellaneous expenses that come up over the course of the move.

Trick of the Trade _____

Some companies will provide educational consultants who are advisors who will help you to choose and enroll your children in the right schools.

Most companies offer to buy at least a portion of your home. This means that, no matter what you sell it for, they will make sure that you walk away with a certain minimum amount. This is called a partial buyout. Other companies might offer a full or guaranteed, *or* 100 percent buyout, or a price guarantee. This means that they will either commit to giving you a set price for your home, no matter what price it sells at, or they will actually buy the home from you directly and then sell it themselves. The company actually becomes the seller.

A guaranteed buyout is great for you because you get to take the equity out of the home no matter what happens. But it is a risk to your employer, because if your home ultimately sells for less than what they paid you, they will actually lose money. For example, if the relocation company buys your home for $600,000 and then it sells ultimately for $575,000, they will be out $25,000.

Seller Alert _____

If you are being relocated after living in your home for only a short time, and home prices have fallen since you bought it, you stand to lose money. If you can, push hard with your employer for a guaranteed buyout or a price guarantee to protect your asset.

Listing Your Home with a Relocation Clause

When you work with a relocation company to sell your home, it will be marketed with a relocation clause in effect. This means that when you list your home, a relocation clause was included in the listing agreement, and, when it sells, the clause will be included in that written contract. It is important for the Realtor who lists your home to disclose this to potential buyers before they make offers. This is because the buyer will be entering into a business transaction with a third party—the relocation company.

Additionally, the relocation company will require certain practices and impose specific rules that will affect just about everybody associated with the deal—the Realtors, the attorneys, the banks or lenders, the appraisers, the buyer, and you, the seller. Some of these practices may slow the deal down or affect its progress. You may feel somewhat frustrated by the constraints of the agreement. But your employer is assuming part or all of the risk in the sale of your home and has the right to manage the process as it sees fit and according to its own guidelines.

Seller Alert _____

If you are selling your home with a relocation clause in effect, it may be difficult for you to hire the local Realtor of your choice. Not only does the relocation company sometimes require final approval of the choice of Realtor, but many Realtors will not work with relocation companies, as they take a huge chunk of the Realtor's commission—typically 35 percent or more. The workload is heavier than it is in a "normal" transaction, as well.

For example, if your company is giving you a guaranteed buyout, it will likely require three appraisals to establish a realistic value to the home. This step alone can take some time. There are also much more administrative requirements and paperwork than in a normal real estate transaction. Even the resolution of the inspection negotiations take longer because the company must have written estimates for and approve any and all repairs or credits.

Having your new employer involved in the sale of your home can be a financially rewarding, wonderful, and freeing experience, as long as you are completely aware of the negatives.

Estate Sales

Estate sales have their own set of challenges. You may have lost a spouse and are the only person who has decision-making power over the estate of the deceased. Or you may have lost a parent and will be sharing the decision-making responsibility with several siblings. On the one hand, it can be a comfort to have others to lean on at this sensitive time. But it can be frustrating to have a committee of people to funnel every single decision through. When there is a group of relatives at the helm, as opposed to one individual, everything takes longer than it should and emotions can enter into the proceedings.

When you have lost a loved one, it's hard enough to cope without having to worry about selling the home. If you can delay the sale without any penalties or loss of equity, we recommend that you do. Having more time to work through your grief without the added pressure of a business transaction is often a better strategy. Speak to an accountant familiar with the tax code and your financial situation first to see if you can delay it and for how long.

Marketing a Home as Part of an Estate

As with the sale of any residential real estate, if you want to get top dollar, all the approaches discussed in this book apply. Even though the owner has passed away and the home is full of his belongings, the home should still be cleaned and staged. The home should still be photographed. It should be exposed to the entire buyer pool and aggressively priced. Find a top Realtor to manage the whole process along with you and your family. In fact, the Realtor's role will now be more important than ever.

Family Roles and the Division of Labor

Hopefully, the deceased had a will and established one person to oversee and manage what's left of the estate. This person is the *executor* and has the power to make decisions on behalf of the estate, open and close bank accounts, write checks, and otherwise disperse money.

def•i•ni•tion

An **executor** is a person who carries out the terms of a will. A female is called an executrix.

In a marriage, the surviving spouse is usually the executor. If there is no spouse but there are several surviving children, it can become more complicated. It is even possible to have more than one executor. Even so, when there are multiple surviving children who may all want to weigh in on their opinions, it can be quite challenging, especially at an emotionally sensitive time. On the flip side, it is very common for one sibling to feel that she is doing all the work, particularly if she lives locally and the others are farther away.

No matter what the situation in your family, there should be only one person communicating and interacting with the Realtor. Other nonlegal tasks can be divvied up amongst the siblings (unless the deceased wished otherwise), but legal duties and communicating with professionals like attorneys, Realtors, and accountants should be placed squarely on one person's shoulders. Otherwise, communication would be a nightmare.

Dispersing the Proceeds of the Sale to Heirs

Proceeds (or money) from the sale of any real estate go to one place only, and that is to the person whose name is on the deed. If that person is deceased, then the check gets written out to the estate of the person's name that is on the deed. It then falls to the executor to deposit it and distribute in any way that he sees fit, legally and in accordance with the will.

If there is a dispute that is intense enough to prevent the money from being forwarded after the sale, the money will be held in an escrow account until the dispute is settled.

Tax Implications for You in an Estate Sale

Taxes paid on income from profits of the sale of a home owned by a deceased person are often referred to as an estate tax or even a death tax. They are paid out of the funds left in the estate itself. The amount of profit that can be taxed is calculated differently than profit on the sale of someone who is living. The profit on the sale of a living person's home is based on what the owner bought it for and the expenses incurred throughout the ownership period. The profit on an estate sale is based instead on what is called the *fair market value* of the home on the date that the person died.

def•i•ni•tion

Fair market value is an estimate of the current value of a home typically determined by a professional and licensed appraiser.

When One Spouse Dies and the Other Is Still Living

When one spouse dies, there is never an estate tax required to be paid by the one who is living. The deceased spouse may have left six homes and $100 million to the surviving spouse, and there will be no estate tax on it. When one spouse dies, the homeownership typically transfers directly to the surviving spouse. The good news is that when the living spouse goes to sell it one day, the way that the government calculates what is actually profit on the sale changes dramatically. The IRS no longer bases the profit on the appreciation from the year that it was first purchased. It now uses the day that the spouse died as the starting point, or basis, to determine how much the home has appreciated. If the couple lived in the home for 30 years, the appreciation (or what the taxes will be based on) will often be a fraction of what it was before the death, when both homeowners were still alive. When the surviving spouse finally sells the home as a single owner, the taxable profit will go way down.

When One or Both Parents Die, Leaving the Children as Heirs

While there may be an estate tax when a homeowner leaves the property to surviving children or *beneficiaries*, the estate tax will be paid by the estate itself before the proceeds are distributed to the children. Because the taxes are paid before the children collect, they are not required to pay income tax on the proceeds. Taxes cannot be paid twice.

def•i•ni•tion

A **beneficiary** is a person named in a will to receive benefits from real estate, insurance policies, bank accounts, retirement accounts, and more from the estate of the deceased.

Additionally, an estate tax is only paid (by the estate) if the estate in question has a total worth of more than a certain amount. As of January 1, 2009, that amount will be $3.5 million. This is a law that is somewhat controversial, but also interesting. When George W. Bush took office, he got legislation passed that set this amount. The amount changes from year to year. It began at only $675,000, then went to $1 million, then $1.5 million, then $2 million, and will change to $3.5 million in 2009. In 2010, it goes back down to zero and in 2011, back up to $675,000.

There are many people in Congress who are trying to change this law—and the amount—as they think it favors the rich. It has been introduced to the floor of Congress many times but has never gone to a vote. Be sure to check with an accountant or tax advisor to find out where the law stands when and if you are in a position to sell a home through the estate of a deceased person.

Calculating the Value of an Estate

The following is an example of how to calculate the value of an estate.

Cash. Money is distributed in accordance with the will after the estate pays any taxes due.

Securities. The executor may decide to simply sell the securities (stocks, bonds, and so on) and divide up the income in accordance with the will. The estate pays taxes on it before it's distributed. However, the heirs may decide not to sell but rather to hold on to the securities as a continued investment.

Life Insurance. By law, the proceeds must go directly to the named beneficiary in the policy; they do not go back into the estate of the deceased. The beneficiary does not pay taxes on the income; they are paid before the income is distributed.

Retirement Funds. These accounts usually, but not always, have named beneficiaries on them and income goes directly to them. The beneficiary does not pay taxes on the income. They are paid before the income is distributed.

Real Estate. Homes are often sold and the estate pays any taxes, commissions, fees, and so on. Any remaining proceeds are then distributed in accordance with the will or wishes of the deceased. Some heirs choose to keep the home and share in its use, particularly with vacation homes. A new deed must be drawn up in that case to show transfer of ownership to multiple parties.

Cash

Securities	Mortgages
Life Insurance	Other Debt
Retirement Funds	Funeral Expenses
<u>Real Estate</u>	<u>Deductions</u>
Total Assets	**Total Debt**

Total Assets – Total Debt = Net Estate Value

Trick of the Trade

The home of the deceased can be sold and the profit used to pay off debt on the estate. An alternative is that after transferring ownership to the heirs, they could borrow money against it in the form of a second mortgage or home equity line of credit. Only an heir whose name is on the deed may borrow money against it.

Power of Attorney

You may be selling a home for a friend or family member who is alive but is somehow unable to execute the sale herself. The seller may be out of the country, or physically or mentally incapacitated. Power of attorney is a legal piece of paper that allows one person to make certain decisions, and to act on another person's behalf. It must be stamped and notarized by a notary public. It is the notary public's job to make sure that the person understands what he is signing. If there is any question (particularly in the case of a mentally incapacitated seller), the notary public should not sign it. Sometimes, it is necessary to go before a judge to get power of attorney.

The Least You Need to Know

◆ The marketing of a home as part of an estate is subject to the same standards as any other home. However, the Realtor's role may become more important than ever if you or your family is still grieving.

◆ It is critical to negotiate a relocation package with your new employer before accepting a job. The package will have a big impact on how much money you make on the sale.

◆ One of the strongest packages includes a 100 percent buyout package, where the new employer pays you the full appraised value of your home, whether it sells or not.

◆ Most wills designate one person to oversee the estate of the deceased. He is called an executor (or executrix, for a woman) and can have the power to sell real estate, open and close bank accounts, write checks, and disperse money.

◆ There is no estate tax between spouses. There may be an estate tax if both parents have died and the estate is worth over a certain amount. Either way, the taxes are paid by the estate and not by the beneficiaries.

◆ Power of attorney is when one living person legally appoints another to make certain decisions and to act on his behalf.

Selling Income-Producing Properties

In This Chapter

◆ Pros and cons of selling income-producing properties

◆ Overcoming obstacles to selling a home occupied by renters

◆ The powerful key to marketing investment properties

◆ How to calculate income for buyers

◆ What really attracts buyers to rental properties

Selling any home that is occupied by renters can present its own special set of challenges. However, these challenges can be overcome with good planning and thoughtful strategies. In this chapter, we examine the decision to sell an investment property, how to work with renters when selling, and how to market rental homes you plan to sell.

Types of Investment Properties

There are several different types of investment properties. Among them are condominium units, multifamily dwellings (buildings with two or more rental units), and private homes that have a rental unit attached to or on the same property. Additionally, you may have a boarder apartment or mother/daughter layout within your own home. All of these types of rentals provide *passive income*. Passive income is another way to make money on your investment, in addition to its increase in value over time.

def•i•ni•tion

Passive income, as defined by the IRS, comes from one of only two sources: a rental property or a business in which the taxpayer does not "materially participate." For example, you might be an investor in a company where you do not work and yet receive repeated ongoing income from the investment. Passive income is received on a regular basis with little or no effort to maintain it.

Deciding to Sell a Home with Rental Income

Unlike your primary residence, the decision to sell investment real estate is less emotional and mainly rooted in dollars and cents. It's much more of a business decision than choosing to sell a private residence and should be evaluated in as objective a manner as possible.

Here are some of the pros and cons of selling an investment property.

Pros of Selling

There are several reasons for unloading investment properties. There may be more than one that applies to you.

- The property is experiencing a negative cash flow. (Your expenses are higher than the income it produces, causing you to lose money each month.)

- The property is not appreciating in value as fast as you would like it to.

- You are tired of maintaining it.

- You are tired of dealing with the hassle of renters.

◆ You need an immediate infusion of cash to manage a financial crisis.

◆ You want to use the proceeds of the sale to do a renovation or buy down (reduce) the mortgage on your primary residence.

◆ You want to buy another or bigger investment property, also known as a *1031 exchange*.

def•i•ni•tion

A **1031 exchange** got its name from Section 1031 of the IRS code. It is a law that allows you to defer federal (and some state) taxes on capital gains from the sale of a property that was used for trade, business, or investment purposes only. However, you must exchange the property for another that is similar in nature and equal to or greater in value than the one you are selling. Also known as a *tax-deferred exchange,* it is based on the premise that when you reinvest proceeds from a sale to another property, you haven't really received funds to pay taxes on—it's only a paper gain. Eventually, you will pay taxes when you sell a property that is not being replaced with another.

Cons of Selling

On the other hand, there are many reasons not to sell. Selling any investment can be a difficult choice to make and you may question that choice for years to come. Real estate, as an asset, has always appreciated in value over time. There have been significant dips and even major market corrections, but prices never go down and stay there. They always rebound and climb higher and higher, historically. This is the strongest argument against selling. Additionally, an investment property can provide a safe harbor for your money when other markets (such as stocks) are more volatile. It spreads the risk in your investment portfolio around. The following are reasons not to sell income-producing real estate:

◆ You will no longer own an appreciating asset—something that is growing in value.

◆ You will no longer have passive income.

◆ Without a real estate investment, you may not be as financially diversified as you should be.

◆ You may pay income taxes on the profit from the sale.

◆ You may lose a powerful tax deduction and/or tax shelter.

◆ You may regret the sale down the road.

Before you decide to sell such an investment, remember what you put into acquiring it in the first place, not to mention what you did to raise its value over the course of your ownership. You had to find the right property, secure a loan, negotiate an inspection, find and screen reliable tenants, and make it to closing. You may have made many capital improvements to the property, such as new appliances; heating, plumbing, and electrical upgrades; landscaping; and possibly even a new roof. It's important to establish if you meant for it to be a *long-term real estate investment*. If so, then you should hang on to it for the long term, if possible. If, on the other hand, you bought it for the short term or to "flip" it, that's another scenario entirely (we cover this in Chapter 14).

def•i•ni•tion

We define a **long-term real estate investment** as one that you hold for 10 years or more. The reason is that the market will fluctuate over the course of your ownership. It can take a dip (even a serious one), but history tells us that the real estate market will always recover within a 10-year time frame. However, the most recent U.S. real estate market crash was so serious that it may temporarily redefine the term "long-term investment." It is possible that you may need to hold on to your investment a little longer.

Selling Homes with Pre-Existing Renters

If you are selling a home that is occupied by renters, you will definitely have some challenges and will be handicapped in your ability to properly market the home. There are several reasons for this. We show you how to overcome them.

One of the first things to establish is whether or not the law in your area states that a renter's lease supersedes the sale of the property. In other words, will the new buyer be forced, by law, to inherit your renters after closing? Some buyers may be quite happy to keep your renters so that the flow of rental income is uninterrupted. Other buyers want to handpick their own renters and may not even consider buying a property that has tenants. Still others may want to live in the house and not rent it at all. Either way, it's important for you to be aware of the state or regional laws.

Obstacles to Selling a Home Occupied by Renters

Most of the obstacles that you face have to do with what is going on in your renters' lives at the time of the sale, their disposition, how they feel about you as a landlord and the nature of your relationship with them, and how they feel about the fact that you are selling the building or unit. Here are some of the most common challenges from renters:

- They fear they will lose their home if you sell.
- They feel inconvenienced by showings and might not cooperate.
- They don't seem to care if you get a good sale price.
- They don't keep the rental unit clean.
- They don't have nice furniture or don't have it arranged well. Even clean, the unit is not staged properly.
- They have pets.
- They have a baby.
- They smoke.
- They don't seem to like you or care about your needs.

Overcoming the Obstacles

There are a few ways to get renters on your team and get them to support your cause. If you don't succeed at getting them to work with you, renters can seriously affect or even sabotage efforts to sell a property. The following sections discuss some ways to create an atmosphere of cooperation between you and your tenants.

Call a Face-to-Face Meeting

So many landlords call their tenants on the phone, usually at night, to inform them that the property is going up for sale. This is one of the worst approaches possible, for three reasons. First of all, most people are tired in the evenings. Their mood is not likely to be particularly open to receiving bad news. The immediate reaction is often negative.

The second problem with this approach is that the message is being delivered over the phone instead of face to face. There is nothing that feels good or safe about getting a phone call announcing that the building you live in is going up for sale.

Finally, it may be hard to communicate all that you want to, and in the way that you want to, over the course of a phone call. You will be perceived as more caring and sensitive to their needs if you meet with them in person.

Sell to Someone Who Will Continue the Lease

This is not always possible, but, technically, you can make the sale contingent upon the new owners honoring your tenants' lease. If this is something you are prepared to do, then share that fact with your tenants and they will feel more secure, and will therefore probably be more cooperative.

Involve Renters in Scheduling Showings

Instead of simply telling them—each day—the time that a particular showing will take place, why not set them up as the point of contact for Realtors who want to bring potential buyers into the unit? They may only be "renters," but your building is where they live. It's their home and if they feel respected and have a sense of control about the process, it will run more smoothly. However, in exchange, they must make every attempt to allow all buyers to get inside for showings and only deny access on the rare occasion, if at all.

Make a Deal

Sometimes you just have to throw a little money at a problem to make it go away. If your tenants are motivated by dollars, knock 5 or 10 percent off the rent while the home is on the market. It's amazing how agreeable and helpful tenants are when they feel they are saving money as a result. And if you are selling the building, it's not likely that a temporary 5 or 10 percent rent rebate will hurt you too much.

However, make it crystal clear what you expect in return for that rent discount. You may simply want the unit kept clean and that the tenants let all potential buyers in as long as they are given reasonable notice. Some sellers get it in writing that the tenants will not do anything that can be interpreted as sabotaging a purchase, such as speaking negatively about the property or about you, the landlord.

If all of the preceding tactics have failed and you cannot motivate your tenants to cooperate, perhaps it's time to just ask outright, "What do you want in exchange for helping me?" Maybe they want their unit painted. Maybe they want to be released early from their lease—or have it extended in writing before you sell. Perhaps they want more parking spaces, or a washer/dryer installed in the basement. If there is something that you can do for them, legally and financially, do it. It's worth it in the end.

The Powerful Key to Marketing Income-Producing Homes

Aside from the basic principles of marketing a home, the key to selling an income-producing property is to spell out the income potential for buyers. The biggest mistake that sellers make is to assume that the buyer (or even his Realtor) understands how to calculate it. Even if he does know how to do the math, you must provide the information. Your buyer may be just beginning to invest in real estate, and your building may be his first purchase. Whomever your buyer, if he doesn't know the income potential, he won't see the value; if he doesn't see the value, he's not buying.

We recommend that you do the math for him! Write out the specific expenses and earnings, both on the listing itself and on paper, that can be forwarded to any buyer who comes through. Remember, buyers of investment properties are motivated by different factors than buyers shopping for a private residence. The income potential is the driving force behind the purchase. It's your story to tell, and you must tell it clearly and simply.

There is usually a section on a listing where this information should go, but we find so many listings in the MLS's that leave the entire section blank or even filled out incorrectly.

Once you have told your story about income potential, your home should be marketed as any other following the principles of SALE (discussed in Chapter 9). It should be staged and aggressively priced, you should lead the deal, and you should expose the property to the entire buyer pool.

Trick of the Trade _____

When preparing your taxes each year, you likely made the annual income from your renters look lower than it really was by deducting certain legally allowable expenses on the property, such as depreciation. As the owner of an investment property, you probably already know that depreciation is a "paper expense," as you don't actually pay for it out of your pocket. In fact, it's a tax law that allows you to offset income from an investment property from taxation each year by claiming wear and tear and physical deterioration on the property—but only on the building, not the land. The law further states that you must take depreciation on residential investment properties in equal amounts every year for 27.5 years (called *straight-line depreciation*). At that point, the property is "fully depreciated." What you may not know, however, is that if you experienced losses on the property (real or "on paper") instead of gains, you may be able to deduct the accumulated losses at the time of sale. You may also be able to deduct closing costs as well. Check with an accountant or tax expert to see what you may legally claim.

Calculating Property Income for Your Buyers

There are three key areas when calculating rental income on a property. They are universally accepted by buyers, lenders, insurers, and appraisers. Some of these groups can take the math to a much more complicated level, but we boil it down to its basic elements. Even someone who has a tough time with math should be able to tackle this. If you haven't already done the math on your income-producing property, we strongly urge you to do so. It will have a major impact on your ability to get the best sale price—and your ability to attract all buyers, no matter their level of expertise.

The three key areas are based on annual numbers:

GOI = Gross Operating Income (total potential rental income before expenses)

TOE = Total Operating Expenses

NOI = Net Operating Income (adjusted rental income after taking out operating expenses)

 Seller Alert

Mortgage payments are not considered to be an expense of an income-producing property. However, for personal tax purposes, the interest on the mortgage is typically deductible.

To calculate your gross operating income (GOI), let's assume that you have two units in one building and each unit is renting for $1,500. This will give you a combined monthly rental income of $3,000. When you multiply $3,000 by 12 months, your GOI is $36,000.

Total Operating Expenses (TOE)

Annual Taxes:	$3,000
Annual Insurance:	$1,100
Annual Maintenance:	$600 (landscape, snow removal)
Annual Repairs:	$500
Annual Management Fee:	$1,100 (at 5%)
Annual Administrative Fees:	$300 (advertising, tax prep)
Annual Utilities:	$900 (if paid by landlord)
TOE:	$7,500

Net Operating Income (NOI)

Net operating income is figured by subtracting your expenses from your total income on the property: GOI – TOE = NOI.

$36,000	GOI
– $7,500	TOE
= $28,500	NOI

Trick of the Trade _____

Some savvy buyers may want to know your rental yield. This is expressed as a percentage; divide the net operating income by the total value of the property. If the property is worth $300,000, then the rental yield is 9.5 percent.

$28,500	Annual Income
÷ $300,000	Property Value
= 9.5%	

What Really Attracts Buyers to Investment Properties?

As we have discussed, buyers of income-producing real estate are motivated differently than buyers looking for a home to actually live in. These buyers evaluate hard numbers, as we've just seen, but they also look closely at amenities and their effect on getting good rents. You may have more amenities than you realize. It's important to capitalize on them and highlight them when selling.

The factors that they consider include some or all of the following:

◆ Rental income history

◆ Future potential income

◆ Proximity to public transportation

◆ Proximity to shops and restaurants

◆ Proximity to local or regional universities, hospitals, or business centers

◆ Availability of parking

◆ On- or off-site laundry

◆ Separate outside building entrances for tenants

- Condition of the building

- Safety of the neighborhood

- Bylaws about pets (for condos and co-ops)

- Accessibility for persons with disabilities

Many renters do not have cars and must walk or use public transportation to get to work, school, entertainment, or laundry facilities. Landlords often rent their units to students, medical residents, teachers, and transplanted business people. It's important to include information about the close proximity of your rental units to services, entertainment, and academic or business hubs. This will allow potential buyers of your property to quickly see that they can keep the units occupied and at higher rents than other buildings.

Trick of the Trade

Share with potential buyers any research you may have already done about ways to increase the value of the property, such as creative ideas to expand parking or possibly convert the attic to another rental unit.

On-site conditions and amenities are also important. Having private parking, laundry in the unit or within the building, a doorman, health facilities, or common rooms can be important for rental income. If the building has more than one entrance, tenant privacy is enhanced and the building is worth more. If you have made upgrades to the structure and the units during your ownership, describe them. All of these issues impact the value of your building and should be highlighted.

Attached Rental Units, Mother/Daughter, and Boarder Apartments

Selling a private home with an attached rental unit, carriage house, mother/daughter layout, or boarder apartment is trickier than selling a straightforward rental property. For one thing, the rental unit may not be legal. Mother/daughter layouts imply that there is another wing or section of the home, often with its own entrance, where extended family may reside. But creating a lease for it and taking in rental income may not be legally allowed in your neighborhood. A boarder apartment may be legal, but perhaps only as long as you do not have certain appliances within it that constitute a fire code violation, such as a kitchen stove. If you market the property as having legal rental income and it turns out to be illegal, you could find yourself in a difficult position with your buyer and you may lose the deal altogether.

If you did not check the legality of the unit with the local zoning board at the time you purchased the rental unit, you should do so now. You may not hear what you want to hear, but it's better to find out now that you're violating a code or ordinance than to find out after you have spent time and money marketing the property and having gone into escrow with a buyer.

Showing Rental Properties

As we said earlier, it may be easier on everyone to allow your renters to be the direct point of contact for showings. If you make yourself the contact, then you will be the constant go-between, receiving calls from Realtors and then calling tenants to get permission for every single showing. If your tenants have been properly motivated by you, they will do the right thing and let buyers in whenever possible. To be sure that your tenants are granting access, put a note in the MLS listing itself that instructs Realtors to call you if they have trouble getting an appointment to see the unit.

You can also get creative in other ways if you have problem tenants. For example, if your building has two identical units and one tenant is more flexible or at home less often than the other, see if the buyers are willing to view just one of the units. If there is strong interest, then schedule another showing to see the other unit. It's not ideal, we grant you, but it may be your best option when dealing with difficult tenants. It's the same principle as a new condo development that takes all buyers through one model unit. If a buyer expresses keen interest, then another showing is scheduled to see the other units.

The Least You Need to Know

- ◆ Income-producing real estate is a valuable long-term asset, and the decision to sell should be carefully weighed.

- ◆ It can be challenging to conduct showings of units occupied by renters. Incentivize them to get their cooperation.

- ◆ To demonstrate potential income to buyers, subtract the property's operating expenses from the rental income to come up with net operating income.

- ◆ To calculate the percent that represents rental yield, divide the annual income by the total value of the property.

◆ Key factors that buyers will use to evaluate your property include proximity to public transportation and business centers, as well as amenities such as on-site parking and laundry facilities.

◆ Before putting it on the market, check to be sure that your rental units are legally zoned—especially carriage houses, boarder apartments, and mother/daughter layouts.

Flipping Homes

In This Chapter

◆ What you need to know to flip homes

◆ The formula for successful flipping

◆ Working with contractors and partners

◆ Choosing the right upgrades

◆ How to market a flipped home

◆ Measuring your financial profit

Flipping homes is a practice that has been around a long time but has become popular in recent years. When home values were rapidly rising and the cost of borrowing money went down, the business attracted a lot of people looking to capitalize on the climate. Home sales of all kinds exploded and flipping homes became another way to make a big profit quickly. Television programs were created that showed how it could be done, and they made it look easy.

But flipping homes is *not* easy. It's difficult, and even seasoned experts in the field can suffer some losses from time to time. If you think that you want to flip homes, there is such a thing as a formula for success. In this chapter, we share it with you. Our overall advice is to proceed with great caution, do your homework, be prepared, and create a financial safety net.

What Is Flipping?

Flipping is the practice of buying a property for a bargain price and then selling it quickly for a profit. If the real estate market is rising extremely rapidly, some flippers will do nothing to improve the home and still make a profit when they sell. But most flippers will make some upgrades in an attempt to make an even healthier gain.

Should You Get into the Business of Flipping?

There are pros and cons, benefits, and risks associated with any investment. Flipping is among the riskiest but also among the most profitable and rewarding. You can make a large amount of money in a very short time. If you have the skills required of a successful flipper, you will also have a wonderful creative outlet in your life.

On the downside, you can lose great sums of money; even experienced flippers sometimes suffer losses. If you are inexperienced and don't have the proper skills, the risk is even greater. The stress levels are high in this business, and a project can temporarily be all consuming and take over your life.

The Necessary Skills to Flip Homes

There are certain skills and characteristics that all successful flippers share. Here is a list and a description of those skills.

Strong knowledge of the local real estate market. To make money when buying and selling homes quickly, it is crucial for you to have a keen sense of what different types of homes are worth in the region, what sort of upgrades are necessary, and the average amount of time homes take to sell. If you miscalculate, it can wipe out your profit. To educate yourself, attend public open houses and/or work with a Realtor to get inside as many homes on the market as possible. When you learn what these homes eventually sell for, you will become knowledgeable and have a realistic expectation of what your flip will sell for.

An understanding of buyer expectations in the area. When choosing certain upgrades to make to the home, you may overestimate the interest, need, or demand for them among buyers. In other words, get to know the group you're selling to, as well as their expectations. For example, creating new bathrooms is very expensive and you may not need as many as you think. Why build four bathrooms when most homes in the neighborhood have only two and a half? Perhaps you want to add a two-story addition, but that may make the home dwarf others on the street, making it appear overimproved for the neighborhood. Fulfill buyer expectations without spending unnecessarily.

The ability to work with all types of contractors. Depending on how much of a transformation you're making to a property, you will be dealing with several types of contractors, including architects, engineers, demolition workers, plumbers, electricians, masons, insulators, painters, landscapers, and roofers. You must have an understanding of what's involved with each upgrade, the order in which the work is to be done, how long it takes to complete, the costs associated with it, and how it's billed.

An understanding of finance and math. To flip homes, you must be able to obtain swift financing for a loan; understand how the mortgage business works to your advantage; understand how to calculate projected costs, profit margins, tax implications, fees and commissions; know measurements for ordering materials; and more. Some of the number crunching needs to be done quickly and under pressure. When you find a home that is a perfect candidate for a flip, you must have as many of your ducks in a row as possible. Speak to mortgage brokers, accountants, tax experts, contractors, Realtors, attorneys, or anyone who is in a position to give you an education on numbers, as early in the process as possible.

A love and knowledge of architecture and décor. This part of the process of flipping should be pure fun. After all, if you're getting into the business, a main reason should be for the love of homes and making them better than when you found them. But it's not enough to just love homes. You need to be well versed in what types of décor appeal to a wide audience and you should have enough knowledge of architectural styles and building periods to preserve, or even restore, the "authenticity" of the structure. Paint colors, countertop choices, appliances, fixtures, flooring, moldings, exterior accents, and even landscaping are part of the whole package when trying to improve the value of a flipped home.

A personality type that is calm and unafraid of risk. Perhaps the most prominent personality trait among successful flippers is that they are not afraid of risk. Flipping is one of the riskiest investments because you stand to make or lose tens (and even hundreds) of thousands of dollars. If mistakes are made, or the market doesn't go your way, it can rattle not only your finances but your self-confidence as well.

Expect that there will always be at least one or two things that will not come out the exact way that you envision. Maybe cabinetry was hung an inch lower than you pre-ferred or the paint color did not turn out to be the perfect shade. If you want to stay on budget and on schedule, decide which obstacles might require work to stop or slow down in order to be addressed and which can be overlooked. Always keep the project moving forward. Successful flippers are called upon to make lightning-fast choices on a constant basis and remain calm throughout the process.

The Formula for Successful Flipping

There are five ingredients to a successful flipping formula. To remember them, think of the acronym LUCKY.

Location

Upgrades

Contractors and Partners

Kickoff and Timeline

Yardsticks for Success

Location

When most of us hear the word "location" as it relates to real estate, we immediately think of the best (or one of the best) neighborhoods in town. But when it comes to flipping, you need to completely change your thinking, and this is what makes the business so fun and unique. You can flip a home anywhere you want to: in good or bad areas, expensive or inexpensive, suburban or urban, safe or unsafe, residential or com-mercial.

Don't get us wrong; location is important. But when evaluating it for flip, the thing you absolutely must focus on is finding a home that has become significantly less valu-able than other homes in the immediate area, either because it has been neglected or has not experienced updating in quite some time. To be clear, a good place to find a flip is in almost any location, but always in one where the other homes around it are worth considerably more money. Why? Because the home can be bought for a bargain price and, by making cost-effective upgrades, it will be intelligently transformed into something as valuable as the properties around it. If you have real talent, it may sell for even more money than others around it of equal size and condition.

Trick of the Trade

When you think you've found a great candidate house, give yourself the quick "flip test." It may sound simple, but it's powerful. We have seen so many flippers lose money because it was obvious that they didn't take this simple step. Stand on the front lawn or even across the street. Look at the structure and the property. Look at the size of the structure, the condition of the exterior walls, the roof, the size of the lawn, the depth of the property, and the style. Then look at each house around it. Go back and forth with your eye from house to house. Will the flip be as good as these homes when you're done? Forget the interior for the moment—and even cost. They don't matter right now if the house candidate doesn't pass this test. If you think it does pass, then go on to the next step, figuring the cost of making the house as good as the neighbors—on the interior as well as the exterior.

Upgrades

Upgrading a home while keeping costs down is probably the most difficult part of flipping. It's not making them that is hard; it's choosing the right upgrades to make. And the choice is not just rooted in cost. The key is in understanding the expectations of buyers in the region. Which upgrades do they "need"; which ones do they "want"; and which ones will they pay good money for in a home?

This is another moment when a Realtor's counsel can be invaluable. The advice you get can save you from huge losses and help you to realize very big profits.

Seller Alert

There are some rare professional investors who flip properties without making a single upgrade. They are essentially betting on the market to go up soon after they purchase and they believe that the profit will offset the temporary carrying costs of the property. Carrying costs are regular ongoing expenses associated with home ownership such as mortgage payments, taxes, maintenance, and insurance. This is an extremely risky way to flip that relies heavily on the market going your way. We strongly recommend making at least some improvements to a home before you flip. It's important to build additional value into the asset, as markets are unpredictable and can turn on a dime.

The amount of upgrading that goes into flips varies wildly from project to project. But no matter how many or how few you make, the profits should be proportionate to what you spend. We'll get into the specifics of measuring your return on investment dollars later in this chapter. For now, let's talk about the size and scope of your project. There are three broad categories that refer to the amount of work associated with flips and they are as follows.

The Structural Overhaul

Structural renovations usually refer to dramatic improvements that change the actual size and/or the architectural style of a home. They usually go hand in hand with changes or upgrades in the systems of the home, such as plumbing and electric.

Some flippers make a fundamental change to a home by converting it from one style of architecture to another. This requires a massive amount of work and is probably the highest level of expense. It is usually done by professional home renovators or builders who not only know how to build (or rebuild) fast, but who also have that keen sense of the local real estate market, its buyers, and what they want and will pay for certain types of homes.

One of the more popular projects among professional home renovators is to take a ranch and turn it into a large colonial. Ranches tend to have a big footprint because they only have one floor of living space, so it's pretty easy to simply "build up" by adding a second or even a third floor. One of the reasons that it's popular is because many communities populated by colonials have ranches that are randomly sprinkled among them. Taking a run-down ranch amid a sea of colonials and turning it into yet another polished colonial is considered to a relatively safe bet. If the predominant style in town is that of the colonial, then buyers obviously buy there because they like colonials. Therefore, the run-down ranch house is often a natural candidate for flipping after structurally overhauling it to a colonial.

Another popular structural overhaul is to expand a *Cape Cod–style home* or fully convert it to a colonial. Because Capes have limited space on the second floor, they represent another top candidate for people looking to flip. But be careful. Capes were typically built in clusters by developers and their sizes are usually pretty uniform, which means their sale prices can be uniform as well. If you try to flip one of them by changing the structure, you might turn off buyers who are afraid to pay more to own the biggest home on the block. If you can't flip it at a good number, or flip it at all, then you have made a mistake in your choice of renovations. As we said earlier, be very aware of the other homes around your "flip project."

def•i•ni•tion

Cape Cod–style houses built in colonial times (1600s–1700s) were small, one-floor symmetrical homes with a steep-pitched roof and a centered chimney. They were built primarily in the New England region of the United States. In the 1930s and 1940s, thousands of Cape Cod revivals were built all over the United States, but particularly in Michigan, Ohio, and Pennsylvania. These revivals consisted of one-and-a-half-story homes with no more than one or two bedrooms and sometimes a bathroom on the second floor.

Putting an addition onto a home before flipping it is expensive, but it can make great financial sense when the home is significantly smaller than its peers. This can be a fabulous moneymaker for you when you find that rare breed of tiny home that somehow got mixed up in a neighborhood full of giants. The home may have actually been the servant's quarters to one of the neighboring properties over 100 years ago. It was also quite common in the eighteenth and nineteenth centuries for fathers to build small houses nearby for newly married daughters and sons. In any event, it's a great opportunity to use the imposing homes around it as the motivating force to expand the size of the home and dramatically bring up the value of your flip project.

Seller Alert

Be mindful of scale when putting on an addition. We have seen so many flip projects where the addition is so gigantic that it literally dwarfs the rest of the home. It is not any buyer's dream to buy a home with a tiny entry hall and living room leading into a cavernous addition slapped onto the back or side of the house. It ruins flow and makes the home seem lopsided. Another mistake is when the addition eats up too much of the property, making the house disproportionately large compared to the yard.

The Restoration

The restoration project is a more accessible project to flippers because it's less expensive than a structural overhaul and because many flippers are able to do much of the work themselves, saving on labor costs. No walls are being moved. There is less demolition involved. The roof and exterior walls of the property remain intact. And it can be done faster than a structural overhaul. In some ways, a restoration is also the most fun, especially if you love to roll up your sleeves and get involved in the improvements that are usually rewarding.

Restorations typically cost less than a structural overhaul, but make no mistake about it: they can still be expensive. Because your money will be spread out on upgrades all over the home, it's sometimes more complicated and difficult to keep tabs on cost, if you're not experienced. Putting on an addition is like starting from scratch; you can anticipate costs better because it's building from the ground up with all new plumbing and wiring. But in a restoration you can find new and unexpected problems each time you take down a light fixture or move a pipe. Your costs can unexpectedly go up considerably.

The restoration home might be in need of many major upgrades, including the following:

◆ New kitchen

◆ New bathrooms

◆ Refinished wood floors

◆ Restored or replaced moldings

◆ New or restored windows

◆ Repairing serious foundation cracks or compromises

◆ New furnace

◆ Updated electrical wiring and electric panel

◆ New plumbing

The Diamond in the Rough

We call a diamond-in-the-rough home one that is essentially a good home that just shows quite poorly. But when you look closely, you see that it is only in need of *cosmetic improvements*. All that is required to flip this house is some polishing up in order to make it attractive for a buyer. But do not be fooled by your low costs and fast turn-around time!

Flipping a diamond in the rough is yet another example of something in the business of real estate being simple but not easy. The challenge here is in knowing which cosmetic improvements to make. When you are strategic about the upgrades, you can keep your costs low, yet at the same time transform the home and make it look as though you spent much more money than you actually did.

def•i•ni•tion

Cosmetic improvements are any upgrades made to a home that are superficial and inexpensive relative to structural improvements. They improve the aesthetic appearance of a home in most cases. For example, painting, refinishing floors, and replacing light fixtures are considered to be cosmetic improvements.

A typical diamond-in-the-rough home often has these characteristics:

♦ It is equal to or greater in size than other homes on the same street. In other words, there is no need for an addition; it's already large enough.

♦ There is no need to spend money on big-ticket items such as a new roof, siding, or a heating system.

♦ The interior construction is good and it has charm. The house is generally well built, solid, and perhaps has great architectural details.

♦ Still, the home appears to buyers to be in great disrepair. They perceive the property to have been neglected and in need of vast amounts of money to fix. But it's an illusion. In reality, the neglect is only cosmetic in nature. There is a hidden potential in the home that won't be seen by the average buyer because he or she is so distracted and turned off by what is perceived as a lot of work.

Some examples of cosmetic problems that can scare off buyers are overgrown weeds and shrubs, old and faded wallpaper, superficial cracks in walls, floors that are in need of refinishing, dirty or stained wall-to-wall carpeting, and dated light fixtures. When they exist altogether, these repairs can seem to add up and become overwhelming to a buyer. However, to a flipper, it's a gold mine because he or she understands that it will take very little money to correct these minor sins and make the home beautiful again. It's just a diamond waiting to be polished and sold at auction.

It's a fact of real estate that the majority of buyers will pay a premium for a home in move-in condition. Updated homes sell for more money; therefore, you will make more when you flip it.

Contractors and Partners

Unless you happen to be a contractor yourself, you will likely be hiring one to make your upgrades. The way you communicate and work with this person is crucial to your success. You may also have a partner with whom you plan to flip homes. That person could also be your contractor, a passive investor, or even a spouse. In this section, we discuss all of these relationships.

Contractors

You will be working with the contractor, either as a temporary employee or as a partner. With either form of relationship, the contractor is still your key "point person" and you will likely be communicating on a daily basis, making hundreds of decisions together. The following are three things that you need to make the relationship work, in order of importance.

◆ **Trust** is the most important dynamic between you and the contractor. This person may have the biggest impact on your profit or loss, success or failure. He will be at the property every day, and quite often while you are not there. There is usually a lot of money at stake with a flip. You should feel you can trust him to show up every day, to do good work, to keep costs down, to be ethical, and to forewarn you when he thinks you are about to make a mistake.

One area where trust between the both of you can impact cost is that of upgrades. You might expect him to warn you that a choice you're making is foolish and costly, but not all contractors for hire will do that. Let's say that you want to add an extra bathroom. You may not realize that the diameter of the sewage pipe going out to the street isn't wide enough to accommodate another bathroom in the house. Replacing that pipe is an enormous cost, but the contractor may not forewarn you of this if the nature of your relationship is such that he simply does what he's told.

◆ Obviously, you should feel that the contractor has **talent**—that he's good at his job. But we're not just referring to how well he can frame out a new addition. You should feel that he has a broad view of what a home needs or doesn't need as well as being a clear-headed, solution-oriented person. Many contractors are quite good at telling you what you cannot do instead of proactively offering ideas about what you can do.

Trick of the Trade

Another plus for sharing profits with the contractor is that you may be able to pay him less up front and save on your pre-project, out-of-pocket expenses. You could also give him a combination of profits and a small weekly salary.

◆ **Incentive** is your personal insurance policy. We strongly urge you to create incentive for the contractor to keep costs down, do the job fast, and do it well. The easiest way to incentivize him is to cut him in on the profits. Now, by definition, this makes him a partner and maybe that's not such a bad idea. You'll be sharing a portion of the profits when the project is finished but there will likely be more profit to share as he will be sure to come in under budget and on time, if he's motivated. Here's one small example. In the demolition phase, dumpsters will be loaded and hauled away. There is a charge to you each time another one is hauled. But some contractors will not fill the dumpster up all the way, creating additional and unnecessary expense. You may not be aware that the dumpster fees are higher than they need to be. A contractor who is motivated to keep costs down will fill those dumpsters to the brim before taking them away.

Partners

If you are just getting into the business of flipping, taking one or more partners can be a good idea. Depending on what kind of a partner you have (limited partner versus general partner), it can be helpful to divvy up the work and spread the risk around so that you don't have to shoulder all the responsibility of the investment. There are two broad types of partnerships in any business: a general partner and a limited partner. A limited partner invests money in the venture or business but has nothing to do with the day-to-day operations. If the business should fail, he is not liable or exposed for any more money than his initial investment. However, a general partner is legally liable for any debts or even legal action that the business may face.

On the downside of partnerships, while you have reduced your risk, responsibility, and liability, you must also share your profits. Partnerships are also susceptible to conflict which can be very bad for business, not to mention your personal friendship. Take the time to evaluate your need for a partner and who the best candidate would be.

Seller Alert

Flipping will have tax implications for you. Regardless of whether or not you make this your profession or just a side activity, profits will be taxed by the IRS as income. But the IRS wants to know what "kind" of income it is. For example, if flipping homes is your job, then the IRS will tax your profits as *active income*. If it's something you do on the side as a hobby, it will be taxed as *passive income*. This matters because if you are running it as a business (and receiving active income), then you must pay social security taxes. If you have employees, you must also pay payroll taxes and worker's compensation, too.

Further, if you take on a partner, be sure that he or she is labeling the income the same way that you are. For example, let's say that you have taken your contractor on as a general partner. Not only has he invested in the project, he is working on the project as well. Plus, he has assigned employees to work on the project. While you may claim it as passive income, he may claim it as active income, coming in through his contracting company. The IRS will pick this up.

Kickoff and Timeline

You will begin the process of selling a flipped home the minute that your offer to buy it is accepted. Even though you may not close on the purchase for several weeks or months, you will need to set your plans in motion so that you can begin work the day after closing.

Speed is one of the most important considerations when flipping a home. The goal, whenever possible, is to sell the property in the same market cycle in which you bought it. Market cycles are periods of time over the course of a year where many homes tend to go up for sale. For example, many communities in the United States consider the "spring market" to be the most desirable time to sell. The spring market typically begins in January and ends in June.

Home values (and the speed at which homes sell) are always moving and changing. It is easier to predict future value within one given market cycle, such as the one between January and June. It's much riskier to buy in one cycle and then wait to sell it in the next, because your prediction may be way off.

This business is about hedging your bets and having built-in safety nets. A universally accepted safety net in the home flipping business is to work swiftly in order to sell the home in a market period similar to the one in which you bought it.

Like any renovation or construction project, you should have a master timeline to keep you focused, on time, and therefore on budget. Time is money! There are so many marks to hit and they must be hit in a certain order, too. This is the area of flipping homes where it is most important to understand construction, each specific upgrade, how long each will take, and how each one impacts another. You could almost compare a home to the human body. Both have "systems" running throughout. Plumbing and electrical wires are like the veins of a home. The ceiling, floors, and walls are the bones. As soon as you mess with one part, it has an effect on other parts.

To create your timeline, begin with a master list of all your upgrades, how long they will take to complete, and in what order they will be done. The following is a sample chronological list of improvements that may be made when flipping a home and the order in which they should be made.

Trick of the Trade

The following are just three examples where timing and order really do matter and how upgrades affect one another:

- ◆ Update the electric before renovating anything, especially kitchens and baths. The new outlets get placed and wired long before paint gets applied, and moldings, tile backsplashes, and appliances get installed.

- ◆ Never paint interior walls before refinishing floors. The fine dust from sanding embeds itself in the fresh paint. Depending on how many layers of stain and polyurethane you're applying, allow as many as five or six days for floors to cure, or dry.

- ◆ Do landscaping after you paint the exterior, not before, as it's very difficult to get all the scrapings from the old paint up from grass and around shrubs. Exterior painting should be scheduled for when temperatures will be at least 50°F; above 60°F is even better, but no higher than 85°F.

Tasks	Permit Opened	Inspections/Permit Closed
1. Demolition		
2. Replace plumbing pipes		
3. Replace electric panel		
4. Frame out new walls		
5. Install new electric wiring		
6. Put up drywall		
7. Install electric outlets and switches		
8. Install ceiling		
9. Install light fixtures		
10. Install crown molding		
11. Install countertops		
12. Install tubs, sinks, showers, and toilets		
13. Install new flooring		
14. Install kitchen appliances		
15. Refinish wood floors		
16. Install base moldings		
17. Paint interior		

When the renovation and upgrade work is completed, you should build about a week or so into your schedule to have the home staged, photographed, and generally prepared for sale. In order to do this in a timely manner, you should have already completed the process of researching, interviewing, and choosing a Realtor, if you are using one to market your flipped property.

Seller Alert _____

When you schedule your final inspections with the local municipality and pass them, your permits will then be closed. After your permits close, your property taxes may be raised as a result of the improvements you have made. Most Realtors (and many buyers) know this and wonder what your new assessment is. Be prepared to share the new tax bill with potential buyers when you sell the home.

Yardsticks for Success

Calculating sheer profit is what most of us might think is the only measurement of success that matters when you flip homes. After all, that's the goal, isn't it? Not always.

Learning the Business

If you are just getting into the flipping business and working on your first project, you might set realistic goals. For example, the goal may be to get through your first flip and learn as much as you possibly can without "losing" money (just breaking even). If you accomplish that, then you were successful. Most experienced flippers would say that breaking even your first time out "ain't bad." The learning curve in flipping is so incredibly steep that we can guarantee you'll still be learning on your fiftieth flip.

Return on Investment (ROI)

Return on investment (ROI) is a common term that reflects how much money you made compared to how much you invested. It shows profit or loss on an investment and it is a number that is expressed as a percentage. Many flippers aim for 20 percent return on their money but may be quite happy if they end up with a 10 percent return. Going below 10 percent is still showing a profit, of course, but the margin for error is getting thin and if something goes wrong, you could easily shift from showing profits to showing losses. Shooting for 25 to 30 percent is ambitious and not typically realistic. It's not that it can't happen, but it's a very talented flipper indeed who can get that kind of ROI on a consistent basis!

To calculate the ROI on a flip, begin by tabulating all your costs, including the purchase of the home, to establish your total investment. Let's assume the flip will be purchased for $200,000 and you have $50,000 to use as a down payment. Your plan is to flip the home within three months, and you expect to sell it for $275,000 when you're done.

How to Calculate ROI on a Flip

Item	Cost
Down Payment on Home Purchase	$50,000
Mortgage Payoff	$150,000
Closing Costs	$3,000
Materials	$,000
Labor	$,000
3 Mos. Mortgage Payments	$3,300
3 Mos. Property Taxes	$900
3 Mos. Homeowner's Insurance	$210
Permit	$300
5% Real Estate Commission on Sale	$13,750
Closing Costs on Sale	$700
Realty Transfer Tax	$850
Total Investment	$248,010

Your "income" will be the price for which the flip sells. Let's assume that your prediction was correct and the property sells for $275,000. To calculate your ROI, divide the income (or sale price) by your investment (or costs associated with flipping):

> $275,000 Sale Price (or income on the investment)
>
> ÷ 248,010 Investment (or cost associated with flipping)
>
> = 1.1088, or an 11% return

Trick of the Trade _____

A fantastic way to boost your profit even more is by living in the home as you make the upgrades or renovations. This is hard to do if you have a family whom you do not want to move around from property to property. But if you are a mobile-type person or perhaps single and can reside in the home you are flipping, you will save by eliminating the cost of renting a place (or paying mortgage and taxes) to live in another location.

How to Market a Flipped Home

A flipped home should be marketed like any other home using the principles of SALE (see Chapter 9), but with two specific additions: sell the upgrades themselves, and emphasize the contractor's level of work to potential buyers.

To review, SALE stands for the following:

S = Stage

A = Aggressively Price

L = Lead the Deal

E = Expose the Property

Lead with the Best

On almost every level of marketing (MLS, brochures, and the like), tell potential buyers what you have done to transform this home. Many of the buyers and probably all of the Realtors will remember the property's condition from when you bought it just a few short months ago. Make it clear immediately that this is a "new and improved" version. You're saying to the buyer pool, through your marketing channels, that if you haven't seen this home lately, you haven't seen it—come see it with a fresh perspective.

Sell the Contractor

Quality of workmanship will be extremely important to potential buyers because they may be wary of flippers out to make a fast buck using cheap materials and shoddy labor. Deal with this fear head on by educating everyone to the level of workmanship of the contractor. You must establish credibility and buyer confidence in your construction team. If the contractor has a strong reputation locally and has done other good work, direct buyers to those other properties as well as providing testimonials from past clients.

The Least You Need to Know

- ◆ Flipping is the practice of buying a property and quickly selling it for a profit, usually after making some improvements.

- ◆ Flipping requires a deep understanding of the local real estate market, buyer expectations, construction, finance, architecture, décor—and a willingness to assume risk.

◆ The five ingredients to a successful flipping formula can be remembered by thinking of the acronym LUCKY, which stands for **L**ocation, **U**pgrades, **C**ontractors and Partners, **K**ickoff and Timeline, and **Y**ardsticks for Success.

◆ The three types of flips are structural overhauls, restorations, and diamonds in the rough.

◆ There are two broad types of partnerships. A limited partner has no responsibility or liability beyond his initial investment. A general partner is legally liable for any debts or legal action that the business may face.

◆ To determine your return on investment, divide your income from the project (sale price) by your investment (costs associated with flipping) to come up with a percentage.

Part 3

Negotiating and Closing the Deal

Part 3 of this book addresses what to do from the time that you receive an offer all the way to the time of closing. An offer must be properly evaluated and can be negotiated to be more beneficial to you, as well as to protect you. We show you how to assess the quality of the offer and negotiate it by making "counteroffers" until you and your buyer come to an agreement. Then, we walk you through the stages of a deal such as the home inspection, environmental issues, appraisal, mortgage contingencies, and final walk-through. Finally, we show you how to calculate your profit, detail your preclosing responsibilities, and talk about everything that happens at the closing table, as well as offering a simple guide to packing and moving.

Evaluating and Accepting an Offer

In This Chapter

- The four elements of an offer
- Interpreting terms and provisions
- Evaluating financing letters
- The buyer's profile
- How to accept an offer

Congratulations! You have an offer! It's a great feeling when a buyer loves your home enough to make an offer. Not only does it validate the way you feel about your home, but there is such a feeling of relief after all the planning and preparation. It's even more rewarding if you are able to sell in a falling or down market. When you get an offer that is at or near full list price, you obviously have done a good job in pricing it, presenting it, and exposing it to the buyer pool.

While most people think mainly of price, there are actually four important elements to an offer:

♦ The price

♦ The terms (provisions of contract)

♦ The source (quality and profile of buyer)

♦ The presentation

In this chapter, we discuss all four elements. Some of the issues relating to them will be clearly written into the offer and others will not. You and/or your Realtor will evaluate them, and by doing so you will negotiate a stronger deal. You may also save yourself from the stress of having the deal fall apart for certain unforeseen reasons.

Price

From the time that you first decided to sell, you likely had a price in mind that you hoped to get. Now is the moment of truth, when you find out if you've gotten it or not. An offer will come in one of three ways: below list price, above list price, or right at the list price. Let's discuss all three scenarios—how to interpret them as well as how to respond in the best way possible.

Below the List Price

When an offer comes to you below list price, it's understandable for a seller to feel insulted or to take it personally. Resist the urge to do this. This is a critical point in time for you where you can either engage this buyer in a negotiation or throw a potentially solid contract out the window. It's possible that this buyer will not budge on his price. Then again, he might come up to an acceptable number. But you will never know unless you—or your Realtor—respond to his offer and engage him in a negotiation.

Now, let's talk about your approach when this buyer will not budge off his below list price. Again, the natural tendency for many sellers would be to reject the offer. Before you do that, you should be 100 percent sure that the buyer is wrong about the value of your home. The way to be sure is to go back to square one with your Realtor and examine updated (up-to-the-minute) comps to find out what the market has been doing since you first priced it. If your updated analysis shows that this buyer is, in fact, wrong, then perhaps you are correct in rejecting his offer.

But what if he is right about the value of your home, and his low offer is an accurate reflection of the marketplace? This will be disappointing to you and you will likely go through a form of grief. However, think long and hard about rejecting him. If you do, you could be passing up the highest price you will ever receive in this market cycle.

There is a silver lining in this scenario. If the value of your home fell because the market is heading downward, it's probably going to continue in that direction. Therefore, this number may look good when you look back six months from now.

 Seller Alert _____

Never forget the six- to nine-month rule! A seller cannot truly understand how well he did on the sale of real estate until approximately six to nine months have passed. Just like the stock market, it is impossible to know when the market has hit the bottom—or the top—until the moment is well behind us. Until a seller reflects back on the market conditions at the time of the sale, she cannot make a concrete judgment. At the time, she may have thought that she gave her home away. Yet, six to nine months later, the market may prove that she actually did quite well.

Full-Price Offers

When an offer comes in right at list price, most sellers are thrilled to get what they asked for. This is called a full-price offer. It's a great feeling and worthy of celebration.

Surprisingly, some sellers reject full-price offers. Perhaps these sellers were only testing the waters in the market to see what price they would get. When they actually got the price they wanted, they doubted themselves and worried that they had undersold it. Sometimes the decision to sell was just not well thought out. The sellers may have had nowhere to go, or they simply realized how much they like the home and wanted to stay in it after all.

Whatever the reason, problems can arise when a seller refuses to sell to a buyer who has met the full list price. The buyer feels duped and that his emotions have been played with because he has fallen in love with something he cannot have. Time, money, and energy have also been spent by attorneys, Realtors, and the seller herself.

If you receive a full-price offer and then change your mind, believing that your home is worth more, you have three ethical choices.

♦ Try to reopen the negotiations. Go back to the buyer who made the offer and ask for more money. However, it is extremely difficult to get a buyer to give you more than what you asked for, particularly if he is not competing against other buyers. Good luck!

◆ Accept the full-price offer. If you do not accept the offer, you are gambling. You are betting on the fact that you are going to make more money with the next buyer, if there is one. If you don't make more money, you will have rolled the dice and lost.

◆ Raise the list price. Reject the full-price offer and change the list price to a higher number. This approach is unusual and sends a negative message to buyers about the seller's ability to follow through on an agreement. They're afraid to get into a deal with a seller who may raise the number again once they make an offer at the new price. The buyers have lost trust and the seller is in danger of losing her credibility.

The point, which we make again and again in this book, is that you, as a seller, should approach the pricing of your home with extreme thought and care. It is essential that you have gone over this number with a fine-tooth comb and that you are truly willing to accept an offer at the number you have chosen.

Above the List Price

This is obviously a terrific situation for any seller. It usually happens when there is more than one buyer competing for your home. This is also known as a multiple bid or, more commonly, a bidding war.

If you have a bidding war on your home, it is crucial that you set up ground rules for all the buyers involved. If you do not, there can be serious consequences. It is your responsibility (along with your Realtor's) to make sure that the playing field is level for everyone and that the rules are crystal clear. Buyers are cautious by nature. If a buyer suspects that he is not being dealt with in a straightforward and fair manner, he will often walk away from the negotiation and the home itself. Losing a potential buyer in this manner is so unnecessary. To avoid this, take the time to have a lengthy discussion with your Realtor about what the rules will be and how they will be communicated. We have shared what we have experienced to be the best approach to handling bidding wars in Chapter 11.

Terms

A term is a provision in the contract. These provisions may apply to the duties or obligations of the seller and buyer; your rights as well as those of the buyer; and the dates by which responsibilities need to be met, such as forwarding deposit monies and performing inspections.

There will be many terms in the contract. Some of the most important are discussed in the following sections.

If the Buyer Needs to Sell Property Before Buying Yours

Many buyers need to sell and get the money from the sale of one home in order to buy another home. This is often a matter of choreography where two closings happen on the same day. Your buyer will take the money she made on her home and use it to secure the loan to buy your home. Much of the time it works out, but timing is everything.

The potential problem for you, as a seller, is when the buyer makes a written provision in the contract that the purchase of your home is based on (or contingent upon) her selling her property first. This is a dangerous term for you. You should avoid it if you can. When the deal on your buyer's own home falls apart, your deal will fall apart, too! It's a domino effect. When one deal goes down in this manner, usually every deal associated with it goes down. If you accept a contingency like this one, you assume the liability of your buyer.

Ask the buyer outright if she needs to sell any real estate in order to buy yours. If the answer is no, that's great—but have it confirmed in writing that she will close with or without the money from her own home. If you have to accept this contingency because it's your only option, then proceed with great caution. Ask a lot of questions about the status of the other deal, how far along and how secure it is. Many buyers can also arrange some type of bridge financing—a short-term loan taken out to buy your home that is to be paid back when the buyer sells her own home.

Closing Date

Closing dates are the most common term to be negotiated when accepting an offer. They are usually pretty straightforward. You and the buyer can either coordinate your schedules or you cannot. One way or another, a mutually acceptable date gets negotiated.

The problems arise when something unexpected comes up later on in the deal, well after you've signed and accepted the contract. Sometimes the buyer decides that he wants to move in sooner than he'd stated. Or perhaps there is an inspection repair issue, or an environmental or financing issue that delays the closing. But these scenarios usually come as a surprise and cannot be known or negotiated when you receive the offer.

Seller Alert

When you and the buyer sign off on an anticipated closing date in the contract, keep in mind that the exact date does not always have to be met, legally. Contracts often have closing date language that reads like this: "The closing will take place on or around May 5th." This means that either party can delay it for a short time—perhaps a few days—without violating the contract. In some states, when a number of days have passed beyond the closing date, either the buyer or seller can have an attorney send a "time is of the essence" letter that notifies the other party that they are in danger of violating the contract. Overall, be careful to build in a backup plan for a delayed closing date.

Deposit Monies

Ideally, a down payment on a home should be 20 percent or more. Banks don't like to loan more than 80 percent of the value of a home. They want to see buyers personally invested in the property and they also want to limit their liability. However, buyers routinely put down less. Some will put down 15 percent, 10 percent, 5 percent, and even less.

Until closing, deposit money is usually held in an escrow account of an attorney or title company, or in the listing Realtor's agency account. If you or the buyer back out of the deal for a fair reason that is in accordance with one of the provisions in your contract, then the deposit money is returned to the buyer. But if the buyer backs out for reasons that violate the provisions in the contract, then she may lose her deposit money to you.

For example, the buyer can get out of the deal if her financing falls apart and she is unable to secure a loan—assuming that the contract stated the purchase was contingent upon her getting a loan. Most contracts do state this, by the way. (This is why it's so important to review the preapproval letter from her lender that was attached to the contract. Later in this chapter we discuss how to evaluate preapproval letters.)

On the other hand, if a buyer simply changes her mind about wanting to buy your home after all the contract provisions have been met, then you may be able to keep her deposit money and sell the home to someone else.

Deposit monies usually arrive in three sections and on three different dates.

- ◆ First deposit: Also known as the earnest money deposit, this comes with the offer itself. Earnest money can be anywhere from a dollar to tens of thousands of dollars.

◆ Second Deposit: Typically comes a few days or weeks into the transaction, depending on how real estate is practiced in your area. It goes into the same escrow account as the first deposit, ideally.

◆ Final Deposit: The last portion of the deposit comes on closing day, along with the loan money from the buyer's bank.

To calculate the percent that your buyer is putting down, add up all three payments and divide it by the purchase price.

Seller Alert

There are stages in the transaction when a buyer can legally back out of the deal and the deposit money will be refunded. However, sometimes a buyer will back out after she is legally allowed to, according to the contract. In those cases, the seller keeps the first deposit and, if the second deposit was already made, the buyer stands to lose that, too.

Calculating Percent Down on Offer

First Deposit:	$1,000
Second Deposit:	$36,500
Third Deposit:	$37,500
Total Deposit:	$75,000
Divided by	$375,000 Sale Price

= 20% Down

The amount of deposit that the buyer is putting down on your home may not be spelled out in percentage form, but rather in exact dollars. It is important for you and your Realtor to calculate the percentage because the more cash she is putting down, the less of a financial risk she is going to be.

Mortgage Contingency

Most buyers borrow money in the form of a mortgage. When you receive an offer, the buyer will not yet have this mortgage in place. What he should have is a letter from a bank, lending institution, or mortgage broker stating that he has been preapproved for a loan. A copy of this letter should be included with his offer.

Unfortunately, some of these letters are not worth the paper they are printed on. In the years leading up to the subprime crash in 2007 and 2008, it was easy to get a letter even if a buyer was a poor risk. Some say it's still easy to get one of these letters. In any event, the following sections discuss some tips for how to read between the lines and fact-check letters from lenders.

The Difference Between a Prequalification Letter and a Preapproval Letter

When a buyer contacts a lender to get a letter stating that she is able to get a loan, she receives what's called a "prequalification" letter or a "preapproval" letter. Too many buyers out there, and even some Realtors, use the term "preapproval" to describe both types.

A prequalification letter can be obtained—via fax—without the buyer ever having met a representative of the bank or lender. She may only have spoken to the representative on the telephone. The buyer gives the lender a Social Security number and a verbal description of her income and assets. The lender will then run a credit check on the buyer to come up with her credit score. Based on this credit check and verbal statement of income and assets, a letter of prequalification can legally be given to the buyer. The letter doesn't automatically make her a bad risk, but it certainly doesn't ensure that she is a good risk, either.

A preapproval letter, on the other hand, requires giving the lender actual documents that prove income and assets, such as the previous year's taxes, employment pay stubs, and original bank statements. In this scenario, the buyer has demonstrated more of a commitment to this lender, and to you, by taking a concrete step in the pursuit of a loan. The documents that she provided cannot be forged and she has given a more complete financial profile to the bank.

The objective, for a seller, is to know what type of letter you are holding in your hand. Surprisingly, many prequalification letters are labeled as preapproval letters. Here are two ways to distinguish between these letters.

- Ask, or have your Realtor ask, the buyer if she has provided employment pay stubs, W-2s, last year's taxes, and bank statements to her lender. Most buyers answer the question without realizing how revealing the answer is. If the answer is no, then perhaps you should not sign the offer until she has done so.

- Ask the buyer's Realtor if you may call the lender directly to verify the information. If she has nothing to hide, she shouldn't have a problem with this. If she does, that may be a red flag.

When a Buyer Puts Down Mostly Cash

Some buyers put down a huge chunk of money—40 to 80 percent of the purchase price. If your buyer plans to do that, then the loan is a lesser issue and the fact that he really has that kind of cash is the greater issue.

In this case, he should provide an original bank statement showing that he has that much money readily available. If he'd rather not do that, then he should provide a letter from a third party stating that he has the money. It could be a letter from his own accountant, attorney, or bank representative.

When a Buyer Takes the Mortgage Out of the Deal

When a buyer waives the mortgage contingency or "takes the mortgage contingency out of the deal," she is still borrowing money to buy your home, but she is not making the sale contingent upon her obtaining a mortgage. In other words, she is saying that, even if she is unable to secure a loan, she will still commit to buying your home no matter what. She is trying to show that her finances are strong and that you do not need to worry that she will be a financial risk to you, the seller. However, it's risky for her, the buyer, to waive the right to back out of the deal because ultimately, she can be required to buy a home that she cannot afford.

 Seller Alert _____

> There is one way for the buyer to legally back out of the deal even if she has waived the mortgage contingency, and that is if her Realtor or attorney put a clause in the offer stating that she can withdraw if your home "does not appraise." If this clause is not there, she cannot back out even if the bank appraiser says that your home is not worth the amount she offered. Technically, she would be required to make up the difference between the sale price and the appraised value out of her own pocket because she waived her rights.

Inspection Contingency

Almost every buyer will perform an inspection of your home. Some buyers may waive the right to perform one, but they are the exception and not the rule.

In some states, the inspection is done before the buyer makes an offer. In other states, it is done after the offer is signed and accepted. If the inspection reveals something that the buyer wants repaired and the seller does not wish to repair it, then the buyer can legally back out of the deal. Quite literally, the purchase is *contingent* upon the inspection being satisfactory to both parties. If it is not, the buyer can walk away and will have his deposit money returned to him.

However, if his offer is a good one, try to work with this buyer. Perhaps you can negotiate a term or provision in the contract that satisfies you both. Maybe the buyer will agree to only address big-ticket items such as structural problems or environmental issues. These are items that you would have to address with any buyer, so why not do them for this buyer, now? Or maybe you don't want to make any repairs but will give the buyer a credit at closing—a dollar amount to cover the cost of the repairs.

Seller Alert

Certain environmental and structural issues must be addressed and/or corrected because they are a safety or code violation, or the buyer's lender requires it as a condition of the loan.

Another type of inspection provision is called an inspection cap. This is where a buyer and seller agree to a maximum dollar amount for repair credits. Sometimes, a buyer will make it an "individual item" cap. She may agree, in the contract, not to address any single repair item valued at less than $500. The buyer is saying, in essence, that she does not want to nickel and dime you on small repair items. She just wants to be sure that she can address major problems with the house, like a leaking roof or cracked foundation.

The Source of the Offer

It is also helpful to know as much about the buyer as possible. Sometimes, you can actually predict how smoothly a real estate transaction will go when you understand someone's motivation, level of knowledge, and a bit of their history.

If the buyer's Realtor is good at her job, she will draft and attach a cover letter to the offer with background information on her client. If the following information is not included in the letter, then ask questions. Here are some pertinent ones:

- How long has the buyer been looking for a home? If he has just begun his search, he may not be as strong a buyer as you'd like. When a buyer has been looking for a while, he has seen many homes, enough to know when he's found the right one—and he understands value, too. When a buyer is thoroughly educated to the local real estate market, he will be more confident that he is paying a fair price because he's been at it for a while. Additionally, the deal is more likely to stay together because he is probably tired of shopping and ready to buy. After a while, buyers get tired of giving up their weekends to home searches. We went further into the buyer thought process in Chapter 10.

- Has the buyer recently put an offer in on another home? If so, what happened? It's amazing how honest and forthcoming a buyer will be when you ask a direct question. If she has put in an offer(s) before, she has demonstrated that she is a motivated buyer and is not afraid to step up to the plate when she finds the right home. On the other hand, maybe she frivolously puts offers on homes that appeal to her but has no intention of following through. Either way, by asking this question, you will learn something about her that could be helpful.

- How long has the buyer been at his current job? You shouldn't necessarily hold it against him for being new to his current job—but it can be quite reassuring to hear that he has been at one job for a decade. It's probably further proof of his financial stability.

- Does she currently rent or own? If she's a renter, that can be good news because there are no worries about having to sell property first. On the other hand, if her lease is not up for several months, she may not have the same sense of urgency that you do to close.

- How long has the Realtor known, or been working with, this buyer? If the Realtor has only been working with the buyer for a very short time, the relationship won't be as strong as if they'd been working together for a long time. You are depending on his guidance of the buyer as well as the buyer's trust in the Realtor. If they have a brand-new relationship, the Realtor may not have had enough time to build up the trust needed to guide the buyer and manage the transaction as well as it could be managed. It does not mean that the deal will fall apart, but added to the list of other pertinent questions, you can build a pretty good profile of this buyer and her merits.

The Presentation

The offer should be presented in a legible, clear, and professional manner. It always amazes us when we see purchase contracts come in that are incomplete, confusing, and difficult to read. The following sections discuss the basic elements of a good offer.

Cover Letter

Cover letters are not a legal requirement to making an offer on a home, but they have a positive effect on the presentation. Sometimes, a seller will get two—one from the buyer and one form the buyer's Realtor. The buyer's letter will often say something about who he is, where he comes from, and why he wants to buy the home.

The Realtor's letter will introduce the buyer and will summarize the best points of the offer. These letters also have the effect of putting the seller in a positive mindset before she reads the actual contract.

Here is a sample cover letter from a Realtor:

Property: 100 Main Street, Anytown, USA
Buyers: John and Jane Doe
Date: March 28, 2009

Dear Mr. and Mrs. Seller:

I represent John and Jane Doe in their offer to purchase your beautiful home. They fell in love with it the moment they stepped inside. It was clear to them that you have put a great deal of care into it over the years. They particularly love the unique architecture and open floor plan.

I have been working with the Does for six months in their search for the perfect home. I have come to know them quite well. They have seen dozens of properties and are very educated about the marketplace. They are also very motivated and qualified buyers.

Their offer is quite strong and is summarized as follows. Details can be found in the attached contract.

- Their offering price is $421,000
- They plan to put down a 25 percent deposit
- They are fully preapproved for a mortgage with XYZ Bank
- They have no property to sell in order to purchase yours
- They can close whenever you wish
- They hope to execute as smooth a transaction as possible

I hope that you will seriously consider their offer.

Regards,

Buyers' Realtor

As you can see, the main deal points are clearly outlined and Jane and John Doe have made it clear that they are ready, willing, and able buyers.

The Actual Contract

The contract, or purchase offer, is usually about five or six pages long. It outlines the price being offered, the closing date, the amount of the deposits, the amount being borrowed from a lender, the dates by which certain obligations must be met (such as inspections), items included in the sale, environmental and regional laws, and a signature page.

NEW JERSEY ASSOCIATION OF REALTORS ® STANDARD FORM OF REAL ESTATE CONTRACT
© 1996 New Jersey Association of REALTORS®, Inc.

THIS FORM MAY BE USED ONLY IN THE SALE OF A ONE TO FOUR FAMILY RESIDENTIAL PROPERTY OR VACANT ONE FAMILY LOTS. THIS FORM IS SUITABLE FOR USE ONLY WHERE THE SELLER HAS PREVIOUSLY EXECUTED A WRITTEN LISTING AGREEMENT.

THIS IS A LEGALLY BINDING CONTRACT THAT WILL BECOME FINAL WITHIN THREE BUSINESS DAYS. DURING THIS PERIOD YOU MAY CHOOSE TO CONSULT AN ATTORNEY WHO CAN REVIEW AND/OR CANCEL THE CONTRACT. SEE SECTION ON ATTORNEY REVIEW FOR DETAILS.

CONTRACT OF SALE

1 **1. PURCHASE AGREEMENT AND PROPERTY DESCRIPTION:**
2
3 _____   _____ , Buyer,
4
5 whose address is _____
6
7 **AGREES TO PURCHASE FROM**
8
9 _____   _____ , Seller,
10
11 whose address is _____
12 **THROUGH THE BROKER(S) NAMED IN THIS AGREEMENT AT THE PRICE AND TERMS STATED**
13 **BELOW, THE FOLLOWING PROPERTY:**
14
15 Property Address:_____
16 Shown on the municipal tax map of _____
17 County _____
18 As Lot _____ Block _____ Approximate size of lot _____
19
20 **THE WORDS "BUYER" AND "SELLER" INCLUDE ALL BUYERS AND SELLERS LISTED ABOVE.**
21 **2. PURCHASE PRICE: THE TOTAL PURCHASE PRICE IS:** $ _____
22
23 **3. MANNER OF PAYMENT:**
24   (A) **Deposit paid** by Buyer on signing of this Agreement to ☐ Listing Broker or ☐ Participating $ _____
25 Broker, by ☐ cash or ☐ check, for which this is a receipt:
26
27   (B) **Additional deposit** to be paid by Buyer on or before _____ (date): $ _____
28   **All deposit monies paid by the Buyer shall be held in escrow in the NON-INTEREST BEARING**
29 **TRUST ACCOUNT of** _____ , **Escrowee, until closing of**
30 **title, at which time all monies shall be paid over to the Seller.** The deposit monies shall not be paid over
31 to the Seller prior to the closing of title, unless agreed in writing by both the Buyer and Seller. In the event
32 the Buyer and Seller cannot agree on the disbursement of these escrow monies, the Escrowee may place the
33 deposit monies in Court requesting the Court to resolve the dispute.
34
35   (C) **IF PERFORMANCE BY BUYER IS CONTINGENT UPON OBTAINING A MORTGAGE.**
36   The Buyer agrees to apply immediately for a mortgage loan through any lending institution of the
37 Buyer's choice or the office of the Listing Broker or the Participating Broker. The application shall be
38 furnished by the Buyer in writing on an application form prescribed by the lending institution to which the
39 application shall be submitted. Buyer shall also furnish, in a timely manner, such other documents and
40 information as is usually required by said lending institution. Failure of Buyer to comply with the
41 foregoing, in good faith, shall be deemed a breach of this Contract of Sale. The amount of mortgage loan
42 required by the Buyer is $ _____ and will be what is commonly known as the ☐ (F.H.A.)
43 ☐ (V.A.) ☐ (Conventional) ☐ (A.R.M.) _____ year direct reduction plan with interest at not more
44 than _____ % and not more than _____ Points. Buyer agrees to pay not more
45 than _____ Points. Seller agrees to pay not more than _____ Points. **IF THE**
46 **MORTGAGE LOAN HAS NOT BEEN ARRANGED, OR IF THE BUYER HAS NOT NOTIFIED**
47 **SELLER OF BUYER'S DECISION TO COMPLETE THE TRANSACTION WITHOUT**
48 **OBTAINING A MORTGAGE COMMITMENT, ON OR BEFORE** _____
49 **(Date) THEN EITHER BUYER OR SELLER MAY VOID THIS AGREEMENT BY WRITTEN**
50 **NOTICE TO THE OTHER PARTY.** The method of notifying the other party shall be in accordance
51 with Section 21 of the Agreement. $ _____
52
53   (D) **BALANCE OF PURCHASE PRICE.**
54 The balance of the purchase price shall be paid by cash, certified check or Attorney's Trust Account check
55 on delivery of a _____
56 (Type of Deed). Title to the Property will be free from all claims or rights of others, except as described in
57 Sections 6, 7 and 8 of this Agreement. The deed shall contain the full legal description of the Property.
58 Payment of the balance of the purchase price by Buyer and delivery of the deed and affidavit of title to
59 Seller occur at the "Closing." The Closing will take place on or before_____ , at
60 the office of _____ or such other place as the Seller
61 and the Buyer may agree. $ _____
62
63   **TOTAL PURCHASE PRICE:** $ _____
64
65
66 NJAR form-118-5/04 Page 2 of 8   Buyer's Initials:_____   Seller's Initials:_____

67 **4. BUYER FINANCIALLY ABLE TO CLOSE:**
68   Buyer represents that Buyer has sufficient cash available (together with the mortgage referred to in Section 3) to
69 complete this purchase.
70
71 **5. ACCURATE DISCLOSURE OF SELLING PRICE:**
72   The Buyer and Seller certify that this Contract accurately reflects the gross sale price as indicated on line
73 sixty-three (63) of this Contract. The Buyer and Seller **UNDERSTAND AND AGREE** that **THIS INFORMATION**
74 **SHALL BE DISCLOSED** to the Internal Revenue Service as required by law.
75
76 **6. TENANTS, IF ANY:**
77   This sale is made subject to the following tenancies. The Seller warrants that these tenancies are not in violation of
78 existing Municipal, County, State or Federal rules, regulations or laws.
79 **NAME   LOCATION   RENT   SECURITY DEPOSIT   TERM**
80
81
82
83 **7. QUALITY OF TITLE:**
84   This sale will be subject to easements and restrictions of record, if any, and such state of facts as an accurate survey
85 might disclose. Generally, an easement is a right of a person other than the owner of Property to use a portion of the
86 Property for a special purpose. A restriction is a recorded limitation on the manner in which a Property owner may use
87 his/her/their Property. The Buyer does not have to complete the purchase, however, if any easement, restriction, or
88 facts disclosed by an accurate survey would substantially interfere with the use of the Property for residential
89 purposes. The sale will also be made subject to applicable zoning ordinances.
90   Title to the Property shall be good, marketable and insurable, at regular rates, by any title insurance company
91 licensed to do business in the State of New Jersey, subject only to the claims and rights described in this section and
92 Section 6. Buyer agrees to order title insurance commitment (title search) and survey if necessary and to furnish copies
93 to Seller. In the event Seller's title shall contain any exceptions other than as set forth in this paragraph, Buyer shall
94 notify Seller and Seller shall have 30 days within which to eliminate those exceptions. If Seller cannot remove those
95 exceptions, Buyer shall have the option to void this Contract or to proceed with closing of title without any reduction
96 in the purchase price. If Buyer elects to void this Contract, as provided in the preceding sentence, the deposit money
97 shall be returned to Buyer and Seller shall reimburse Buyer for search and survey expenses not exceeding
98 _____ dollars.
99
100 **8. BUILDING AND ZONING LAWS:**
101   The Buyer intends to use the Property as a _____ family home. The Seller states, to the best
102 of the Seller's knowledge, that this use does not violate any applicable zoning ordinance, building code or other law.
103 The Seller will pay for and obtain Certificate of Occupancy, Certificate of Land Use Compliance or other similar
104 document required by law and will arrange and pay for all inspections required to obtain such document. **SELLER**
105 **AGREES TO CORRECT ALL VIOLATIONS, AT THE SELLER'S OWN EXPENSE, PRIOR TO THE**
106 **CLOSING OF TITLE.**
107
108 **9. ITEMS INCLUDED IN SALE:**
109   Gas and electric fixtures, cooking ranges and ovens, hot water heaters, linoleum, T.V. antenna, screens, storm sash,
110 shades, blinds, awnings, radiator covers, heating apparatus and sump pump, if any, except where owned by tenants,
111 are included in this sale. All of the appliances shall be in working order as of the closing of title. **This provision shall**
112 **not survive closing of title.** This means that the Seller **DOES NOT GUARANTEE** the condition of the appliances
113 **AFTER** the deed and affidavit of title have been delivered to the Buyer at the "Closing". **The following items are**
114 **also specifically included:**
115
116
117
118
119 **10. ITEMS EXCLUDED FROM SALE:**
120
121
122
123 **11. ASSESSMENTS:**
124   All confirmed assessments and all unconfirmed assessments which may be imposed by the municipality for public
125 improvements which have been completed as of the date of Closing are to be paid in full by the Seller or credited to
126 the Buyer at the Closing. A confirmed assessment is a lien (legal claim) against the Property. An unconfirmed
127 assessment is a potential lien (legal claim) which, when approved by the appropriate governmental body, will become
128 a legal claim against the Property.
129
130 **12. FINAL INSPECTION:**
131   Seller agrees to permit the Buyer or the Buyer's duly authorized representative to examine the interior and exterior
132 of the Property at any reasonable time immediately before Closing.
133
134 **13. NEW JERSEY HOTEL AND MULTIPLE DWELLING HEALTH AND SAFETY ACT:**
135   If the New Jersey Hotel and Multiple Dwelling Health and Safety Act applies to the Property, the Seller represents
136 that the Property complies with the requirements of the Act.
137
138 **14. NO ASSIGNMENT:**
139   This Agreement shall not be assigned without the written consent of the Seller. This means that the Buyer may not
140 transfer to anyone else his/her/their rights under this Agreement to buy the Property.
141

Buyer's   Seller's
Initials:_____   Initials:_____

142 | **15. RISK OF LOSS:**
143 | The risk of loss or damage to the Property by fire or otherwise, except ordinary wear and tear, is on the Seller until
144 | the Closing.
145 |
146 | **16. ADJUSTMENTS AT CLOSING; RIGHTS TO POSSESSION:**
147 | Rents, water charges, sewer charges, real estate taxes, interest on any existing mortgage to be assumed by Buyer,
148 | and fuel are to be apportioned as of the date of actual closing of title. The Buyer shall be entitled to possession of the
149 | Property and any rents or profits from the Property, immediately upon the delivery of the deed and closing of title. The
150 | Seller shall have the privilege of paying off any person with a claim or right affecting the Property from the proceeds
151 | of this sale at the time of Closing.
152 |
153 | **17. MAINTENANCE AND CONDITION OF PROPERTY:**
154 | The Seller agrees to maintain the grounds, buildings and improvements, in good condition, subject to ordinary
155 | wear and tear. The premises shall be in "broom clean" condition and free of debris on the date of Closing. Seller
156 | represents that all electrical, plumbing, heating and air conditioning systems (if applicable), together with all fixtures
157 | included within the terms of the Agreement now work and shall be in proper working order at the time of Closing.
158 | Seller further states, that to the best of Seller's knowledge, there are currently no leaks or seepage in the roof, walls or
159 | basement **UNLESS OTHERWISE INDICATED IN THE ADDITIONAL CONTRACTUAL PROVISIONS**
160 | **SECTION (Section 34) OF THIS AGREEMENT. ALL REPRESENTATIONS AND/OR STATEMENTS**
161 | **MADE BY THE SELLER, IN THIS SECTION, SHALL NOT SURVIVE CLOSING OF TITLE.** This means
162 | that the Seller DOES NOT GUARANTEE the condition of the premises **AFTER** the deed and affidavit of title have
163 | been delivered to the Buyer at the "Closing".
164 |
165 | **18. LEAD-BASED PAINT DOCUMENT ACKNOWLEDGMENT: (Applies to dwellings built before 1978)**
166 | Buyer acknowledges receipt of the EPA pamphlet entitled "Protect Your Family From Lead In Your Home."
167 | Moreover, a copy of a document entitled "Disclosure of Information and Acknowledgment Lead-Based Paint and
168 | Lead-Based Paint Hazards" has been fully completed and signed by Buyer, Seller and Broker(s) and is appended to
169 | this Agreement as Addendum "A" and is part of this Agreement.
170 |
171 | **19. LEAD-BASED PAINT AND/OR LEAD-BASED PAINT HAZARD CONTINGENCY CLAUSE:**
172 | **(This paragraph is applicable to all dwellings built prior to 1978. The law requires that unless the Buyer and**
173 | **Seller agree to a longer or shorter period, Seller must allow Buyer a ten-day (10) period within which to**
174 | **complete an inspection and/or risk assessment of the Property. Buyer, however, has the right to waive this**
175 | **clause in its entirety.)**
176 | This Agreement is contingent upon an inspection and/or risk assessment (the "Inspection") of the Property by a
177 | certified inspector/risk assessor for the presence of lead-based paint and/or lead-based paint hazards. The Inspection
178 | shall be ordered and obtained by the Buyer at the Buyer's expense, within ten (10) calendar days after the termination
179 | of the Attorney Review period set forth in Section 24 of this Agreement (the "Completion Date"). If the Inspection
180 | indicates that no lead-based paint or lead-based paint hazard is present at the Property, this contingency clause shall be
181 | deemed to be null and void. If the Inspection indicates that lead-based paint or lead-based paint hazard is present at the
182 | Property, this contingency clause will terminate at the time set forth above unless within (5) days from the Completion
183 | Date, the Buyer delivers a copy of the inspection and/or risk assessment report to the Seller and Broker(s) and (a)
184 | advises Seller and Broker(s), in writing, that Buyer is voiding this Agreement; or (b) delivers to Seller and Broker(s) a
185 | written amendment (the "Amendment") to this Agreement listing the specific existing deficiencies and corrections
186 | required by the Buyer. The Amendment shall provide that the Seller agrees to (a) correct the deficiencies; and (b)
187 | furnish the Buyer with a certification from a certified inspector/risk assessor that the deficiencies have been corrected,
188 | before the date of Closing. The Seller shall have _____ days after receipt of the Amendment to sign and return it to
189 | Buyer or send a written counter-proposal to Buyer. If Seller does not sign and return the Amendment or fails to offer a
190 | counter-proposal, this Agreement shall be null and void. In the event Seller offers a counter-proposal, Buyer shall
191 | have _____ days after receipt of the counter-proposal to accept it. If the Buyer fails to accept the counter-proposal
192 | within the time limit provided, this Agreement shall be null and void.
193 |
194 | **20. INSPECTION CONTINGENCY CLAUSE:**
195 | (a) **Responsibilities of Home Ownership**
196 | The Buyer and Seller acknowledge and agree that because the purchase of a home is one of the most significant
197 | investments a person can make in a lifetime, all aspects of this transaction require considerable analysis and
198 | investigation by Buyer before closing title to the Property. While the Broker(s) and Salesperson(s) who are involved in
199 | this transaction are trained as licensees under the License Law of the State of New Jersey, they readily acknowledge
200 | that they have had no special training or experience with respect to the complexities pertaining to the multitude of
201 | structural, topographical and environmental components of this Property. For example, and not by way of limitation,
202 | the Broker(s) and Salesperson(s) have no special training, knowledge or experience with regard to discovering and/or
203 | evaluating physical defects including structural defects, roof, basement, mechanical equipment such as heating, air
204 | conditioning, electrical systems, sewage, plumbing, exterior drainage, termite and other types of insect infestation or
205 | damage caused by such infestation. Moreover, the Broker(s) and Salesperson(s) similarly have no special training,
206 | knowledge or experience with regard to evaluation of possible environmental conditions which might affect the
207 | Property pertaining to the dwelling such as the existence of radon gas, formaldehyde gas, airborne asbestos fibers,
208 | toxic chemicals, underground storage tanks, lead, mold or other pollutants in the soil, air or water.
209 |
210 | (b) **Radon Testing, Reports and Mitigation**
211 | **(Radon is a radioactive gas which results from the natural breakdown of uranium in soil, rock and**
212 | **water. It has been found in homes all over the United States and is a carcinogen. For more information on**
213 | **radon go to www.epa.gov/iaq/radon/pubs/hmbyguid.html or www.state.nj.us/dep/rpp/radon/index.htm or call**
214 | **the NJ Radon Hot Line at 1-800-648-0394 or 1-609-984-5425)**
215 | If the Property has been tested for radon prior to the date of this Agreement, Seller agrees to provide to the
216 | Buyer, at the time of the execution of this Agreement, a copy of the result of the radon test(s) and evidence of any
217 |
218 |

Buyer's
Initials:_____   Seller's
Initials:_____

219 subsequent radon mitigation or treatment of the Property. In any event, Buyer shall have the right to conduct a radon
220 inspection/test as provided and subject to the conditions set forth in subparagraph (C) below. If any test results
221 furnished or obtained by Buyer indicate a concentration level of 4 picocuries per liter (4.0 pCi/L) or more in the
222 subject dwelling, Buyer shall then have the right to void this Agreement by notifying the Seller in writing within seven
223 (7) calendar days of the receipt of any such report. For the purposes of this Paragraph 20, Seller and Buyer agree that
224 in the event a radon gas concentration level in the subject dwelling is determined to be less than 4 picocuries per liter
225 (4.0 pCi/L) without any remediation, such level of radon gas concentration shall be deemed to be an acceptable level
226 ("Acceptable Level") for the purposes of this Agreement. Under those circumstances, the Seller shall be under no
227 obligation to remediate, and this contingency clause as it relates to radon shall be deemed fully satisfied.
228   If the Buyer's qualified inspector reports that the radon gas concentration level in the subject dwelling is four
229 picocuries per liter (4.0 pCi/L) or more, Seller shall have a seven (7) calendar day period after receipt of such report to
230 notify Buyer in writing that the Seller agrees to remediate the gas concentration to an Acceptable Level (unless the
231 Buyer has voided this Agreement as provided in the preceding paragraph). Upon such remediation, the contingency in
232 this Agreement which relates to radon shall be deemed fully satisfied. If Seller fails to notify Buyer of Seller's
233 agreement to so remediate, such failure to so notify shall be deemed to be a refusal by Seller to remediate the radon
234 level to an Acceptable Level, and Buyer shall then have the right to void this Agreement by notifying the Seller in
235 writing within seven (7) calendar days thereafter. If Buyer shall fail to void this Contract within the seven (7) day
236 period, the Buyer shall have waived his right to cancel this Contract, and this Contract shall remain in full force and
237 effect, and Seller shall be under no obligation to remediate the radon gas concentration. If Seller shall agree to
238 remediate the radon to an Acceptable Level, such remediation and associated testing shall be completed by Seller prior
239 to the closing of title.
240
241
242   (c) **Buyer's Rights To Inspections**
243   The Buyer acknowledges that the Property is being sold in an "**AS IS**" condition and that this Agreement is
244 entered into based upon the knowledge of the Buyer as to the value of the land and whatever buildings are upon the
245 Property, and not on any representation made by the Seller, the named Broker(s) or their agents as to character or
246 quality. Therefore, the Buyer, at the Buyer's sole cost and expense, is granted the right to have the dwelling and all
247 other aspects of the Property, inspected and evaluated by "qualified inspectors" (as the term is defined in paragraph (f)
248 below) for the purpose of determining the existence of any physical defects or environmental conditions such as
249 outlined above. If Buyer chooses to make the inspections referred to in this paragraph, such inspections must be
250 completed, and written reports must be furnished to the Seller listed in Section 1 and Broker(s) listed in Section 26 of
251 this Agreement within _____ calendar days after the end of the Attorney Review Period set forth in Section 24 of this
252 Agreement. If Buyer shall fail to furnish such written reports to the Seller and Broker(s) within the time period
253 specified in this paragraph, this contingency clause shall be deemed waived by Buyer, and the Property shall be
254 deemed acceptable by Buyer. The time period for furnishing the inspection reports is referred to as the "Inspection
255 Time Period."
256
257   (d) **Responsibilities to Cure**
258   If any physical defects, or environmental conditions (other than radon) are reported by the inspectors to the
259 Seller within the Inspection Time Period, the Seller shall then have seven (7) calendar days after the receipt of such
260 reports to notify the Buyer in writing that the Seller shall correct or cure any of the defects set forth in such reports. If
261 Seller shall fail to notify Buyer of Seller's agreement to so cure and correct, such failure to so notify shall be deemed
262 to be a refusal by Seller to cure or correct such defects. If Seller shall fail to agree to cure or correct such defects
263 within said seven (7) day period, or if any part of the dwelling is found to be located within a flood hazard area, or if
264 the environmental condition at the Property (other than radon) is incurable and is of such significance as to
265 unreasonably endanger the health of the Buyer, the Buyer shall then have the right to void this Contract by notifying
266 the Seller in writing within seven (7) calendar days thereafter. If Buyer shall fail to void this Contract within the seven
267 (7) day period, the Buyer shall have waived his right to cancel this Contract and this Contract shall remain in full
268 force, and Seller shall be under no obligation to correct or cure any of the defects set forth in the inspections. If Seller
269 shall agree to correct or cure such defects, all such repair work shall be completed by Seller prior to the closing of title.
270 Radon at the Property shall be governed by the provisions of Paragraph (b), above.
271
272   (e) **Flood Hazard Area (delete if not applicable)**
273   Buyer acknowledges that the Property is within a flood hazard area, and Buyer waives Buyer's right to void this
274 Agreement for such reason.
275
276   (f) **Qualifications of Inspectors**
277   Where the term "qualified inspectors" is used in this Contract, it is intended to refer to persons who are licensed
278 by the State of New Jersey for such purpose or who are regularly engaged in the business of inspecting residential
279 properties for a fee and who generally maintain good reputations for skill and integrity in their area of expertise.
280
281 **21. NOTICES:**
282   All notices as required in this Contract must be in writing. All notices shall be by certified mail, by telegram,
283 telefax or by delivering it personally. The telegram, certified letter or telefax will be effective upon sending. The
284 personal delivery will be effective upon delivery to the other party. Notices to the Seller shall be addressed to the
285 address that appears on line fifteen (15) of this Contract. Notice to the Buyer shall be addressed to the address that
286 appears on line five (5) of this Contract.
287
288 **22. MEGAN'S LAW STATEMENT:**
289   **UNDER NEW JERSEY LAW, THE COUNTY PROSECUTOR DETERMINES WHETHER AND HOW**
290 **TO PROVIDE NOTICE OF THE PRESENCE OF CONVICTED SEX OFFENDERS IN AN AREA. IN**
291 **THEIR PROFESSIONAL CAPACITY, REAL ESTATE LICENSEES ARE NOT ENTITLED TO**
292 **NOTIFICATION BY THE COUNTY PROSECUTOR UNDER MEGAN'S LAW AND ARE UNABLE TO**
293 **OBTAIN SUCH INFORMATION FOR YOU. UPON CLOSING, THE COUNTY PROSECUTOR MAY BE**
284 **CONTACTED FOR SUCH FURTHER INFORMATION AS MAY BE DISCLOSABLE TO YOU.**
295

Buyer's   Seller's
Initials:_____   Initials:_____

23. NOTICE ON OFF-SITE CONDITIONS: (Applicable to all resale transactions)
   PURSUANT TO THE NEW RESIDENTIAL CONSTRUCTION OFF-SITE CONDITIONS DISCLOSURE ACT, P.L. 1995, C. 253, THE CLERKS OF MUNICIPALITIES IN NEW JERSEY MAINTAIN LISTS OF OFF-SITE CONDITIONS WHICH MAY AFFECT THE VALUE OF RESIDENTIAL PROPERTIES IN THE VICINITY OF THE OFF-SITE CONDITION. PURCHASERS MAY EXAMINE THE LISTS AND ARE ENCOURAGED TO INDEPENDENTLY INVESTIGATE THE AREA SURROUNDING THIS PROPERTY IN ORDER TO BECOME FAMILIAR WITH ANY OFF-SITE CONDITIONS WHICH MAY AFFECT THE VALUE OF THE PROPERTY. IN CASES WHERE A PROPERTY IS LOCATED NEAR THE BORDER OF A MUNICIPALITY, PURCHASERS MAY WISH TO ALSO EXAMINE THE LIST MAINTAINED BY THE NEIGHBORING MUNICIPALITY.

24. ATTORNEY REVIEW CLAUSE:
   (1) **Study by Attorney**
      The Buyer or the Seller may choose to have an attorney study this Contract. If an attorney is consulted, the attorney must complete his or her review of the Contract within a three-day period. This Contract will be legally binding at the end of this three-day period unless an attorney for the Buyer or the Seller reviews and disapproves of the Contract.

   (2) **Counting the Time**
      You count the three days from the date of delivery of the signed Contract to the Buyer and Seller. You do not count Saturdays, Sundays or legal holidays. The Buyer and the Seller may agree in writing to extend the three-day period for attorney review.

   (3) **Notice of Disapproval**
If an attorney for the Buyer or the Seller reviews and disapproves of this Contract, the attorney must notify the REALTOR ® (S) and the other party named in this Contract within the three-day period. Otherwise this Contract will be legally binding as written. The attorney must send the notice of disapproval to the REALTOR® (S) by certified mail, by telegram, or by delivering it personally. The telegram or certified letter will be effective upon sending. The personal delivery will be effective upon delivery to the REALTOR® (S) Office. The attorney may also, but need not, inform the REALTOR® (S) of any suggested revision(s) in the Contract that would make it satisfactory.

25. ENTIRE AGREEMENT; PARTIES LIABLE:
   This Agreement contains the entire agreement of the parties. No representations have been made by any of the parties, the Broker(s) or his/her/their agents except as set forth in this Agreement. This Agreement is binding upon all parties who sign it and all who succeed to their rights and responsibilities.

26. BROKER'S COMMISSION:
   The commission, in accord with the previously executed listing agreement, shall be due and payable at the time of actual closing of title and payment by Buyer of the purchase consideration for the Property. The Seller hereby authorizes and instructs the Buyer's attorney, or the Buyer's title insurance company or whomever is the disbursing agent to pay the full commission as set forth below to the below mentioned Broker/Brokers out of the proceeds of sale prior to the payment of any such funds to the Seller. Buyer consents to the disbursing agent making the said disbursements.

COMMISSION IN ACCORD WITH PREVIOUSLY EXECUTED LISTING AGREEMENT, LESS PARTICIPATING BROKER'S COMMISSION (IF ANY)

_____
Listing Broker

_____
Address and Telephone #

_____   _____
Participating Broker   Commission

_____
Address and Telephone #

27. FAILURE OF BUYER OR SELLER TO SETTLE:
   In the event the Seller willfully fails to close title to the Property in accordance with this Contract, the Buyer may commence any legal or equitable action to which the Buyer may be entitled. In the event the Buyer fails to close title in accordance with this Contract, the Seller then may commence an action for damages it has suffered, and, in such case, the deposit monies paid on account of the purchase price shall be applied against such damages. In the event the Seller breaches this Contract, Seller will, nevertheless, be liable to the Broker for commissions in the amount set forth in this Contract.

28. CONSUMER INFORMATION STATEMENT ACKNOWLEDGMENT:
   By signing below the sellers and purchasers acknowledge they received the Consumer Information Statement on New Jersey Real Estate Relationships from the brokerage firms involved in this transaction prior to the first showing of the property.

Buyer's Initials:_____   Seller's Initials:_____

373 **29. DECLARATION OF LICENSEE BUSINESS RELATIONSHIP(S):**
374
375   (a) _____ , (name of firm) AND
376
377 _____ (name(s) of licensee(s)), AS ITS AUTHORIZED
378 REPRESENTATIVE(S), ARE WORKING IN THIS TRANSACTION AS (choose one) ☐SELLER'S
379 AGENTS ☐BUYER'S AGENTS ☐DISCLOSED DUAL AGENTS ☐TRANSACTION BROKERS
380
381   b) **INFORMATION SUPPLIED BY** _____ (name of
382 other firm) HAS INDICATED THAT IT IS OPERATING IN THIS TRANSACTION AS A (choose one)
383 ☐SELLER'S AGENT ☐BUYER'S AGENT ☐DISCLOSED DUAL AGENT ☐TRANSACTION
384 BROKER
385
386 **30. NEW CONSTRUCTION RIDER:**
387   If the property being sold consists of a lot and a detached single family home (the "House") to be constructed
388 upon the lot by the Seller, the "Rider To Contract of Sale of Real Estate - New Construction" has been signed by
389 Buyer and Seller and is appended to and made a part of this Agreement.
390
391 **31. PRIVATE WELL TESTING:**
392   **(This section is applicable if the property's potable water supply is provided by a private well located on the**
393 **property (or the potable water supply is a well that has less than 15 service connections or does not regularly**
394 **serve an average of at least 25 individuals daily at least 60 days a year).)**
395   Pursuant to the Private Well Testing Act (N.J.S.A. 58:12A-26 to 37) and regulations (N.J.A.C. 7:9E - 3.1 to 5.1), if
396 this Contract is for the sale of real property whose potable water supply is provided from a private well and the
397 analytical results of prior water tests no longer are valid, a test on the water supply must be performed by a laboratory
398 certified by NJDEP. Seller agrees to procure the test, at Seller's sole cost and expense and to provide a copy of the test
399 results to Buyer within seven (7) calendar days after receiving the report(s). Seller shall order the new test or, if
400 applicable, provide Buyer with the valid prior water test within seven (7) calendar days after the end of the Attorney
401 Review Period set forth in Section 24 of this Agreement. The test shall cover the parameters set forth in the Act and
402 regulations. As required in the Act, prior to closing of title, Seller and Buyer shall each certify in writing that they
403 have received and read a copy of the water test results.
404   If any of the water tests do not meet applicable standards at the time Seller provides the water test results to the
405 Buyer, Seller shall notify Buyer, in writing, that Seller agrees to cure or correct said conditions in the water test
406 results. If Seller shall fail to notify Buyer of Seller's agreement to cure or correct, such failure to so notify shall be
407 deemed to be a refusal by Seller to cure or correct. If Seller shall fail to agree to cure or correct any of the conditions
408 set forth in the water test results within seven (7) calendar days or if the condition is incurable and is of such
409 significance as to unreasonably endanger the health of the Buyer, the Buyer shall then have the right to void this
410 Contract by notifying the Seller in writing within seven (7) calendar days thereafter. If Buyer shall fail to void this
411 Contract within the seven (7) day period, the Buyer shall have waived his right to cancel this Contract and this
412 Contract shall remain in full force, and the Seller shall be under no obligation to correct or cure any of the conditions
413 set forth in the water test results. If Seller shall agree to correct or cure such conditions, all such remediation shall be
414 completed by Seller prior to the closing of title.
415
416 **32. MEGAN'S LAW REGISTRY:**
417   Buyer is notified that New Jersey law establishes an Internet Registry of Sex Offenders that may be accessed at
418 www.njsp.org .
419
420 **33. SMOKE DETECTORS, CARBON MONOXIDE ALARM AND PORTABLE FIRE EXTINGUISHER**
421 **COMPLIANCE:**
422   The Certificate of smoke detectors, carbon monoxide alarm and portable fire extinguisher compliance
423 (CSDCMAPFEC) as required by law, shall be the responsibility of the Seller.
424 **As of November 1, 2005 there is a new law in effect that requires that upon the sale, lease or transfer of**
425 **a building with fewer than three units, each unit be equipped with at least one portable fire extinguisher.**
426 **Seasonal rental units are excluded. The law further requires that the extinguisher is to be provided at the**
427 **expense of the seller, landlord or transferor of the property. The law defines portable fire extinguisher as**
428 **"an operable portable device, carried and operated by hand, containing an extinguishing agent that can be**
429 **expelled under pressure for the purpose of suppressing or extinguishing fire, and which is: (1) rated for**
430 **residential use consisting of an ABC type; (2) no larger than a 10 pound rated extinguisher; and (3) mounted**
431 **within 10 feet of the kitchen area, unless otherwise permitted by the enforcing agency."**
432
433 **34. NOTICE TO BUYERS CONCERNING INSURANCE**
434 **Buyers should obtain appropriate casualty and liability insurance for the Property. Your mortgage lender will**
435 **require that such insurance be in place at time of closing. Occasionally there are issues and delays in obtaining**
436 **insurance. Be advised that a "binder" is only a temporary commitment to provide insurance coverage and**
437 **is not an insurance policy. You are therefore urged to contact a licenced insurance agent or broker to**
438 **assist you in satisfying your insurance requirements.**
439
440 **35. ADDITIONAL CONTRACTUAL PROVISIONS(if any):**
441
442
443
444
445
446
447
448
449   NJAR form-118-11/05 Page 7 of 8

                                       Buyer's   Seller's
                                         Initials:_____   Initials:_____

35. ADDITIONAL CONTRACTUAL PROVISIONS (concluded):

I hereby acknowledge receipt of the Affiliates Relationship Disclosure.

BetterHomes Premium Services can make your home buying or selling experience smooth and effortless. Premium Services is available to coordinate your mortgage financing, title insurance, and homeowner's insurance to expedite your closing, giving you a peace of mind. In addition, our Home Protection Plan is available through Premium Services. Ask your BetterHomes sales associate to introduce you to our professional staff for details on these and other services for an effortless closing. BetterHomes... the Better Way.

The best time to contact me regarding these services is at: am/pm, at phone# _____________

_____ Yes! I wish to take advantage of the BetterHomes Premium Services.

36. INDEX

1. PURCHASE AGREEMENT & PROPERTY DESCRIPTION
2. PURCHASE PRICE
3. MANNER OF PAYMENT
4. BUYER FINANCIALLY ABLE TO CLOSE
5. ACCURATE DISCLOSURE OF SELLING PRICE
6. TENANTS, IF ANY
7. QUALITY OF TITLE
8. BUILDING & ZONING LAWS
9. ITEMS INCLUDED IN SALE
10. ITEMS EXCLUDED FROM SALE
11. ASSESSMENTS
12. FINAL INSPECTION
13. NJ HOTEL AND MULTIPLE DWELLING HEALTH & SAFETY ACT
14. NO ASSIGNMENT
15. RISK OF LOSS
16. ADJUSTMENTS AT CLOSING; RIGHTS TO POSSESSION
17. MAINTENANCE & CONDITION OF PROPERTY
18. LEAD-BASED PAINT DOCUMENT ACKNOWLEDGEMENT
19. LEAD-BASED PAINT CONTINGENCY CLAUSE
20. INSPECTION CONTINGENCY CLAUSE
21. NOTICES
22. MEGAN'S LAW STATEMENT
23. OFF-SITE CONDITIONS
24. ATTORNEY REVIEW CLAUSE
25. ENTIRE AGREEMENT; PARTIES LIABLE
26. BROKER'S COMMISSION
27 FAILURE OF BUYER OR SELLER TO SETTLE
28. CONSUMER INFORMATION STATEMENT ACKNOWLEDGMENT
29. DECLARATION OF LICENSEE BUSINESS RELATIONSHIP
30. NEW CONSTRUCTION RIDER
31. PRIVATE WELL TESTING
32. MEGAN'S LAW REGISTRY
33. SMOKE DETECTORS, CARBON MONOXIDE ALARM AND PORTABLE FIRE EXTINGUISHER COMPLIANCE:
34. NOTICE TO BUYERS CONCERNING INSURANCE
35. ADDITIONAL CONTRACTUAL PROVISIONS (if any):
36. INDEX

IN THE PRESENCE OF:

____________________ ________ ____________________(L.S.)
Date BUYER

____________________ ________ ____________________(L.S.)
Date BUYER

____________________ ________ ____________________(L.S.)
Date SELLER

____________________ ________ ____________________(L.S.)
Date SELLER

NJAR form-118-11/05 Page 8 of 8 **Better Homes NJ, VRI Realtors**

Financing Letter

There should be a letter from a bank, lender, accountant, or financial advisor attached to the offer. This letter should state that the buyer has the funds necessary (either in cash or through a loan) to purchase your home at the price outlined on the contract.

As discussed earlier in this chapter, when the buyer is using a loan to buy your home, note whether he is offering a prequalification letter or a genuine preapproval letter. There is a difference, and the one that the buyer actually presents to you will have an impact on his ability to borrow.

Disclosure Forms

Each state has different requirements for which disclosures a seller must legally provide to a buyer. Some states require a broad seller's disclosure form, which is essentially a checklist pertaining to every area and system of the home, including electric, plumbing, the foundation and structural integrity, environmental hazards, pests, water leakage, underground tanks, remodeling projects, and more. The seller fills out the form and discloses whether there are any problems in these areas. The buyer then reads it, signs it, and includes it with her offer.

Other disclosure forms that may be required in your state are those that pertain to the possible presence of lead in the home, the advisability of using an attorney, and a *dual agency* form. All of these forms explain the ethics and obligations of those involved—buyer, seller, attorneys, Realtors, agencies, etc.

def•i•ni•tion

Dual agency exists when the real estate agency that represents you has also found, brought in, and is representing the buyer. Both buyer and seller must understand its meaning and agree to sell the home through this agency, which is representing both sides of the deal.

Copy of Earnest Money Check

It is typical for the buyer's Realtor to include a check—or a copy of a check—from the buyer showing that he has earnest money to put down right away, in the event that you accept his offer. The check helps to convey his seriousness about following through on the purchase, hence the use of the word "earnest."

Accepting an Offer

You can accept an offer verbally, and there is such a thing as a legal verbal contract. But, in some states, it is only a written and signed contract that is recognized in a real estate transaction. Once you sign it, you have, in essence, accepted the offer. It doesn't mean that the deal will make it all the way to closing, but it does formally begin the process.

What to Do After You Have Accepted

Offers, or purchase contracts, presented to you have probably been written up and filled out by a Realtor and then signed by the buyer. If you accept the offer by signing it, the contract should then be forwarded to your representative for review. You are hopefully being represented by an attorney. If you have no representation, then unfortunately you are on your own. We advise against this.

Some states have an attorney review period which often lasts three business days. In that time period, either party—buyer or seller—has the right to change her mind and back out of the contract for any reason … or, for no reason at all. Once this period ends, it is more difficult for the buyer to get out of the agreement without using one of the provisions in the contract, like the inspection or mortgage financing.

When Other Offers Come in After You Have Accepted

This is quite the dilemma for a seller, especially when the new offer is higher than the one that you already signed. If you live in a state that provides a way to easily back out of a signed contract, as in an attorney review period, this scenario can be quite common. We have witnessed it hundreds of times. It can be bumpy and can end badly.

A buyer who would come in and encourage you to break a valid contract with someone else is someone who probably isn't used to playing by the rules. His motives may be ego-driven. Once he enters into a contract with you and satisfies his need to win, he—quite easily—could decide that he no longer wants your home. When you dropped the first buyer, you likely angered him and will not get him back to the negotiating table. And when the second buyer backs out, you find yourself in the unenviable position of having no buyers at all. If an offer comes in on your home after you have accepted another, think long and hard before you break that first contract.

The Least You Need to Know

◆ Price is not always the most important element of an offer. Consider all the provisions or terms of the contract as well as the overall profile of the buyer.

◆ Do not automatically reject an offer that is below your list price. You may be able to negotiate it up to an acceptable number.

◆ Many buyers need to sell their own homes before they can buy another. Make sure that the buyer's offer on your home is not contingent upon that sale of her own home.

◆ Don't confuse a buyer who is fully preapproved for a loan with a buyer who is only prequalified for a loan. A prequalification letter is much less reliable.

◆ Well-presented offers should include a cover letter, finance letter, earnest money check, relevant disclosure forms in your state, and the contract itself.

◆ Proceed with caution when another offer comes in after you've accepted one. It could lead to you losing both buyers.

Chapter 16

The Inspection and Environmental Issues

In This Chapter

- ◆ What gets inspected in your home
- ◆ How to successfully negotiate an inspection
- ◆ What you are required to fix
- ◆ How to deal with environmental inspection issues

Inspections can be a difficult part of a home sale. Buyer and seller are often on edge on inspection day. The buyers don't really want to find something wrong with their new home and yet they want the peace of mind that it is in good condition. They need the inspector's stamp of approval to complete and validate their choice. When they find flaws in the home, they can suddenly change. They still want the home but now they may take an aggressive approach to repair requests and credits for repairs. On the other hand, sellers tend to be anxious about what the home inspector is going to find and what they will be asked to repair. When they receive a repair request, they can become defensive.

Unless you are selling a newly built home where the property is expected to be entirely free of defects, you should take comfort in the fact that your home cannot fail an inspection. It's not how they are structured. An inspection is an objective visual assessment of your home, its structure, and its systems.

Among the items that are found to be in need of repair, it is up to you to negotiate which requests are reasonable. If you're selling in a down market, you may want to keep this buyer happy and work it out with him. If you don't, and the buyer walks away, the next buyer may ask for the same repairs to be made anyway.

In this chapter, we cover everything you need to know to understand, navigate, and successfully negotiate the inspection on your home.

What Gets Inspected and When Is It Done?

An inspection covers just about everything in your home. Structurally, the things to be assessed are the roof, foundation, exterior and interior walls, floors, ceilings, doors, windows, attic and basement, drainage, sidewalk, walkways, driveway, and garage.

The systems of the home to be evaluated are plumbing, electric, heat, and central air (season permitting).

And, finally, there will be an environmental and pest inspection. These can sometimes be inspected separately by specialists. In the case of an environmental consideration, some testing may be required for radon, mold, wells, underground oil, and septic tanks. We discuss environmental issues one by one later in this chapter.

Seller Alert

Make sure that the Realtors get the inspection scheduled as quickly as possible. If there is going to be a negotiating problem between buyer and seller, it's best to know about it right away so that the sale is not in limbo (or in jeopardy) for too long.

In some states, the inspection is performed before an offer is even made by the buyer. This takes the item-by-item haggling out of the process altogether because the buyer's offer reflects what was assessed in the inspection.

In other states, the inspection is done a week or two after the offer has been accepted by the seller. The inspection becomes a contingency in the contract. If you cannot negotiate successfully, the buyer can get out of the deal and not buy the home at all.

What You Are Required to Fix

There are two broad categories of repairs that you must make: items mandated by law and items listed in the contract.

Items Mandated by Law

Depending on where you live, there are certain laws and safety codes that you must abide by in order to sell. Some of these requirements include having working smoke and carbon monoxide detectors, a dryer that is vented to the exterior of the home, railings along the side of a certain number of steps, and other code regulations. If you do not have a Realtor to guide you, then you can find out what the requirements are in your community by contacting your local town hall. Some of the safety codes are available through the planning and building department. Others, like smoke and carbon monoxide detector requirements, are known by the fire department.

Some communities require a municipal inspection to ensure that these items are all in good working order and that the home is safe to occupy. There may be a small fee associated with these inspections and, if you pass, the city or town will issue you a certificate of occupancy (a "CO" or C of O) or a certificate of continued use (CCO). If your community requires these inspections, then you cannot legally sell your home without this certificate.

Seller Alert

Don't leave the scheduling of the town or city's inspection to the last minute. There is usually a backlog, and if you cannot get them into your home in time, you cannot legally close.

Items Listed in the Contract

The standard contract form used in your region specifically lists items that must be in working order to sell a home. They may include the systems of the house like plumbing, electric, heat, and central air. The contract may also refer to the home as being in a clean, livable condition, free of pests and abandoned underground tanks, and the like. So, contractually, repair items related to any of these areas must be fixed in order to sell your home.

Items Negotiated

Some buyers confuse their home inspection with a "repair list." We have found that when buyers present a laundry list of repairs to be made or request a dollar credit for them, the buyer usually feels as if he paid too much for the property. He is experiencing a form of buyer's remorse. He'll then use the inspection as a bargaining tool to lower the sale price.

If you are pleased with the sale price, you may want to actively negotiate the repair items with him. It is often more financially prudent to work with the buyer you have than it is to put your home back on the market. It may take weeks or months to find another buyer and, when you do, he may present you with an equally long repair list. He may also offer a lower sale price.

Negotiating repair items is an area where a good Realtor is very important. Some of the best negotiations are done Realtor to Realtor. For example, an inspector may tell the buyer that the roof is old. It's not leaking and it's not unsightly, but the buyer may ask for a new one anyway. Naturally, the seller will think it's absurd to fix something that isn't broken and firmly deny the request. The Realtors may call in a professional roofer to analyze it more closely, which may calm the buyer's fears. However, to keep the deal together, the listing agent may convince the seller to offer a credit anyway for a portion of the cost of replacing the roof. Or the buyer's Realtor may counsel the buyer to withdraw the request if the seller has already agreed to other repair credits. In the end, it's all about the Realtors communicating effectively with each other and being able to educate and manage the emotions of the buyer and seller. Not all Realtors are good at it but, when they are good, they are invaluable.

How to Negotiate Inspections

The good news is that the buyer begins the inspection negotiation. There is an old saying that goes, "The first person to speak in a negotiation loses." That's because both parties in a negotiation expect to go back and forth before coming to a middle ground. It's implied. So, the person who goes first has tipped her hand, so to speak. If she comes in lower than what you were prepared to pay, she's a fool. If she comes in too high, you'll know that she has padded her number and will go lower. Be glad that, in this negotiation, you start out with the upper hand. Negotiating is an art, and home inspection haggling is no exception.

Once the inspection is completed and the buyer has the report, she will then communicate the items she wishes you to repair. You must decide whether or not to make these repairs. If you refuse, the buyer typically has the right to be legally released from the contract without penalty.

Trick of the Trade _____

If you want to be proactive and avoid the nail-biting during the inspection phase, you could have an inspection performed on your home before you put it on the market. This also gives you an automatic "second opinion" to your buyer's inspection report, as well as the chance to repair unknown defects in advance. We talk about how to hire an inspector in Chapter 1.

Receiving the Buyer's Request for Repairs

Upon receiving this list of repairs, you may feel insulted or even angry. This is common. After all, you've been living in this home for years and it was good enough for you. How dare this buyer send you a laundry list of defects and flaws! Follow these steps to keep yourself objective and in control.

1. The first thing to do once you receive a repair list is tell yourself that this isn't personal; it's business. The buyer is trying to secure the best deal for himself, as are you. Try not to get angry and let emotion rule your actions.

2. Break down the repairs item by item. When 2 items out of 10 seem outrageously inappropriate, they can make the other 8 look unreasonable, as well. Evaluate each one as though it were the only repair that the buyer is requesting. Some of them are bound to be legitimate.

3. Choose the items that you are willing to fix.

4. If you do not have the time or ability to make the repair, decide instead if you would offer a dollar credit for the amount of the repair(s). This is a convenient solution. You won't have to give the buyer a check; the credit would come out of the proceeds of the sale at the closing table.

5. If you decide that one particular item has no merit at all and you refuse to even address it, ask yourself how far you're willing to take it. If you feel strongly about the item not needing repair yet it's apparently important to the buyer, are you prepared to lose the whole deal over it? In the big picture, which is more important—that one repair or the sale?

Responding to a Buyer's Request for Repairs

There are two kinds of responses that you can make to your buyer: productive ones and counterproductive ones! Put more simply, there are good responses and bad responses. Following is an example of each.

Bad Response

"I will not address any of these items. The house is in good working order and overall condition. The buyer should know that no home is perfect. That's what home ownership is about. Take my house 'as is' or nothing."

When a seller draws a line in the sand, refusing to make any repairs, the buyer doesn't really have anywhere to go in terms of a response. He has been backed into a corner and may have a strong negative reaction. The negotiation has been stopped dead in its tracks and it's very hard to resurrect it from there.

Good Response

"I will address some items but will not address others."

For the sake of this discussion, it doesn't really matter which items the seller will address. What's important here is that the seller is addressing some of them. By doing so, she has shown that she is listening to the buyer and has demonstrated a willingness to bargain. The fact that the seller responded will keep this negotiation alive.

The rest of the negotiation will likely be a simple "point-counterpoint" until a middle ground is reached. Buyers go into a negotiation expecting the seller to refuse some repairs. They expect to haggle. So, haggle! Choose some repairs to make. Throw the buyer a bone. Everybody likes to go home feeling like they got something, that they were heard, that their needs were met, and that they didn't get ripped off.

Trick of the Trade

When you feel yourself digging your heels in and refusing to make a certain repair, take out a calculator and figure out how much the repair costs you versus how much it will cost you to lose the buyer; keep the home on the market; pay carrying costs such as mortgage payments, insurance, and maintenance; and the possibility of receiving a lower offer later. Mathematically, it may make more sense to give this buyer what he wants.

Environmental Issues

When you sell a home you are required, by federal law, to disclose the existence of any potentially hazardous conditions. We discuss the various types of environmental issues that come up in relation to home ownership. Some of them can have serious effects on your health. It's important to both understand what they are and what your legal obligation is to your buyer.

Most environmental problems in the home can be cleaned up and removed quickly and safely, even while you are in the midst of selling. Many are relatively inexpensive to address as well. Some sellers do find themselves in a terrible situation where they must spend tens of thousands of dollars to correct a problem or, worse, when a family member becomes ill as a result of its presence. But again, the lion's share of environmental problems can be corrected without too much heartache, stress, or money.

Asbestos

Asbestos is a fiber that has been used in home materials and home products for decades. People who have been exposed to it, in elevated levels and over time, are at increased risk of certain types of lung cancer. It can be found in many places including roofing, siding, insulation, the back of vinyl sheet flooring, wrapped around hot water and steam pipes throughout a home, and even around some furnaces. It is most dangerous when it is damaged or crumbling and the fibers become airborne.

The only way to positively identify it is to have it tested by an expert. There are two remediation solutions for asbestos. One is to have asbestos remediation experts remove it entirely and the other is to have it professionally wrapped, like a cast on a leg, so that particles cannot escape. Some homeowners and experts feel that it is safer not to disturb asbestos at all, while others prefer to have it removed from their homes.

 Seller Alert

If you plan to finish the basement in order to get more money on the sale, we recommend removing the asbestos. Once the walls or sheetrock, drop ceiling, and carpeting are installed, it is much more difficult to access and have removed. More important, some buyers will not want to see that a basement has been finished around asbestos—covered or not.

Radon

Radon is a cancer-causing radioactive natural gas that comes from uranium in the earth. You cannot smell it, see it, or taste it. It enters your home through cracks or openings in the foundation. While it is the second leading cause of lung cancer in the United States, it is highly avoidable. The solution to radon is ventilation. All you have to do is have your home tested (at little or no cost). If you have more than 4 picocuries of radon (the EPA's maximum exposure level), your buyers may insist that you install a radon remediation system, which is essentially a high-tech fan. In fact, many homeowners enjoy the security of having the fan device as it monitors radon levels at all times. Most homeowners are unaware what their radon levels are unless they test every year or so.

Do-it-yourself radon test kits are available from several sources. Free test kits are sometimes available from local or county health departments, or from state radon programs. Discounted low-cost radon test kits are also available from the National Safety Council (www.nsc.org/issues/radon) or call 1-800-SOS-RADON (1-800-767-7236). Do-it-yourself radon test kits are also available from some local or state branches of the American Lung Association (www.lungusa.org) and some home improvement stores. For general information on radon and most home-related environmental hazards, visit www.epa.gov.

Underground Oil Tanks and Septic Tanks

The most common underground tanks are septic tanks for waste disposal and oil tanks for home heating. Both can be hazardous to the environment and human health.

A septic system treats and disposes of waste right on your property. They are used in places where people rely on groundwater for drinking water. They do not pose a health hazard unless they are damaged or poorly maintained. Your septic system will be inspected as part of the process of selling. If the integrity is compromised, you will be required to repair or replace the system in order to complete the sale.

If you have an underground oil tank, expect that the buyer will have it tested for leaks. Underground oil tanks corrode over time and may leak into the soil. The leak can spread to the water table, taking the toxic material to other properties and locations and contaminating them as well.

If the tests reveal that your tank is leaking, you will be required to replace or remove the tank altogether. This is a costly and time-consuming procedure which can cause your deal to fall apart at worst or delay it at best. If you are getting ready to put your home on the market, we strongly urge you to have your tank preinspected, tested, serviced, and insured (if not removed altogether). If it's not leaking now, it probably will one day, and many buyers know this. Place the tank inside your basement or consider converting to gas.

Additionally, if you live next to or near a gas station, there can be contamination of your property and drinking water from the underground gas storage tanks.

> **Seller Alert** _____
>
> For more information on properly managed septic systems, visit the EPA's Office of Wastewater Management's septic systems site.
>
> For more information on underground oil tanks, visit the EPA's Office of Underground Storage Tanks or www.epa.gov/oust.com.

Lead-Based Paint

Federal law dictates that sellers must disclose known lead paint hazards in their home and provide buyers with a 10-day window to assess the presence and extent.

Lead-based paint can be hazardous to human health and development, particularly for children. It is the most common source of lead poisoning in children, and can cause irreversible brain damage and affect mental functioning in general. If there are loose paint chips anywhere in your home or dust particles containing lead, it is easy for children to ingest them. Small children may eat the paint chips directly. But even if they only handle the chips or touch the dust, once they put their hands in their mouths, they have consumed lead.

You are not required to remove lead hazards from your home. You are simply required to disclose its presence when you know it to be there. Many sellers do not know if they have lead in their homes. They are not required to know. But, if they have assessed their home and have reports that show that lead is present, they are required by law to share them.

For more information on lead paint and other lead hazards in the home, call 1-800-424-LEAD or visit www.epa.gov and click on "Lead."

Water Wells

Private well water was commonly used for drinking water a few decades ago. It is still common in rural areas, but overall fewer and fewer homes are relying upon it. When a home is being sold with a private well on the property that is used for drinking (and not just lawn watering), many states require by law that the water be tested.

Often, both the buyer and seller must receive a copy of, review, and sign the report.

If your private well fails the test, the deal can be saved by either cleaning (or shocking and flushing) the system or, if necessary, replacing the system. Many wells that fail bacteria tests do so as a result of poor maintenance, not bad water. Your local or regional health department will have guidelines for you.

Wet Basements

Having a wet basement will not prevent you from selling your home. However, you have an ethical obligation to disclose this condition to a buyer. If you do not disclose it up front and evidence of having had water in the basement presents itself in the inspection, the buyer may lose trust and actually back out of the deal.

The wetness itself in a basement is not an environmental hazard, but the condition can cause loss of property and give rise to environmental hazards such as mold, bacteria growth, and sometimes exposure to raw waste.

There are a number of ways to fix a wet basement. The least expensive, though not always effective enough, is using a waterproof paint on the floor and walls. In Chapter 2, we discuss sump pumps and French drains, which have a considerable cost associated with them. Sump pumps take water out of your basement but French drains usually prevent the water from coming inside at all.

Mold

Mold is a serious problem in some parts of the nation. It can creep inside walls and under floor boards. They are tiny spores that can grow on surfaces that are wet. You may not even be aware that it is in your home. There are many different types of mold, but not all of them are dangerous. Some people are particularly sensitive to mold. It can cause asthma attacks in people with asthma and can irritate people who are sensitive to allergens.

If your buyer tests your home for mold and it turns out to be present, you should remediate it. If you hire a contractor, make sure that he has experience removing mold from homes. Information on mold can also be found at www.epa.gov.

Carpenter Bees

Carpenter bees are those big fat bees that you might see flying around near your home. They may seem frightening but they do not really attack and, contrary to popular belief, they do not eat your wood, either. Like carpenter ants, they tunnel into wood and simply nest there. Because the tunnels and nests are so close to the surface, the damage is mainly cosmetic.

Like any infestation, when carpenter bees are found during an inspection, the seller will need to have the problem remediated through a licensed pest control expert.

Carpenter Ants

The myth about carpenter ants is that they eat wood, too. They do not. They damage wood when they excavate and nest in it. They also rarely target new, dry wood, but are attracted to wood that has already been moisture damaged.

Nevertheless, you need to address them as you would any pest infestation that comes up in an inspection. Any pest control expert can treat them.

Termites

Termites do eat wood, and it can lead to massive structural damage of your home. The cellulose in wood is their nutrition and when they find it, they eat 24 hours a day.

When signs of active termite infestation turn up in your home inspection, it may be a simple and relatively inexpensive treatment. However, if their presence has resulted in structural damage to your home, you will need to make those structural repairs. They could include rebuilding a new porch, exterior stairs, a garage foundation, or other more serious renovations.

Termites are far easier to pretreat than they are to treat once they become active. It's a great idea to have your home inspected for termites and all pest infestations before you sell. For a few more dollars, you can offer a one-year warranty to the buyers as an added incentive.

> **Trick of the Trade**
>
> Look for a pest control company that offers a one-year warranty on most pest treatments, free of charge, as part of their service. Many good companies do this, and it gives the buyers a feeling of security. Make sure it's transferable to new homeowners, though.

Other Pest and Rodent Infestations

There are all kinds of critters that can gain access to a home, including squirrels, raccoons, bats, fleas, bed bugs, and more. If you have any kind of infestation, you'll need to treat it before selling.

The Least You Need to Know

♦ In general, an inspection covers the structure of the home, the systems of the home, and environmental issues.

♦ When an inspection is done after you have accepted an offer, it is possible for the buyer to back out if you refuse to make certain repairs.

♦ You are required to fix items that are mandated by law in your state, that are listed in the contract, and what you and your buyer negotiate to have fixed.

♦ Negotiations are not personal; it's business. Try and give a little on some repair items to keep the negotiations alive and moving forward.

♦ Your home may be tested and inspected for certain environmental hazards such as radon, underground oil or septic tanks, mold, termites, and private water wells.

Chapter 17

The Final Walk-Through

In This Chapter

- ◆ The purpose and execution of the walk-through
- ◆ The condition of your property
- ◆ Items that cannot be removed from the property
- ◆ Items that should be removed from the property
- ◆ Nice things to do for the new homeowners

It may be many weeks or months since your buyer first saw your home. As a courtesy, you may have allowed him to come back in several times over the course of the transaction, with family members, contractors, or decorators. Now that closing is upon you, the buyer is entitled to visually inspect the premises one more time. This inspection is brief and is known as a walk-through. Its purpose is to confirm that the property is in the same condition that it was when the buyer made his initial offer; that all systems and appliances are in good working order; that all of your belongings have been removed; and that the premises are "broom clean" and free of debris. Believe it or not, deals can and do fall apart at this stage. It's silly and it's rare, but it happens. If you are prepared for your walk-through, it will be smooth.

In this chapter, we discuss the entire walk-through process and some of the more common issues and problems, as well as how to rectify them.

The Walk-Through

The ideal time for a walk-through is right before the closing takes place, preferably within an hour or two. A buyer will sometimes do it the day before the closing, for personal scheduling reasons. This is not uncommon but not ideal, either. There is some inherent risk to performing it a day in advance, as the property could sustain damage of any kind in the 24 hours between the walk-through and the closing. There could be a storm that evening where a tree falls on the house, a pipe could burst, or it could be vandalized.

Overall, if there are any problems with the property or with its condition at the walk-through, the closing can be seriously delayed. If this happens, it's usually because of some small dispute that comes up in the walk-through. The disputes are often relatively minor in nature—in theory, they should be highly negotiable—but in reality they may become more problematic than they need to be, because it's an emotionally charged day for the buyers. Home ownership is imminent for them now. Small issues may appear to be bigger or more important than they really are. What may seem insignificant to you could be a big deal to the buyer.

Seller Alert

At the time of the walk-through, make sure that you are reachable at least by phone. It is very common for there to be at least some minor issue or question that the buyer may have that needs to be resolved or answered before the closing can take place.

As a seller, it's important to remember two things. First, try not to minimize the particular concerns of your buyers on this very important day. Second, you are legally and ethically obligated to deliver the property in a certain condition. Sellers often end up negotiating credits to the buyer when the walk-through does not go well. We want to help you avoid unnecessary and avoidable costs.

The Condition of the Property

On a walk-through, the buyer and his Realtor will cover the entire property, inside and out, to confirm that the condition has not deteriorated or changed, and that everything is in its place and suitable for closing. There are many areas that are inspected as part of a thorough and properly executed walk-through.

Floors

Now that your home is empty and the area rugs have been removed, the floors will be completely exposed. If an unusually large scratch, gauge, stain, or flaw is revealed in the walk-through, you may have a problem. It is disheartening for a buyer to walk into her new and empty home only to see a big gash in the center of a room's floor. Some buyers will ask for a dollar credit before they will agree to close. Their thinking is that the seller should have disclosed the defect, particularly because it was hidden by a rug, and they deserve money to fix or restore the floor.

The overall point is that if you have a flaw in your floor (which was covered while your home was being shown), it should be disclosed to the new owners, at some point, well before closing. Or correct the defect yourself, before you put the home on the market. The cost may be lower than the credit you end up giving to the buyers at closing.

Walls and Ceilings

Walk-through problems with walls usually have to do with holes, chips, and marks resulting from your move. Another is when the buyer objects to leftover nails and picture frame holders. Some don't bother to address this, usually because they plan to repaint anyway. But others do care and expect the walls to be spackled and touched up. Your response should be crafted in the context of the big picture. If everything else has gone relatively smoothly so far, and this is the only thing holding up the closing, we recommend giving the buyer a small credit to correct the problem.

Dishwasher, Washer, and Dryer

This surprises some sellers, but in a thorough walk-through, these items will be turned on to be sure that they work properly. Broken dishwashers come up all the time. In fact, sometimes they start leaking water all over the place as soon as you flip the switch, even very expensive ones. If there is any appliance in your home that is not working properly, have it serviced or at least disclose the problem to the buyer in advance. It will save you much stress at the walk-through.

Trick of the Trade

If there is a quirk or trick to turning on an appliance, leave a note on the appliance explaining it. This might save you some time, energy, and maybe even some money if the buyer cannot make it work and assumes that it's broken.

Stoves and Ovens

One of the smallest but most common problems with stoves and ovens is when the pilot lights—or more often the burners—don't fire. There is usually a simple explanation such as clogged jets or being wet from a recent cleaning. Some first-time buyers can be very nervous about home ownership and repair, and ask you to fix it before closing, or to give them a credit instead. If you do not want to give them a credit, then run over to the property and actually light them yourself. If you are not physically in the area, ask your Realtor or a relative to do it.

Toilets, Sinks, Tubs, and Showers

If the walk-through is being conducted in a thorough manner, every single toilet and faucet will be turned on to check water pressure, that there is hot water coming through, and that the drains are not clogged up.

Make sure that the toilets flush and are not running, that the drains are open, and that the hot water has not been inadvertently turned off. As far as water pressure goes, if you have a bona fide pressure problem, it would have come up on the general inspection report. If the buyer's inspector did not pick up on it and make it a negotiating point back then, it's really no longer on the table for discussion.

The Lawn

Some sellers move out of the home several weeks before closing. They can forget to assign someone to provide maintenance for the lawn. By the time closing comes around, the once beautiful lawn is either completely overgrown or dead from lack of water.

Your buyer may have a valid case on closing day if he finds a dead or out-of-control lawn that was green and manicured when he made his offer. You're actually in better shape if it's just overgrown as you can mow it yourself that day or give him a nominal amount to hire a mower. But if the lawn is dead, you're in a bit of a pickle. Unless there was a verifiable water shortage (which is a form of a state of emergency) where lawn watering was temporarily prohibited, you owe the buyer a lawn that is in the same condition it was in when he made the offer. In this case, you will likely be asked for enough money to reseed or resod.

Broom Clean

While you are not required to hire a cleaning service or to make the home sanitized and spotlessly clean, you are required to deliver it (in most states) in broom-clean condition. If the buyer can make a case that the home is being turned over in a filthy condition, you may be called upon to give a dollar credit for a cleaning service.

For a buyer to make her case on this point, she would likely need to take pictures to convince a third party—either your Realtor or attorney—that it is, in fact, unacceptably dirty. This is a very subjective dispute. We recommend that you follow the advice of your Realtor or attorney.

No Debris

This may be the most common issue associated with walk-throughs. There are so many items that sellers feel are okay or even good to leave for the new homeowner. The problem is that the buyer may not agree. One man's treasure is another man's trash. The last thing that a buyer wants to do on his first day as a new homeowner is to pay to have stuff he doesn't own, or want, hauled away. In fact, he may even expect you to foot the bill.

In most states, you are required to deliver the premises free of debris. We define "debris" as "just about anything that is not nailed down." If it's not a part of the structure, take it with you.

What You Are Not Allowed to Take

There is so much confusion about what sellers may or may not remove from the home when they leave. There is almost always at least one thing that gets miscommunicated in a real estate sale. The buyers get to the walk-through and find that the seller took something he wasn't supposed to, or left something that the buyers didn't want. Here are the most common items that sellers take that they shouldn't.

Wall and Ceiling Light Fixtures

As a seller, you cannot take light fixtures, wall sconces, or chandeliers that are electrically wired into the walls unless you stipulated in the listing that they are exclusions in the sale. This means that you communicated, as far back as when the home was being shown to all potential buyers, which items would be taken and which would be included in the sale.

Even when you legally remove certain electrical fixtures, you must replace them with another, or at least cap the opening. You cannot leave electrical wires hanging out of a wall or ceiling where a chandelier or a sconce used to be. The replacement pieces don't have to be expensive or even pretty; they just need to work and be safe.

> **Seller Alert** _____
>
> If the light fixtures make a significant contribution to the style of your home, be sure that you really want or need them in the location to which your are moving. It can be a hassle (not to mention expensive) to have them removed and replaced with something else and, if they look good, it's nice to leave them for the buyers.

Built-In Appliances

Microwaves, coffee and espresso makers, flat-screen TVs, and even hot tubs that are built in, mounted, or affixed to a wall or deck become the property of the new homeowner unless you have excluded them from the sale before the contract was signed. If these items are freestanding, and not mounted or affixed to a wall, then you may take them. Otherwise, they are considered to be part of the structure.

Replacing Appliances

This one really happens! Believe it or not, when sellers include the refrigerator in the sale, some of them will take it with them anyway and replace it with a dumpy, old, or far inferior brand. When the buyer notices in the walk-through (and she will), she can be incredulous and there may be a real battle between buyer and seller. The seller may feel that he promised the buyer a refrigerator and he gave her one. However, unless you expressly excluded it, the buyer is entitled to the exact refrigerator that was in the kitchen at the time of her offer. When you are called upon to remediate the problem, it could end up costing you more money than if you just left the original.

Doorknobs and Cabinet Hardware

These items have value and also contribute to the style and look of the home. If you take them, the buyer will very likely notice and want them reinstalled. Original doorknobs can be of particular importance in old homes of a certain style, such as Victorians or Craftsman's. When they are removed and replaced with less expensive contemporary fixtures, it devalues the whole home.

Shutters and Flower Boxes

Shutters and flower boxes are clearly mounted and affixed to the exterior of a home and therefore stay with the property. They are not only part of the structure, they are an integral part of the curb appeal. They cannot be removed without replacing them with the same pieces.

Trick of the Trade

There are some types of flower boxes that can be legally removed if they are not affixed to the home but instead rest on a grate or hook onto a railing.

Porch Swing

A porch swing is part of and clearly affixed to the structure of the home. It can be a major attraction in the curb appeal, and the seller cannot dismantle and remove it unless it was labeled as an exclusion on the listing.

We've personally seen this scenario unfold. The seller removed the swing because he had a personal and emotional attachment to it. When the buyer, at the walk-through, discovered it missing, she was crushed. She stated that the swing was one of the factors in her decision to buy the home. The buyer asked for a credit and was awarded it because the swing was unlawfully removed.

Swing Sets

Swing sets are a negotiable item. The buyer is sometimes glad to have it but also retains the right to refuse it. If the buyer refuses it, the seller is required to remove it from the premises. We can't tell you how many sellers we have seen attempt to get rid of swing sets. They are difficult to dismantle and transport, which is why so many sellers prefer to leave them behind.

We have tried to help some of our sellers find a new home for their swing sets with charitable organizations catering to children. But these organizations often do not have a budget for a truck to transport it or to hire someone to take it apart. If you can find someone to take it away for free, you may already be ahead of the game. Many sellers end up paying a fee to have the swing set hauled away and disposed of.

Mailboxes, Flag Poles, and Sheds

Mailboxes, flag poles, and sheds are also fixtures that cannot be taken without advance disclosure. They are physically attached to or part of the property and if the seller plans to take them, he must have it written into the listing itself to avoid a conflict with the buyer on closing day.

> **Seller Alert** _____
>
> Some sellers want to remove landscape features from the property. Perhaps a small tree or rose bush has some sentimental value. It may have been planted on a child's first birthday or in memory of a deceased loved one. Nevertheless, they are rooted in the ground and are a part of the property. You should disclose your intentions either in the listing or at least before you sign the contract. Flower pots, lawn art, or other decorative outdoor items that are not rooted in the ground can be taken.

What You Should Take in Order to Avoid Problems

Sellers sometimes leave behind a laundry list of items, thinking that the buyer will find them useful. Sometimes the buyer does appreciate the gesture; unfortunately, he may not want them at all. The problems arise when the seller just leaves the items and only learns, at the walk-through, that the buyer has no interest in them and considers them debris to be removed from the premises. Be sure to communicate with the buyers, well in advance of closing, which items you may leave and which ones they prefer that you take. This will not only help to avoid closing table disputes, but it will give you time to dispose of very heavy or hazardous materials.

Paint Cans, Stains, and Epoxy

These come up at some point in almost every deal. And it's amazing how many paint cans a homeowner can acquire over the years! Some sellers may have as many as 50 or 60 cans in their basements or garages. What happens is that the sellers have leftover cans and assume that the buyer will want them for touch-ups. But unless the home has just been freshly painted and the buyer happens to love the colors, they usually don't want the paint. Begin to get rid of your extra old paint cans well before the walk-through. It will save you the stress of trying to get rid of them all at once on the day of the walk-through.

Seller Alert

Paint cans are not simple to dispose of properly, which is another reason why sellers may find it easier to leave them behind. There are two kinds of paint that you are likely to have: oil-based and water-based. Water-based paint is the safer of the two. Oil-based paint is considered a hazardous material. There are rules and regulations about how to dispose of paint and paint cans. Contact your local sanitation, recycling, or public works departments about how to do it correctly.

Air Conditioners

A used air-conditioning unit is an extremely common item that causes problems at the walk-through. Too often, sellers just assume that the buyers will want the units, but the buyers do not. Air conditioners are also difficult to dispose of, which may be another reason why they are often left behind. For one thing, they can be extremely heavy to move. But, more importantly, the man-made chemical or liquid refrigerant within them is a hazardous material which has been blamed for depleting our ozone layer. The chemical, which has the trade name Freon, is also present in refrigerators, car air conditioners, and dehumidifiers. They must (and should) be disposed of carefully whereby a professional removes the refrigerant before the unit itself is discarded and recycled. (Again, contact your local municipality about how to properly dispose of them.)

We see sellers and buyers haggling over used air-conditioning units on closing day all the time. If you choose to leave them behind without the buyer's prior consent, you could be in the forced position, after the walk-through, of hauling several units away with very little notice, and nowhere to take them.

Firewood

Firewood can be a welcome gift to leave behind for the buyers—but don't assume that. Ask them in advance. Some people like the look of fireplaces but don't use them. We've also seen some homes where the seller left a mountain of firewood that turned out to be rotted or infested with insects. The seller usually needs to have it hauled away (or give a credit) before the buyer will close.

Second Refrigerators and Freezers

Many homeowners keep a second refrigerator or freestanding freezer in the basement or garage. There seems to be constant confusion about whether or not these items should stay or go. If the buyer does not want them, they must go. But often, they will want them. The problem lies in the communication because it is usually verbal instead of being written into the contract. We've seen sellers try and do the right thing by hauling them away, only to learn at the walk-through that the buyer actually wanted them.

On the flip side, when a buyer prefers that they be removed, the seller left them on the premises. Be sure to have the Realtors or attorney include them in the contract. Distinguish them from the appliances in the kitchen by naming them as "basement refrigerator" or "garage freezer."

Garden and Workshop Tools, Lawn Mowers, and Trash Cans

If you are selling to first-time homeowners, they may want your garden or shop tools. As always, check with them first. If they do not, your attempt at goodwill can result in a last-minute garage clean-out.

First-time homeowners may appreciate lawn mowers or snow blowers, but if they are old and in precarious condition, the buyers may want them removed. They may be interested in buying brand-new machines for themselves.

Garbage cans are items that first-time homeowners forget that they will need. Renters use outdoor receptacles which are supplied by the landlord, so they don't think of buying them. But put this on the list of things to ask about leaving or not.

Hangers

Technically, hangers should be removed, but we've never had a deal where hangers left in closets were an issue at the walk-through. As long as you aren't leaving hundreds of them, it's probably okay to leave some behind.

Nice Things to Do for the New Homeowners

We hope that you will have a good relationship with your buyers throughout the sale process, particularly if you have lived in your home for many years and raised a family there. The home probably has great meaning for you, and it will be nice to have a cordial relationship with the new owners. The issues that often cause friction during a walk-through, or at the end of a deal, are usually small and may become even less important when looking back months or years later. There are many things that you can do, which cost little or no money, to welcome the buyers into their new home. The goodwill that you will create may come back to you in the future. Here are some things that you can do or leave in the home for your buyers to create a good feeling:

- Instruction manuals and warranties for appliances and systems of the home
- A list of your contractors and service people with contact information
- A nice "feel-good" welcome note with information about why you loved living there so much
- A bottle of champagne or wine in the refrigerator
- Fresh flowers
- Cookies or candies
- Sketches, paintings, or very old photographs of the home
- Information about community services
- Garbage and recycling pick-up schedules
- One interior garbage receptacle with a garbage bag
- Paper towels in the kitchen
- Toilet paper in the bathrooms

The Least You Need to Know

- The closing can be delayed, postponed, or even canceled as a result of problems associated with the walk-through. The more prepared and informed you are, the smoother it will be.
- The purpose of the walk-through is for the buyer to confirm that you have moved out entirely, that the property is in the same condition as when she made her initial offer, and that it is broom-clean and free of debris.
- The walk-through should happen as close to the closing as possible, preferably within an hour or two.

◆ In a walk-through, just about everything gets inspected: the floors, walls, ceiling, lighting fixtures, sinks, toilets, showers, tubs, dishwasher, stove, washer and dryer, and even the lawn.

◆ You should not remove anything that is hardwired into or affixed to the wall or building structure, including chandeliers and wall sconces, unless you have clearly excluded them—in writing—from the sale.

◆ There is often confusion about whether or nor a seller should leave behind paint, air conditioners, second refrigerators or freezers, and big stashes of firewood. Reach out to the buyers well before the walk-through to avoid this.

Chapter 18

At the Closing Table and After

In This Chapter

- ◆ What happens at the closing table
- ◆ Calculating profit and loss
- ◆ Tax implications
- ◆ Liabilities after closing
- ◆ Sample documents

If you've made it to the closing table, you've come to the end of the road. Congratulations! This is the moment when you will legally sign over ownership (and the keys) to your home. Hopefully, a great deal of money will be deposited directly into your account or you will physically be handed a large check. But it's also a bittersweet moment because, after the closing has concluded, you may not go back to that property unless as an invited guest.

While it's rare, there are certain circumstances that may cause the journey in selling your home to extend beyond closing. We discuss some examples of those unusual scenarios. We also discuss how to prepare for closing, what actually happens at a closing table, important documents and fees, the tax implications of selling a home, and how to calculate your profit or loss on the sale (we're assuming it's a profit!).

We genuinely hope that closing day will be a joyful one for you, as well as for your buyers. It is a wonderful thing when the seller and buyer have a smooth deal, become friends, and stay in touch, particularly if the seller lived in the home for many years and feels a deep connection to it. The home will always be something that the two of you and your families will have in common.

What Happens at the Closing Table

The main thing that happens at the closing table is the transfer of ownership from you to the buyers. It is a legal transaction which is recognized, and recorded, by the local or municipal governments and state and federal governments, including the IRS.

When both buyer and seller are represented by attorneys (which we very strongly recommend), the closing typically takes place at the office of the buyer's attorney. As the seller, you do not necessarily need to attend your own closing. It can take place in your absence, as long as you have presigned the necessary documents. The buyers usually need to attend the closing, as they must sign dozens of mortgage documents required by their bank or lender.

Closings can take up to a couple of hours or as little as 10 minutes. Much of the time is eaten up by getting all those signatures from the buyers on the loan documents. However, if the buyers have signed them prior to the closing as well, then the process will be much shorter. A closing can also be delayed if there are problems with the walk-through and the buyer and seller are having a hard time negotiating a resolution. We discussed some of these in Chapter 17.

The Seller's Responsibilities at the Closing

Obviously, your biggest responsibility is to move out. This may seem obvious but you would be surprised how many sellers think that they can go back to the property after the closing to finish moving. Legally speaking, if a seller does that, it would be called trespassing. Ownership has transferred to the buyers after the closing is complete. We now cover the rest of your responsibilities for closing.

Certificates for Use

Most cities and towns require a seller to apply for a certificate that shows that the home may continue to be used and occupied in accordance with local law. If a certificate is required in your area, a seller cannot close on the property without one. The seller must typically have an inspection of his home done and pay a fee of approximately $10 to $100, and then he receives the certificate. The names of these certificates and the guidelines attached to them vary from community to community.

Here are some of the more commonly named certificates:

- Certificate of Occupancy (or a C of O)
- Certificate of Continued Use (CCU)
- Certificate of Continued Occupancy (CCO)
- Zoning Certificate
- Smoke Certificate

The first three certificates are typically given after a city or town official has inspected the property to make sure that everything on the exterior and interior of the home meets local building and safety codes. For example, if the front stoop has more than two steps and no railing, this can be a safety code violation. If the sidewalks are uneven, causing a tripping hazard, your home can fail this inspection. If the stove or clothes dryer are not properly vented, if the sump pump is not properly irrigated, or if there are more than two layers of shingles on the roof, you could fail the inspection and not receive a certificate. The building and safety codes vary by town and by state. In fact, some communities don't have any requirements at all, only recommended codes. But if there are requirements in your area, until you rectify the problem and pass a new inspection, you cannot sell your home.

A smoke certificate is a blanket term used in communities that require a home to have working smoke detectors on every level, working carbon monoxide detectors on sleeping levels, and perhaps even a working fire extinguisher in or near the kitchen. The inspection for this type of certificate is usually done by the local fire department.

A zoning certificate is when the local government wants to be sure that your home will continue to be zoned appropriately for the location. For example, if your neighborhood has nothing but single family homes

Trick of the Trade

If you find that the process of scheduling the inspections and getting the correct certificates is complicated, enlist the help of your Realtor. We have often reached out to the local fire department, building department, and other branches of local government on behalf of clients. It's a small thing to ask and your Realtor should be glad to oblige.

in it, it will be zoned as such. There may be no mixed-use zoning allowed in that location. This is when there may be a mixture of single family homes with multifamily homes, rental apartments, and even commercial or retail spaces. If you had turned your home into a multifamily while you lived there, but it is zoned solely for single family homes, then you are required to convert the home back to a single family before selling it. The inspector for this type of certificate can come from the zoning department, building and planning, or whomever the community designates.

And finally, if you are selling a condominium or co-op, there may be an additional inspection required by the board of directors. Their guidelines and requirements should be made known to you before you sell the unit.

Pay Off the Mortgage and Other Liens

You are required to pay off your mortgage and all *liens* when you sell your home. Because the bank or lender will no longer have equity (or ownership) in it, they will want and expect their money back at the time of the sale. You do not have to come up with the money and pay it off before the closing. The loan will be paid off as a result of closing. When the buyer pays for the home, those proceeds will be forwarded to your bank.

def•i•ni•tion

A **lien** is a legal claim on a property where the property is used as security for a debt. Liens must be paid off when selling real estate.

You may have other debt or liens on the home besides your mortgage. A common lien is a home equity loan or home equity line of credit (HELOC). This is simply another type of mortgage (also known as a second mortgage). This is when you already own the home but need an infusion of cash, so you "borrow against it." Let's say that you borrowed $200,000 when you first purchased the home, in the form of a mortgage. During your ownership, you may have needed some cash—perhaps to make a major improvement on the home. Let's say that you took out a $50,000 home equity loan. Your debt went from $200,000 up to $250,000. If you believe that your home is worth $500,000, then you have 50 percent equity in it. You happen to own the home 50/50 with the bank.

Let's say that home prices have fallen and it is now only worth $450,000. When you sell, you must still pay back the $250,000 you borrowed from the bank. The bank will get its money. If the sale price is $450,000, the bank receives the $250,000 owed on it by you. You receive only the $200,000 that is left over. You actually lose $50,000, probably more when you factor in the expenses involved with selling. This is why borrowing against a home can be financially dangerous to a seller. The bank always gets paid first. If you can't pay it, it takes the home and you go into foreclosure.

Liens can be placed upon your home from many different sources. The IRS can place a lien on your home for failure to pay income taxes. The state, county, or municipality can place a lien on your home for failure to pay property taxes. A judge can place a lien on your home for failure to pay child support. Even a general contractor or a landscaper can place a lien if you haven't paid him for a job. These liens come up when the buyer's title search is performed so they will be found, and they must be cleared or paid off in order to sell.

Pay Taxes

You may pay taxes on the sale of your home. How much you will pay depends on the state in which you live, how long you lived in the home, the sale price, how much profit you made, your income, and your marital status. No matter what state you live in, there is at least one federal form that must be filled out at closing time in order to report the sale, even if you did not make a profit.

IRS reporting forms or tax forms are a requirement at a closing and are for reporting the gross sales price. No matter when you close on the sale, copies should be kept for when the estate files its income tax return.

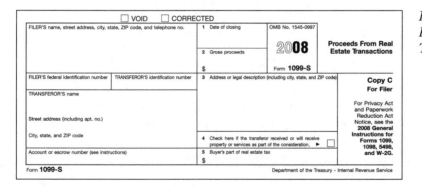

Federal Reporting of Proceeds from Real Estate Transactions.

Check with an accountant or financial advisor about what reporting forms are required by your own state government. Following is a sample from the state of New Jersey.

A. **Settlement Statement**

U.S. Department of Housing and Urban Development

OMB Approval No. 2502-0265

B. Type of Loan

1. ☐ FHA 2. ☐ FmHA 3. ☐ Conv. Unins.
4. ☐ VA 5. ☐ Conv. Ins.

6. File Number:	7. Loan Number:	8. Mortgage Insurance Case Number:

C. Note: This form is furnished to give you a statement of actual settlement costs. Amounts paid to and by the settlement agent are shown. Items marked "(p.o.c.)" were paid outside the closing; they are shown here for informational purposes and are not included in the totals.

D. Name & Address of Borrower:	E. Name & Address of Seller:	F. Name & Address of Lender:

G. Property Location:

H. Settlement Agent:

Place of Settlement:

I. Settlement Date:

J. Summary of Borrower's Transaction		**K. Summary of Seller's Transaction**	
100. Gross Amount Due From Borrower		**400. Gross Amount Due To Seller**	
101. Contract sales price		401. Contract sales price	
102. Personal property		402. Personal property	
103. Settlement charges to borrower (line 1400)		403.	
104.		404.	
105.		405.	
Adjustments for items paid by seller in advance		**Adjustments for items paid by seller in advance**	
106. City/town taxes to		406. City/town taxes to	
107. County taxes to		407. County taxes to	
108. Assessments to		408. Assessments to	
109.		409.	
110.		410.	
111.		411.	
112.		412.	
120. Gross Amount Due From Borrower		**420. Gross Amount Due To Seller**	
200. Amounts Paid By Or In Behalf Of Borrower		**500. Reductions In Amount Due To Seller**	
201. Deposit or earnest money		501. Excess deposit (see instructions)	
202. Principal amount of new loan(s)		502. Settlement charges to seller (line 1400)	
203. Existing loan(s) taken subject to		503. Existing loan(s) taken subject to	
204.		504. Payoff of first mortgage loan	
205.		505. Payoff of second mortgage loan	
206.		506.	
207.		507.	
208.		508.	
209.		509.	
Adjustments for items unpaid by seller		**Adjustments for items unpaid by seller**	
210. City/town taxes to		510. City/town taxes to	
211. County taxes to		511. County taxes to	
212. Assessments to		512. Assessments to	
213.		513.	
214.		514.	
215.		515.	
216.		516.	
217.		517.	
218.		518.	
219.		519.	
220. Total Paid By/For Borrower		**520. Total Reduction Amount Due Seller**	
300. Cash At Settlement From/To Borrower		**600. Cash At Settlement To/From Seller**	
301. Gross Amount due from borrower (line 120)		601. Gross amount due to seller (line 420)	
302. Less amounts paid by/for borrower (line 220) ( )		602. Less reductions in amt. due seller (line 520) ( )	
303. Cash ☐ From ☐ To Borrower		**603. Cash** ☐ To ☐ From Seller	

Section 5 of the Real Estate Settlement Procedures Act (RESPA) requires the following: • HUD must develop a Special Information Booklet to help persons borrowing money to finance the purchase of residential real estate to better understand the nature and costs of real estate settlement services; • Each lender must provide the booklet to all applicants from whom it receives or for whom it prepares a written application to borrow money to finance the purchase of residential real estate; • Lenders must prepare and distribute with the Booklet a Good Faith Estimate of the settlement costs that the borrower is likely to incur in connection with the settlement. These disclosures are manadatory.

Section 4(a) of RESPA mandates that HUD develop and prescribe this standard form to be used at the time of loan settlement to provide full disclosure of all charges imposed upon the borrower and seller. These are third party disclosures that are designed to provide the borrower with pertinent information during the settlement process in order to be a better shopper.

The Public Reporting Burden for this collection of information is estimated to average one hour per response, including the time for reviewing instructions, searching existing data sources, gathering and maintaining the data needed, and completing and reviewing the collection of information.

This agency may not collect this information, and you are not required to complete this form, unless it displays a currently valid OMB control number.

The information requested does not lend itself to confidentiality.

L. Settlement Charges

	Paid From Borrowers Funds at Settlement	Paid From Seller's Funds at Settlement
700. Total Sales/Broker's Commission based on price $ @ % =		
Division of Commission (line 700) as follows:		
701. $ to		
702. $ to		
703. Commission paid at Settlement		
704.		
800. Items Payable In Connection With Loan		
801. Loan Origination Fee %		
802. Loan Discount %		
803. Appraisal Fee to		
804. Credit Report to		
805. Lender's Inspection Fee		
806. Mortgage Insurance Application Fee to		
807. Assumption Fee		
808.		
809.		
810.		
811.		
900. Items Required By Lender To Be Paid In Advance		
901. Interest from to @$ /day		
902. Mortgage Insurance Premium for months to		
903. Hazard Insurance Premium for years to		
904. years to		
905.		
1000. Reserves Deposited With Lender		
1001. Hazard insurance months@$ per month		
1002. Mortgage insurance months@$ per month		
1003. City property taxes months@$ per month		
1004. County property taxes months@$ per month		
1005. Annual assessments months@$ per month		
1006. months@$ per month		
1007. months@$ per month		
1008. months@$ per month		
1100. Title Charges		
1101. Settlement or closing fee to		
1102. Abstract or title search to		
1103. Title examination to		
1104. Title insurance binder to		
1105. Document preparation to		
1106. Notary fees to		
1107. Attorney's fees to		
(includes above items numbers:)		
1108. Title insurance to		
(includes above items numbers:)		
1109. Lender's coverage $		
1110. Owner's coverage $		
1111.		
1112.		
1113.		
1200. Government Recording and Transfer Charges		
1201. Recording fees: Deed $; Mortgage $; Releases $		
1202. City/county tax/stamps: Deed $; Mortgage $		
1203. State tax/stamps: Deed $; Mortgage $		
1204.		
1205.		
1300. Additional Settlement Charges		
1301. Survey to		
1302. Pest inspection to		
1303.		
1304.		
1305.		
1400. Total Settlement Charges (enter on lines 103, Section J and 502, Section K)		

If you are not a resident of the state in which you are selling a home, or are a *nonresident seller*, then you may be subject to a state income tax being withheld from the gross sale proceeds.

The following tax declaration form (from the state of New Jersey) is used to verify the seller's home state and primary residence. Their purpose is to track sellers to make certain that they file a nonresident income tax return and report the sale of a secondary property.

The two most common types of taxes paid on the sale of real estate are realty transfer tax and income tax (as a result of capital gains).

Some states impose the realty transfer tax, while others do not. It is a tax that is based on the sale price (the more you sell it for, the more you pay) and is paid to the state. Here's a hypothetical example of how it works in one state. It is a rather complicated calculation:

> If the home sells for under $350,000, the tax will be $2.00 for every $500 up to the first $150,000. Then, add to it another $3.35 for every $500 between $150,000 and $200,000. Then, add another $3.90 for every $500 up to $350,000.

So, if your home sold for $350,000, the realty transfer tax would be $3,875.

The income tax (often referred to as the capital gains tax) is what you pay when you make a profit on your home, or on the sale of just about anything you own, for that matter. But the sale of a home can bring profits in the hundreds of thousands for millions of Americans. So, the IRS takes it very seriously! And if you are selling a luxury home, your state may impose upon you a *luxury tax*, as well.

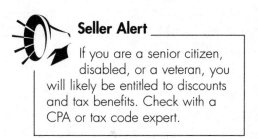

Seller Alert

If you are a senior citizen, disabled, or a veteran, you will likely be entitled to discounts and tax benefits. Check with a CPA or tax code expert.

The tax laws are always subject to change. But, as it stands in late 2008, it is as follows:

> **Married People Who File Jointly:** This group can earn up to $500,000 in profit on the sale of a home and not pay income taxes on the profit if they lived there for at least two years of the last five.

> **Singles:** An individual can earn up to $250,000 in profit on the sale of a home and not pay income taxes on the profit if she lived there for at least two years of the last five.

Note: if you are selling a home as part of an estate sale for a deceased loved one, see Chapter 12 for specific tax implications.

def•i•ni•tion

You may have heard of the **luxury tax,** but it usually applies to buyers of luxury items rather than to sellers. For example, a state may impose a 1 percent luxury tax on the buyer of any home with a sale price of $1 million or more. Check to see if your state has such a tax in addition to taxes which may apply to all properties.

Read and Sign the Settlement Statement

If the buyer borrows money, then both the seller and the buyer must sign a settlement statement (mandated by the U.S. government) that discloses all the charges, fees, credit, debits, taxes, assessments, commissions, attorney fees, and anything else associated with the transaction.

The settlement statement is also known as the HUD or RESPA Statement. Here's why: the document is a requirement made by the Department of Housing and Urban Development (HUD). The legislative act that made it law is called the Real Estate Settlement Procedures Act (RESPA).

The law reads:

> Section 4(a) of RESPA mandates that HUD develop and prescribe this standard form to be used at the time of loan settlement to provide full disclosure of all charges imposed upon the borrower and seller. These are third-party disclosures that are designed to provide the borrower with pertinent information during the settlement process in order to be a better shopper.

For more information on closing or settlement procedures, visit www.hud.gov.

Pay Credits to the Buyer (Inspection Issues)

The seller may need to pay credits to the buyer for a variety of things, including:

◆ Any agreed-upon repairs as a result of the inspection negotiation.

◆ Any special assessments by homeowners' associations or governing bodies that the seller agreed to pay as part of the sale.

◆ Any reimbursements or funds for the remediation of an environmental hazard on the property.

◆ Any excess deposit money that may have been paid.

Receive Credits from the Buyer

The buyer, on the other hand, may need to make payments or credits to you, the seller, for the following areas:

- ◆ Property taxes paid in advance by you

- ◆ Utility payments made in advance by you

- ◆ Condominium, co-op, or other maintenance fees made in advance by you

- ◆ Advance-paid services such as refuse pickup, pool maintenance, landscaping, and others

Pay Commission and Other Fees

With the exception of the commission, many of the fees that you may have heard about in a real estate transaction are actually paid by the buyer, not the seller. Those fees are title services, appraisals, mortgage application fees, inspections, ordering a new survey, and insurance.

You will have your own set of fees and charges associated with the sale. They must all be paid at or before the time of closing. The primary seller's fee is the real estate commission, which is likely to be between 5 and 7 percent of the total sale price. On a $350,000 home, a 5 percent commission would be $17,500. As illustrated in Chapter 3, that commission is split between two real estate agencies: the listing agency and the agency representing the buyer (selling agency). A significant percentage is taken off the top by the agency before giving what's left to the individual Realtor. After the Realtor pays taxes and expenses, she will probably take home less than one third of the total commission.

Other fees include:

- ◆ **Attorney fees:** These are lower for sellers than they are for buyers because there is less legal work to be done on your side of the transaction. The fees vary from state to state, depending on how attorneys bill for their time. Many full-time real estate attorneys charge a flat fee for the whole transaction, while others bill by the hour.

- ◆ **Recording costs:** These are the fees charged by a government party to make an official record of the transfer of ownership and to release any existing liens. The level of government is usually local, such as the county or municipal clerk's office. Fees for recording costs can be anywhere from $75 to several hundred dollars, depending on many different criteria, including how many liens there are or mortgages being recorded.

◆ **Administrative and/or overnight delivery fees:** These fees may be billed to you separately by your attorney. They may be included if the attorney bills by the hour.

Other Documents

The deed is the document that establishes ownership. The names of each and every owner are printed on it. A husband and wife may live in a home together, but if only the husband's name is on the deed, the wife does not own the property, and technically has no legal rights to it. If the couple divorces, she may sue and go after the home or a portion of its value. However, the asset is considered to be her husband's as long as his name alone remains on the deed.

Affidavit of title actually transfers ownership. Do not confuse this with the title on a car or the title on a boat. It's not the same thing. This is a document that is most often prepared by the seller's attorney and given to the buyer for the purpose of recording the sale with the state or local government. People often envision this to be a very old piece of paper with frayed edges. In actuality, a brand-new affidavit of title is prepared each time the property changes owners.

Calculating Profit and Loss on the Sale

Determining whether or not you will make a profit or suffer a loss is a matter of mathematics. After you know what your profit is, you can then know how much of it you'll be taxed on, otherwise known as taxable profit.

How to Calculate Taxable Profit

Step One: Calculate Your Net Sale Price

Sale Price − Selling Expenses (commission, attorney fees, and so on) = Net Sale Price

Step Two: Establish Your Total Basis

Original Purchase Price of Your Home (and old closing costs) + Costs of Improvements Made to Home During Ownership = Total Basis

Step Three: Figure Your Gross Profit

Net Sale Price – Total Basis = Gross Profit

Step Four: Figure Your Taxable Profit According to Current Allowable Deductions

Married, Filing Jointly	Single
Gross Profit	Gross Profit
– $500,000 Deductions*	– $250,000 Deductions*
= Taxable Profit	= Taxable Profit

Seller Alert

For tax purposes, moving costs are not considered as an expense of selling a home.

* These deduction amounts are currently allowable (as of 2008) if the home was your principal residence for at least two of the last five years. Deduction amounts are always subject to change with new legislation voted in by Congress.

Keys

The last thing that happens at a closing is a sort of ceremonial thing, and that is handing over the keys to the buyers. Don't forget to bring them! Even though most buyers have the locks changed right away, it is almost always a touching moment at a closing. It is an emotional act for both the buyers and the sellers, particularly if the buyers are first-time homeowners and the sellers happen to be retiring. That gets us every time.

Seller Liability After Closing

Technically, once the closing has concluded, the seller is absolved of all responsibility associated with the property. There are only three scenarios in which there may be an ongoing liability or any connection to the buyers.

Money Held in Escrow

Sometimes, an issue cannot be resolved in time for the closing, but both parties wish the closing to take place anyway. In this case, money from the proceeds will be held in escrow, or in a trust account of a disinterested third party. It can be the trust account of an attorney, an accountant, the real estate agency, the title company, or the bank. The key thing to remember about money that is held in escrow is that it cannot be taken out of the account and given to either party until both parties give their consent. If the dispute continues for years, then that money will also be tied up for years.

Money can be put into escrow over significant or major disputes or over small or petty ones. The bigger ones include finding an open mortgage or unpaid lien, a leaking in-ground oil tank which may have been removed but the contaminated soil has not yet been hauled away, or an owner named on the deed cannot be found for signatures. These kinds of issues are usually known well in advance of the closing, so appropriate arrangements can be made and everyone involved is forewarned.

Escrow money held for petty issues usually crops up at the final walk-through, where the buyer may feel that an agreed-upon repair was not made, the home has been left in a filthy condition, or there is unwanted debris on the property. Most of the time, these things can be resolved on closing day through a physical action or by the seller offering a last-minute financial credit to the buyer. But sometimes the buyer and seller cannot come to an agreement over the minor issue. In this event, either the closing gets delayed or escrow money will be held. Many attorneys would rather delay the closing than to put money in an escrow account over something so minor, relatively speaking.

Civil Claims or Lawsuits

Even though the seller is legally relieved of any liability on the home after he has sold it, the buyer always retains the right to file a claim or civil lawsuit. However, it is very difficult for the buyer to win such a case. She would likely have to prove that the there was a hidden latent defect with the home which the seller not only knew about, but may also have taken steps to actively conceal from the buyer.

Two stories come to mind. In the one case, a local buyer discovered a leak in the brand-new ceiling that the previous owner had featured in the listing when he marketed the home just a couple months earlier. The buyer called a contractor, who then had to tear open a section of the new ceiling. Inside, just above the ceiling, was a pie plate which had been carefully placed below a leaking pipe to catch water. The previous owner then installed a new ceiling around it and promptly put his home on the market. That buyer may have a case because the seller appeared to willfully conceal a known defect.

In another case, the furnace died one week after the closing. The new homeowner called a plumber. When the plumber arrived, it turned out to be the same one that the seller had used. The plumber said to the new homeowner, "I was here just two weeks ago and I told the seller that this furnace was about to go any minute." And sure enough, he was right. The point here is that, especially in this example, the buyer has clear evidence that that the seller withheld knowledge of a hidden latent defect. A claim or lawsuit could possibly prove successful. But, without clear evidence, it's very hard to prove that the seller knew of, and concealed, flaws in the home.

Use and Occupancy Agreements

Use and occupancy agreements are called U & O agreements for short. It means that the buyer and seller have made an agreement whereby the seller can stay in the home for a period of time after the closing has taken place. The buyers become the new owners and the sellers—in effect, they become "tenants." They have granted the sellers the right to use and occupy the premises.

Trick of the Trade

If you find that, as the closing draws near, you cannot move out in time and need another day or two, it may be easier to delay the closing rather than negotiate a U & O agreement. Since closing dates are not always held to the exact date, you can probably legally just stall a bit. But try to give the buyers some warning so they don't take a financial loss due to penalties with their movers and such.

These agreements often happen when the sellers cannot move out fast enough for the buyers, yet the buyers want to close anyway—usually because their locked-in mortgage loan rate is about to expire. U & O agreements can be complicated legally, financially, and emotionally. The sellers may treat the home as though it is still theirs, the buyers soon feel cheated out of access to their new home, an appropriate monthly rent may be difficult to establish, and if the sellers refuse to vacate, a whole new set of problems arise. If you need a U & O agreement for your home, proceed with care. They can be wonderful, when they work out. But, when they don't, it can get ugly.

The Least You Need to Know

◆ The main thing that happens at the closing table is the legal transfer of ownership of property.

◆ The seller's main responsibilities include moving out completely, paying off the
mortgage, getting a certificate for continued use, reading and signing the settlement statement, paying the real estate commission, and reporting the sale on
federal and/or state tax forms.

◆ When calculating expenses to use in determining profit or loss on the sale, be
sure to include closing costs, attorney fees, real estate commission, and improvements made to the home.

◆ You do not have to pay income taxes (as a result of a capital gain) on the sale of
your home if you are married, filing jointly, made less than $500,000 in profit,
and you lived there for at least two of the last five years. If you're single, it's
$250,000. This law is subject to change at any time.

◆ A seller has no more liability on her home once she sells it unless she leaves
money held in escrow or she has a use and occupancy agreement, or the buyer
files a civil claim against her and wins.

Chapter 19

Packing and Moving Made Simple

In This Chapter

- ◆ Local versus long-distance moves
- ◆ Packing tips
- ◆ Packing materials
- ◆ Movers and estimates
- ◆ Special moving services
- ◆ Moving day

Whether you are moving yourself or hiring a professional moving company, there are many ways to make the process easier on you and your family. Moving is pretty high on the list of the most stressful things that we will do in our lives, but it really doesn't have to be. If you give yourself enough time, have a plan, and take advantage of great cost- and time-saving tips, it can be an organized and efficient move. As they say, there is a hard way to do things and an easy way! Having knowledge and being prepared are the ways to make moving easy.

In this chapter, we cover everything to do with moving, including local versus long-distance moves, the right way to pack, what materials you'll need, how to move yourself, how to hire a good mover and avoid the really bad ones, getting estimates, payment and tipping, licensing, insurance, and other important paperwork you'll need.

Moving Out of State vs. Within the State

There are many moving companies (or carriers) that do only local moves. They tend to be the smaller companies whose trucks you might see around town or in your area. The local companies are required to follow mostly state laws and regulations. The bigger companies, which move people from state to state, must abide by more stringent federal laws. They are called interstate moving companies.

Local Moving

Local moving companies are required to be licensed by the state in which they do business. Generally, they are not allowed to move anyone out of that state. We don't recommend using a local company to move to another state, because it's illegal and the driver and company can be fined. In addition, if the driver gets pulled over and your possessions are in the truck at the time, the vehicle can be impounded. Your best bet is to use a local mover for local moves, and an interstate carrier for moving out of state.

Trick of the Trade _____

There are some occasions when you actually can use a local company when moving from one state to another. This is usually when you are traveling just across the state border to a town or city that is considered to be in the same "commercial zone" as the town or city you left. In this case, federal regulations do not apply. Check with your mover to see if your new community falls within the same zone.

All movers, both big and small, are required to be registered with the Department of Transportation (DOT) in Washington, D.C. You may have noticed that just about any truck on the road will have a DOT number printed on it—usually on the driver's cab door. This number should also be printed on the estimates and other paperwork. Be sure to keep both the state license number and the DOT number in your possession.

Local movers are usually required by their individual state to give you a consumer pamphlet outlining your rights when dealing with a mover. There will also be contact information on it, should you have questions about the process or about how to settle a possible dispute with the company.

Out-of-State Moving

Carriers that do interstate moves are required to have what's called an Interstate Commerce Commission (ICC) license, which is issued by the ICC. This is a blanket license for most or all states in which they do business and which allows them to cross state lines.

When an interstate mover gives you an estimate, the DOT requires that they give you a consumer booklet titled "Ready to Move," or "Your Rights and Responsibilities When You Move." If you want more information on rules, regulations, and your rights, visit www.protectyourmove.gov or call 1-888-DOT-SAFT (1-888-368-7238).

Your Packing Plan

Packing requires a plan! The key to good, efficient packing is all in your approach. Between the two of us, we have moved enough times to have learned from our mistakes. We also interviewed both interstate and local movers for this chapter. Take the time to create a system that everyone in your family will understand and follow; otherwise you will get very frustrated and feel overwhelmed.

Here are some tips and broad strokes to apply in your approach to packing:

◆ Pack the least-used rooms first. These areas are typically the attic, basement, garage, and storage sheds. They are usually filled with items that you do not use every day, so they can be packed weeks in advance of your move. It will force you to sort and to get rid of items that you don't want to take with you to the new home. They are also the hardest rooms to organize, so it's nice to get them over with.

◆ Pack only one room at a time. If you pack several rooms simultaneously, you can easily get overwhelmed with the enormity of the project. Having half-packed open boxes all over the place makes you feel disorganized and confused. When you complete one room before moving on to the next room, you will be able to gauge how much time is needed to finish the whole move and manage your time better. You'll experience a new sense of accomplishment as you finish each one.

◆ Pack all nonbreakables first. Items such as linens, books, and toys are easy to pack. And breakable items such as dishes and glassware often remain in use right up until moving day and should be packed last.

◆ Make a series of pre-moves. If you are moving locally, try bringing a couple of carloads of goods over by yourself, in advance of moving day. This is a terrific way to save money on the professional moving estimate. We like to move highly breakable or valuable things, such as fine china and art, ourselves to be sure that they arrive safely.

◆ Bind tall items to one another. Bundle brooms, mops, rakes, and shovels and tape them together at the top and bottom.

◆ Collect boxes in advance. Your local grocery, liquor, or other retail stores may give you cardboard boxes for free. If you start this process early enough, you may not have to buy any boxes at all. Liquor boxes with the dividers still in them are a fantastic way to pack glasses without wrapping them first.

Trick of the Trade _____

Clear out with a garage sale. Our own editor was an army kid who moved a lot. Each time, her parents gave her garage sale stickers to put on things that she agreed to get rid of while she packed. They were color coded so she could keep track with her siblings of what was sold and her parents let her keep the money to buy new things for her new room. They got rid of more, knowing that they could make more money. You can find more great ideas like this in *The Pocket Idiot's Guide to Garage and Yard Sales.*

◆ Don't forget to bend your knees! Medically speaking, the human back is very expensive. Don't mess with it. Many people bend over from the waist to pick up items, and that is a big mistake. Bend your knees and lower your whole body down to pick up heavy things.

Seller Alert _____

Hazardous materials like propane tanks and gasoline are not allowed to be transported on moving trucks. Moving companies are not insured for them and they are very dangerous, particularly if the truck should get into an accident. Give yourself time to use up the contents or return them to a local facility before you move. You could even give them to your neighbors.

Packing Materials

Boxes and other moving materials can be expensive. There is also the question of what to do with them once you unpack and don't need them anymore. Two quick solutions are to rent some of the boxes from your moving company and to participate in a moving carton exchange program. Renting boxes from a mover usually works best for garment boxes because they are expensive to buy and because they are sturdy enough to be used again and again for consecutive customers. And a way to go "green" is to check with your Realtor to see if the agency (or any local organization) participates in an exchange program whereby you donate your boxes to another family moving out of town at about the same time that you are moving in. It's a wonderful way to use boxes multiple times before sending them to their final destination at the recycling center.

Moving Boxes

There are five basic types of moving boxes or cartons:

♦ **Book cartons.** These are small boxes that are good for anything heavy, including books, canned goods, or tools. They are designed to be filled to the brim.

♦ **Linen or utility boxes.** These are nice wide boxes that are good for all light nonbreakables, including sheets, pillows, toys, games, and even lampshades.

♦ **Dish packs.** In the old days, these were called "china barrels" because they were actually barrels that carried china. This is a tall box designed specifically to transport dishes placed vertically (up and down). The heavier dishes go on the bottom and the lighter ones and glasses go on top of them.

♦ **Wardrobe boxes.** As we said, these are the most popular to rent. They are very tall boxes with a metal rod at the very top for hanging garments. There is usually room at the bottom of the box to toss in shoes and boots, as well.

♦ **Picture cartons.** These are the most expensive boxes and are used for artwork. They are tall and very narrow. They are sometimes made up of two interlocking boxes that adjust to the specific size of your art.

Other Materials

Wrapping items to prevent damage is usually done with bubble wrap, blankets, or paper pads. Paper pads are the best when your possessions, especially furniture, will be in a hot truck for an extended period or if the items will be going into storage. Bubble wrap can trap moisture and we do not recommend it at all for furniture or art unless you prewrap in paper. Additionally, the weight of a blanket, over time, can leave an imprint of its weave on the surface of the item. On the other hand, reusing blankets is better for the environment than paper pads and bubble wrap. Local movers are more prone to using blankets, while long-haul carriers may favor bubble wrap (and charge for it by the foot).

And finally, many movers do not charge to tape up some of your boxes or to secure a blanket around a piece of furniture. Most assume that it is part of the cost of doing business. On the other hand, if you are requesting rolls of tape for your prepacking, they will certainly charge you.

> **Seller Alert**
>
> If a mover provides boxes for free, beware. Boxes are too expensive to just give away. The cost is probably built into the overall moving estimate. In this case, it is more important than ever to get estimates from three movers.

Finding the Right Mover

The approach to finding the right mover is similar to the one for finding the right Realtor. Personal referrals are the best. As Realtors, we have targeted what we think are the best companies and refer them time and again to our clients. Ask your Realtor for any recommendations. Always interview and get estimates from at least three companies and ask for references.

Never book a mover over the phone. They need to come to your home and visually inspect the premises as well as your furniture and other belongings. They cannot give you a sound estimate without this step.

If a company has no local address, uses rental trucks instead of company-owned ones, neglects to give you a written estimate and a booklet outlining your rights, or demands cash from you up front, then you should be very wary.

Getting Moving Estimates

All estimates should be in writing, signed by the mover and given to you before the move. They can be done only after an in-person inspection is performed by the moving company. There are two kinds: *binding estimates* and *nonbinding estimates*.

def•i•ni•tion

A **binding estimate** is a written guarantee of the total cost of the move based upon what is being moved and what specific services you choose or your move requires.

A **nonbinding estimate** is what the mover believes your move will cost. At the time of payment, the amount can be higher or lower, based upon the final weight of the truck or on any unforeseen problems or necessary additional services. You should be prepared to pay 10 percent more than the estimated cost, plus charges for additional services that you requested after the contract with your mover was signed.

Guidelines for Estimates

Many big interstate movers base their moving estimates on the net weight of your possessions, as well as miles traveled. They will weigh the truck before it has been loaded (tare weight) and then weigh it again after your possessions have been loaded (gross weight). The difference is the net weight.

The mover must use a state-approved truck scale and that may be located a long way from your home. You have the right to attend and witness the weighing. He will be given a ticket with a state seal on it that shows the weight. However, if you agree to it, the mover may instead weigh your items on a portable scale or even estimate the weight based on cubic feet. Some interstate movers will not use weight at all but will offer a flat-fee estimate. Some consumers actually prefer this rather than waiting until the truck is loaded and weighed to find out the costs.

Local movers are more prone to giving estimates based on how many hours they think the job will take and how many men it will take to do it. The mover will give you a binding estimate for this. However, sometimes the local mover will not commit to a binding estimate. He may be unsure of what to expect on the other end—where he is unloading. While unloading a truck is much easier and quicker than loading a truck, he may want to keep his options open, just in case there are unforeseen difficulties. You then have two options. One is to ask him to go and inspect the home and location to which you are moving. The other is to ask him to at least give you a cap—a price that he will not go above. Since you are moving locally, he should be able to do one of these two things. If he will not, move on to the next company.

 Seller Alert

Big interstate carriers will sometimes move two or three families' belongings on the same truck. This makes the weighing process much more complicated. It can still be done, but you should at least be made aware of it if your belongings will be transported with those of another homeowner's.

Insurance

There are four main insurance options for assuming liability for your goods. Three of them can be obtained through your mover.

◆ **Full-value protection (FVP).** This is the most comprehensive coverage; if something is damaged or destroyed, the mover can repair it, replace it, or pay to have it replaced.

◆ **Release value of 60 cents per pound per article.** This is the most basic required coverage by any licensed mover. It only gives you 60 cents for each pound that the item weighs. If your 30-pound flat-screen TV breaks, believe it or not, you would only receive $18 for it.

◆ **Separate liability insurance through the mover.** Your mover can, through a third-party insurance company, sell or obtain for you separate liability coverage.

◆ **Your homeowner's insurance.** Your own homeowner's insurance policy may cover moves. If not, you may be able to purchase additional coverage just for the move itself. This may be easier than going through the mover for coverage. If you go through the mover, there will be a separate, and additional, contract between the two of you.

Finally, if you only have one or two expensive items that you're worried about, consider taking out insurance only on them as opposed to paying a large premium on the contents of the whole house.

Moving Day

This may be a long day for you, but even longer for the movers! Here are some insights into what you can expect, your role, how to pay the movers, and how to make it to the end of the day in one piece!

Your Role

First of all, remember that when the moving men arrive, they will probably be seeing your home for the first time. Your estimate came from either the owner or a company representative who previously visited your home. The moving men will want to immediately walk through it with you to get an idea of what they're in for. If there is going to be any kind of problem, they will spot it or anticipate it right away. If you are not finished packing or if a piece of furniture is too big to get through a passageway, this could seriously affect the progress of the day.

Once they begin moving, you want to remain on the premises in case they have any questions, but you also want to stay out of their way. If you and the kids and the dog are underfoot, you will slow them down and add to your costs. Your presence, however, will have the added benefit of keeping the guys working and not slacking off.

Often, the movers will try to load the entire truck before taking lunch. You should not be billed for the lunch hour. When they are eating, the clock stops. We do recommend providing beverages for them, particularly on a warm day. In fact, we have gone so far as to have some form of breakfast food for them when they first arrive. We believe that happy movers are good movers.

Paying the Movers

Many (but not all) big interstate moving companies will expect payment before they unload the truck. You can imagine why that would be important to them. Once your items are off the truck, the driver has little leverage in collecting payment. Local movers tend to be more flexible on this point. Either way, the entire balance is due upon delivery.

A tip for the workers will be expected, but the appropriate amount is sometimes a matter of opinion. We think that a safe window is, depending on how good a job they did, to take 10 to 20 percent of the total cost of the job and divide it among them.

Trick of the Trade

You may be tempted to just add the tip onto the total bill and leave it to the job leader to dispense amongst the workers who moved you. It's better to make it clear how much you wish each worker to receive, or if one or two team leaders deserve a little more so there is no confusion.

Moving Terminology

There are quite a few technical words and phrases used in the moving industry. It is a government-regulated business, after all! Here are some of the most important terms for you to know:

- ◆ **Order for service.** This is not a contract. This is the document that authorizes the mover to transport your belongings. It also indicates the services that the mover will perform, as well as the dates that the goods will be picked up and delivered. If you cancel or delay your move, cancel the order promptly.

◆ **Bill of lading.** This is both a contract and a receipt. The contract is for transport. The receipt is for your actual belongings. You should have a complete copy before the truck is loaded.

◆ **Inventory list.** This is a detailed list/receipt of the number and condition of every item being transported. Keep a copy for yourself.

◆ **Expedited service.** This is an agreement to pay a higher fee to the mover to transport by a certain date.

◆ **Guaranteed service between specific dates.** If the mover does not pick up and deliver between two set dates, you will be reimbursed for delays.

◆ **Exclusive use of vehicle.** This is an agreement whereby you require that your belongings, and no one else's, are on the truck.

◆ **Long carry.** There may be an additional charge when there is a very long distance between the truck and your residence.

◆ **Flight charge.** This is a charge to carry items up and down flights of stairs.

◆ **Storage in transit (SIT).** This is for temporary warehouse storage in the midst of transporting. For example, if the delivery could not happen because no one was present to accept it, the driver can place your belongings in SIT without notifying you.

◆ **Packing service.** This is when the mover packs your items for you. Some movers charge by the hour, while others charge by the carton.

◆ **Photo packing.** This is a newer and emerging service where the mover photographs every item to be transported. It serves to substantiate condition, or for you to prove that damage was done in transit.

The Least You Need to Know

◆ There are two types of moves—local or interstate. Local movers will usually calculate the number of hours and number of men needed for the job. Interstate carriers often use the weight of your belongings to determine the cost.

◆ There are two types of estimates: binding and nonbinding. Nonbinding is a guess at what the total cost will be. A binding estimate is a guarantee.

◆ A mover's basic insurance liability does not cover the total value of your belongings. Check your mover's coverage and supplement it, if necessary.

◆ The five basic types of moving boxes are book cartons, linen or utility boxes, dish packs, wardrobe boxes, and picture cartons.

◆ Bubble wrap traps moisture and is not good for artwork, furniture, or certain items going into long-term storage.

◆ To determine how much to tip the movers, a safe bet is to give them between 10 to 20 percent of the total cost of the job and divide it among them.

Glossary

1031 exchange   Named after Section 1031 of the IRS code, it is a law that allows you to defer federal (and some state) taxes on capital gains from the sale of a property that was used for trade, business, or investment purposes only. However, you must exchange the property for another that is similar in nature and equal to or greater in value than the one you are selling. Also known as a *tax-deferred exchange*, it is based on the premise that when you reinvest proceeds from a sale to another property, you haven't really received funds to pay taxes on—it's only a paper gain. Eventually, you will pay taxes when you sell a property that is not being replaced with another.

absorption rate   This is essentially how long it takes for homes to sell in your area. It is usually referred to in months but, in a hot market, it can be referred to in weeks.

agent   A person who represents someone else in the purchase or sale of real estate and is paid a commission. Commission is not paid directly to the agent, but rather it is paid to the agent's broker.

appraisal   An estimate of value.

attorney review   A period of time when attorneys review the purchase contract only. Buyer or seller has the right to withdraw from the contract without penalty.

back-up offers   Offers in a multiple-bid scenario (or bidding war) that are rejected but can later be accepted if the winning bid falls apart.

beneficiary   A person named in a will to receive benefits from real estate, insurance policies, bank accounts, retirement accounts, and so on.

bidding war   Having several buyers making offers and competing for the same property.

binding estimate   A guaranteed estimate of moving costs, give or take about 10 percent.

broker   The person who legally represents the client and receives a commission. The agent actually represents the broker.

Cape Cod–style   A style of house built in colonial times (1600s–1700s); it's a small, one-floor symmetrical home with a steep-pitched roof and a centered chimney. This type of home was built primarily in the New England region of the United States. In the 1930s and 1940s, thousands of Cape Cod revivals were built all over the United States, but particularly in Michigan, Ohio, and Pennsylvania.

capital gains tax   A tax paid to the government for making a profit on the sale of an item, such as a home.

certificate of occupancy   A document given by an official of the local government that allows a home to be occupied or used according to local rules, regulations, zoning laws, and ordinances.

closing   The final event in the transferring of ownership of a piece of real estate. All relevant documents are signed and funds are transferred, as well.

cloud on the title   An encumbrance, debt, or claim to a property which means that it cannot be legally sold. They are usually uncovered in a title search done by the buyer.

CMA (competitive market analysis)   A study of similar homes in the area that are on the market, have recently sold, or have just gone under contract. The analysis is used as a pricing tool.

commission   A fee paid in exchange for professional services, such as listing and marketing a home.

commission split   How much of the commission the listing agent will share with an agent who brings the buyer.

comparables   Similar homes in the area with regard to size, condition, style, and location.

condominium   A form of ownership whereby someone owns entirely an individual unit in a multiunit building but also owns a part of the common area shared by all the owners in the building. There is usually one master deed.

contingency   A plan of action that addresses an event that may or may not happen. If a contingency in a real estate contract is not met (or "resolved"), the contract ceases to exist.

co-op   A form of ownership in multiunit buildings where individuals do not own any real estate but instead own shares in a corporation and a proprietary lease.

cosmetic improvements   Any upgrades made to a home that are superficial and inexpensive relative to structural improvements. They improve the aesthetic appearance of a home in most cases. For example, painting, refinishing floors, and replacing light fixtures are considered to be cosmetic improvements.

counteroffer   A response to an offer that is neither a rejection nor an acceptance but a suggestion of a new agreement.

credits and debits   Money that is paid to the seller at closing by the buyer for any prepaid taxes or assessments, and money that is paid to the buyer by the seller for repairs or other agreed-upon payments.

curb appeal   A home's level of visual attraction from the street or curb.

death tax   A common term for *estate tax*. A tax on the transfer of property after death.

deed   A written legal document that transfers and demonstrates ownership of a property.

down payment   The part of the sale price that is paid up front, in cash, by the buyer.

dual agency   When a real estate agent or agency represents both sides in a transaction. Unless both parties agree to it, this is unethical. In some states, it is illegal.

earnest money   A small amount of money put down by the buyer, often at the same time the offer is made, in order to show good faith.

equity   Ownership. It is often the net difference between the value of the home and the amount of money owed on it.

escalation clause   A term in a contract where a buyer tries to avoid participating in a bidding war by offering a certain amount of money over the highest bid.

escrow   Money or documents held by a neutral third party until a property closes.

estate sale   The sale of a deceased person's real estate.

estate tax   Also known as a *death tax*. It is a tax on the transfer of property from the deceased to an heir(s) and is paid before the property is distributed to those heirs.

exceptions   When a seller names a party or parties who may purchase the home directly and will not be subject to a paid commission.

exclusive agency   When the seller allows only one agency to both list and sell. If the seller finds his own buyer, a commission does not need to be paid.

exclusive right to sell   When one agency has the sole right to represent the seller regardless of which agency sells it.

executor   The person who carries out the terms of a will. A female is an executrix.

fair market value   The value at which a licensed appraiser estimates a home to be worth. It can also be defined as the price that an able buyer is willing to pay for a home.

feature sheet   A sheet(s) with beautiful photos of a property as well as impressive word descriptions showcasing a property at its best.

final walk-through   The last in-person visit to and inspection of a property by the buyer, which is conducted immediately prior to closing.

fixture   Something that is attached or affixed to a surface such as a chandelier, wall sconce, faucet, washing machine, and so on.

flat-fee listing   A fee the seller pays up front instead of a percentage at closing. It does not matter if the property sells.

foreclosure   A legal process where a seller either loses his interest in the home as a result of not meeting the terms of the loan, or when the sale of the home is forced by the lender.

FSBO (For-Sale-By-Owner)   When a homeowner attempts to sell his home without the aid of a real estate agent.

guaranteed buyout   When an employer or relocation company pays a transferring employee an agreed-upon amount of money for the home, whether it sells or not.

home equity loan   When a seller borrows money and uses his home as collateral. It is also known as a *second mortgage*.

home stager   A person who, for a fee, transforms a home into a condition suitable for selling.

home warranty insurance   Insurance against problems with appliances and the systems of the home, such as heating and plumbing.

homeowner's insurance   Insurance that protects a homeowner from the loss of the home, its value or contents through theft, liability, damage from storms or wind, and other circumstances.

inspection   A review or examination of a home, its structure, and its systems.

inspection cap   When a buyer volunteers or agrees to a cap or limit to the amount of money or credits that he may ask for as a result of an inspection.

keypad   The device that Realtors use to access lockboxes and the keys to a home.

lien   A claim or a debt against a property.

list price   The amount of money that a seller is asking.

listing agent   The real estate agent who is representing the seller.

listing agreement   The contract between the seller and the agency representing him.

listing presentation   When a Realtor makes a case to be hired by the seller to market the home.

listing sheet   The printout from the MLS with the essential information about the property for sale: list price, size, number of rooms, taxes, and so on.

lockbox   A box made of strong material with a combination or electronic code. It houses a key to the property and is attached to a permanent fixture of the home so it cannot be removed from the property by anyone but the listing agent.

long-term real estate investment   An investment that you hold for 10 years or more. The reason is that the market will fluctuate over the course of your ownership. It can take a dip (even a serious one), but history tells us that the real estate market will always recover within a 10-year time frame.

lowball offer   An offer on a property where the amount is considered to be well below the actual value.

MLS (Multiple Listing Service)   An Internet database of homes currently for sale and on the market.

mortgage   A loan that uses a piece of property as collateral.

NAR (National Association of Realtors)   The nationwide trade organization for real estate agents.

net listing   These listings are illegal in some states. The property is listed at an agreed-upon net price. If it sells for more than that, the Realtor takes the balance as commission.

nonbinding estimate   A mover's rough estimate or guess at what a move will cost.

nonresident seller   One who sells property in a state other than the one in which he lives.

notary public   A person who is legally authorized by the government to authenticate and verify signatures and documents. He or she receives the designation through a state-administered exam.

one-step bidding process   When buyers making an offer on a home have one chance to offer their highest offer and best terms, usually without the benefit of a counteroffer or the ability to improve it at a later date.

open listing   Paying a reduced fee to any Realtor who happens to bring a buyer. These are not always in writing.

passive income   Type of income that comes from one of only two sources: a rental property or a business in which the taxpayer does not "materially participate." Passive income is received on a regular basis with little or no effort to maintain it.

point   Equal to 1 percent of the amount of a loan.

power of attorney   A legal authorization to act on someone's behalf.

preapproval letter   After securing certain written documentation from the buyer, a bank or lender issues a letter that states how much money the buyer can borrow.

prequalification letter   A letter that states what a bank or lender believes that a buyer can borrow based on a verbal statement of assets and income by the buyer.

purchase contract   A promise to buy a piece of real estate for a certain amount and under certain terms.

Realtor   A trademarked symbol of membership of a licensed real estate agent who belongs to the National Association of Realtors. They must abide by a strict code of ethics.

realty transfer tax   Usually paid by the seller, it's a state or local tax on the sale of any real estate. It is often a percentage of the sale price.

refinance   When a homeowner pays off one loan and replaces it with a new one, usually for the purpose of paying a lower interest rate.

relocation clause   The clause that a listing Realtor must disclose in a listing to alert buyers that a relocation company will be involved in the transaction.

relocation package   A bundle of services that a company provides for a new employee who will be moving to a new location.

remediation   To correct, clean up, or remove contamination on a property.

seller's disclosure   A written form where the seller shares or reveals to the buyer what he understands the condition of his home to be, specifically with regard to the structure, electrical and plumbing systems, and appliances.

settlement statement   A document that itemizes all costs, fees, and payments in a real estate transaction. It is also known as a *HUD* (*Housing and Urban Development*) *Statement* or *RESPA* (*Real Estate Settlement Procedures Act*) *Statement*.

shopping an offer   When a seller (or Realtor) discloses the amount of one buyer's offer to another buyer for the purpose of obtaining a better offer.

staging   The process of transforming a home through the strategic use of furniture placement, props, and color to create the most appealing visual interest. This enables buyers to take in its best features and to envision themselves living there; it creates the greatest perception of value to potential buyers.

supply and demand   An economic law about the relationship between buyers and sellers and the equalizing effect that price has on quantity and desire.

survey   To measure and establish the legal boundaries of a property.

tare weight   The weight of a moving truck before your belongings are loaded onto it. The gross weight is what it will weigh after it's loaded. The net weight is the difference between the two. Interstate movers will often use net weight to estimate the cost of a move.

tax assessed value   What the local government thinks a home is worth. The worth is used to establish what the property taxes should be.

tax revaluation   The process of reassessing values to homes in a community for the purpose of adjusting property taxes.

taxable profit   The portion of the profit of the sale of a home that can be taxed by the government.

term   A condition in a contract.

title search   A process done by a title company where public records are searched to determine if there are any claims to a property through debt or liens as well as by other unknown owners.

two-step bidding process   The receiving of multiple offers on a home in two stages. Sometimes the first round is responded to by the seller with a blanket counteroffer to all bidders.

under contract   The status of a home that has a signed contract for its purchase but has not yet closed.

use and occupancy agreement   An agreement to allow the buyer to occupy the property before the closing or the seller to occupy it after the closing.

zoning   The regulation (usually by local government) of the various ways that a property may be used.

Appendix B

Resources

American Lung Association
61 Broadway, 6th Floor
New York, NY 10006
1-800-LUNGUSA
www.lungusa.org

For information pertaining to the effects of radon and asbestos on the lungs.

American Society of Appraisers (ASA)
555 Herndon Parkway, Suite 125
Herndon, VA 20170
703-478-2228
www.appraisers.org

Helps the public to find ASA-qualified appraisers. Provides education, accreditation, and other services.

American Society of Home Inspectors, Inc. (ASHI)
932 Lee Street, Suite 101
Des Plaines, IL 60016
1-800-743-ASHI (2744)
www.ashi.org

A not-for-profit organization of inspectors dedicated to building consumer awareness and enhancing professionalism. A resource for both consumers and real estate professionals.

CLR Search
www.clrsearch.com

List your home and find information on schools and communities.

Craigslist
www.craigslist.org

Web-based local classifieds and forums for more than 500 cities in over 50 countries worldwide—community moderated and largely free.

Cyberhomes
www.cyberhomes.com

Provides your home value over the Internet by using software based on publicly available property records. It is not an appraisal. The database covers more than 85 percent of the U.S. population.

Department of Energy
1000 Independence Avenue, SW
Washington, DC 20585
1-800-DIALDOE
www.doe.gov

Provides information about conserving energy and going green at home.

Department of Transportation (DOT)
1200 New Jersey Avenue, SE
Washington, DC 20590
202-366-4000
www.dot.gov

Offers facts and information on interstate moves.

Environmental Protection Agency
Ariel Rios Building
1200 Pennsylvania Avenue, NW
Washington, DC 20460
www.epa.gov

Provides information pertaining to regulations on all environmental issues and remediation. Obtain phone numbers for all agencies at the EPA.

www.epa.gov/greenbuilding

Provides information on the practice of creating and using healthier and more resource-efficient models of construction, renovation, operation, maintenance, and demolition.

www.epa.gov/oust

Updated information relevant to the federal underground storage tank (UST) program.

Federal Motor Carrier Safety Commission
1200 New Jersey Avenue, SE
Washington, DC 20590
1-800-832-5660
www.fmcsa.dot.gov

Responsible for administration and enforcement of safety regulations, licensing, and registration.

FSBO.com
www.fsbo.com

Global For-Sale-By-Owner real estate site on the web, bringing buyers and sellers together.

Google Base
www.googlebase.com

List your home on the Google real estate search engine.

Home Safety Council
1250 Eye Street, NW
Suite 1000
Washington, DC 20005
202-330-4900
www.homesafetycouncil.org

National nonprofit organization dedicated to promoting safety and preventing home-related injuries.

Homes.com
1-888-632-6111
www.homes.com

Provider of real estate services, including property listings, brand advertising, and marketing solutions, both online and in print.

HUD—Department of Housing and Urban Development
451 7th Street, SW
Washington, DC 20410
202-708-1112
www.hud.gov

Government agency that oversees and provides information for home buying and selling, along with programs that are available to consumers involved in real estate.

Insurance Information Institute
110 William Street
New York, NY 10038
212-346-5500
www.iii.org

Attempts to improve public understanding of insurance and how it works.

International Society of Appraisers
230 E. Ohio Street, Suite 400
Chicago, IL 60611
312-224-2567
www.isa-appraisers.org

Not-for-profit, member-driven association, formed to support member needs and serve the public. Offers a search for local appraisers.

IRS
1-800-829-1040
www.irs.gov

Provides information, facts, and frequently asked questions about tax on home sales.

Lycos—Oodle
www.lycos.oodle.com

List your home on the Lycos real estate search engine.

MLS.com
www.mls.com

List your home.

National Association of Realtors (NAR)
430 N. Michigan Avenue
Chicago, IL 60611
1-800-874-6500
www.realtor.org

Membership site for real estate professionals who are bound by the NAR code of ethics. Provides resources for education and reference materials.

National Safety Council
1121 Spring Lake Drive
Itasca, IL 60143-3201
630-285-1121
www.nsc.org

The National Safety Council is a not-for-profit, charitable, international public service organization dedicated to educating and influencing people to promote safety both inside and outside the home.

Protect Your Move
1-888-DOT-SAFT (1-888-368-7238)
1200 New Jersey Avenue, SE
Washington, DC 20590
1-800-832-5660
www.protectyourmove.gov

This a link to part of FMCSC.dot.gov site and is directly related to moves.

Real Estate Espanol
www.realestateespanol.com

Official site of the National Association of Hispanic Real Estate Professionals (NAHREP). Provides Hispanic/Latino home sellers and buyers with up-to-date information on how to find a Realtor and on the process of selling and buying.

Realtor.com
www.realtor.com

Public access to consolidated national MLS listings provided by NAR.

Trulia, Inc.
41 E. 11th Street
New York, NY 10003
www.trulia.com

Trulia is a real estate advertising and search website.

Worldwide ERC
www.worldwideerc.org

An association founded in 1964 to help members overcome the challenges of work-force mobility.

Yahoo! Classifieds
www.realestate.yahoo.com

List your home on the Yahoo! real estate search engine.

Zillow.com
www.zillow.com

Online real estate service that provides real estate tools and information.

Closing and Moving Checklists

The following checklists will help you stay organized as you go through the process of closing on a home and moving:

Closing Checklist

❏ Apply for a certificate of continued use, certificate of occupancy, or smoke certificate at least two weeks prior to closing. Bring original certificate to the closing.

❏ Be sure that all personal belongings are removed from the property (including garage, storage sheds, and lawn).

❏ If you live in a condo or co-op, notify the Board of Directors in advance so that they can schedule their pre-closing walk-through.

❏ Get final utility readings for gas, oil, electric, water, and sewer and get reimbursed by buyers for any payments you have already made.

❏ Get reimbursed by buyers for already-paid condo or co-op monthly maintenance fees and assessments.

❏ Get reimbursed by buyers for prepaid services such as garbage pickup, septic tank, and landscaping.

❏ Pay buyer for agreed-upon inspection items that may be in need of repair.

❑ Pay Realtor's commission, attorney fees, recording fees, and document delivery costs.

❑ Make sure that all mortgages, debts, or liens on the home have been paid and resolved.

❑ Pay realty transfer tax, if applicable in your area.

❑ Calculate your profit (capital gains) or loss and report the sale to the IRS.

❑ Read, approve, and sign the HUD Settlement Statement.

❑ Leave (in the home) instructional manuals and warranty information for appliances and home systems for the new homeowners.

❑ Organize and label all copies of home keys and bring them to the closing.

Moving Checklist

❑ Find, get estimate, hire, and schedule the mover.

❑ Notify post office of address change.

❑ Notify bank, credit card companies, insurers, physicians, schools, and delivery services of the move.

❑ Give yourself enough time to plan for the proper disposal of hazardous waste materials such as paint cans and propane tanks.

❑ Plan for transportation of pets.

❑ Contact utility companies for final readings.

❑ Have enough cash on hand for moving day.

❑ Carry small valuables and important documents yourself in the move.

❑ Have a plan to keep children occupied during the truck loading.

Index

A

absorption rate, 8-9
active comps, 71
additions, 25-26
administrative fees, 268
advertising, 44, 142-143
    agencies, 114
    branding, 143
    buyers, 114
    cost, 114-115
    reasons for, 142
affidavit of title, 268
agencies, advertising, 114
agents, dual agency, 49
aggressive pricing, reasons for, 134
air conditioners, 253
amenities, list price, 76-77
appliances
    built-in, taking, 250
    describing, 106
    dishwasher, 247
    Energy Star, 34
    hidden, attention during showings, 126
    moving, 32
    replacing before walk-through, 250
    showings, 124
    stove/oven, 248
    washer/dryer, 247
appointments for showings, 118-119
appraisals, 16, 58
    list price, 72-73
architect's blueprints left for viewing during showing, 125
architecture
    describing, 62
    flipping homes, 193
    list price, 75

as-is condition, 13
asbestos, 239
attached rental units, 188-189
attic
    captive attics, 126
    staging, 94
attorney fees, 267
attorney review, 15

B

back health and moving, 276
backup offers, 166
bad renovations
    changing style of home, 24
    converting bedroom, 24
    converting yard, 25
    modifying use, 25
    poorly executed, 25
    second kitchen, 24
basement
    finishing, 21
    staging, 94
    wet, 242
bathroom
    staging, 90-91
    updating, 21
bedrooms
    converting, 24
    staging, 91-92
beds, unmade during showing, 125
bidding war, 159
    handling, 160-162
    inspiring, 159
boarder apartments, 188
book cartons, 277

boxes
  book cartons, 277
  collecting, 276
  dish packs, 277
  linen boxes, 277
  picture cartons, 277
  utility boxes, 277
  wardrobe boxes, 277
branding, 143
brochures, 110-111
  showings, 122
broom-clean condition, 249
budget renovations, 29-30
built-in appliances, taking, 250
buyer pool, exposure to, 139
buyer's market
  recognizing, 8
  selling in, 6-7
buyer's remorse, 167
buyers
  advertising, 114
  beliefs during down market, 146
  comfort zone, 135
  credits, seller's responsibilities at closing,
    266-267
  cycles
    chameleons, 136-137
    hunters, 135-136
    tire kickers, 137-138
  fear of missing the market, 157
  fear of paying too much, 147
  flipping homes, 193
  missing market when prices are rising, 157
  myth that they've gone away, 152-153
  offers, 220-221
  overpriced homes, 148-149
  paying premium, 158-159
  Realtors, FSBO and, 60
  sellers present during showing, 121
  selling property before buying, 215
  sense of urgency, 146-147
  urgency, 156
buzz, creating, 113, 140

C

cabinet hardware, 250
candy, showings, 123
captive attics, 126
carpenter ants, 243
carpenter bees, 242
carpeting, 86
cash, 219
ceiling light fixtures, 249
ceilings, 86, 247
central air-conditioning, 21
certificate of continued use, 235
certificate of occupancy, 235
certificates for use, 258-260
chameleon buyers, 136-137
children, discussing with, 111
chips in paint, 85
civil claims, seller liability after closing, 270
cleaning, broom-clean condition, 249
closed comps, 71
closed permits for upgrades and additions, 12
closets, staging, 92
closing, 16
  attorneys, 258
  commission, 267-268
  dates, 215
  deed, 268
  events at, 258
  fees, 267-268
  key handover, 269
  as legal transaction, 258
  seller liability after
    civil claims, 270
    lawsuits, 270
    money held in escrow, 269-270
    use and occupancy agreements, 271
  seller's responsibilities
    buyer's credits, 266-267
    certificates for use, 258-260
    commission and fees, 267-268
    pay off mortgage and liens, 260-261
    settlement statement, 266
    taxes, 261, 265

CMA (competitive market analysis), 56, 70-71
comfort zone, buyers, 135
commission
    closing, 267-268
    exceptions, 53-54
    listing agreement, 52
    payment of, 49
    percentage, 49, 52
    Realtor's income, 49-50
    seller, 52
community services information, 111
comparables (comps), 56
    acquiring, 57
    active comps, 71
    addresses, 57
    closed comps, 71
    list price, setting, 70-71
    secret comps, 71-73
    under contract, 57
condition, describing, 106-107
condo, 6
condominiums, 180, 260
contact person for showings, 118
contract, inspection items listed, 235
contract for offer, 223
contractors
    finding and interviewing, 27
    flipped home marketing, 206
    flipping homes, 193, 200
contracts, FSBO, 62
converting yard, 25
cooking smells at showings, 124
cosmetic improvements, flipping homes, 198
cost of advertising, 114-115
cost-saving strategies for renovations
    footprint of home, 30-31
    general contracting, 31
    moving appliances, 32
    multiple simultaneously, 31
    planning, 32
    stay in home during, 31
    supervision, 32

counteroffer, 151
    second counteroffer, 151
countertops, staging, 88
cover letter for offer, 221-222
curb appeal, 94-95
cycles of buyers
    chameleons, 136-137
    hunters, 135-136
    MLS's, 140
    tire kickers, 137-138
    window for contact, 141

D

date to introduce home, 112
days on market (DOM), 8
deal, managing sale of home
    anticipating problem areas, 139
    emotions and, 138
    information flow, 138
    timeline, 138
debris left behind, 249, 252-254
deck/patio, 23
    staging, 96-98
décor, flipping homes, 193
deed, 12, 268
delaying showings, 140-141
demand water heaters, 33
deposits, 15, 216-217
    cash, 219
describing home, 104-105
    appliances, 106
    condition, 106-107
    FSBO, 61
        amenities, 62
        architecture, 62
        condition, 61
        location, 61
        size, 61
    location, 105
    size, 105-106
diamond in the rough, flipping homes, 198
dining room, staging, 86-87

disclosure forms, 230
dish packs, 277
dishes in sink, showings, 125
dishwasher, 247
DOM (days on market), 8
doorknobs, 250
dormer, 23
down market
  buyers' beliefs, 146
driving up price, 158-159
drop in value, trading up and, 5
dual agency, 49

E

earnest money, 216
  copy of checks in offer, 230
emotions
  deal and, 138
  negotiations and, 150
Energy Star appliances, 34
energy-saving renovations, 32
  geothermal heat, 33
  LED lighting, 34
  radiant heat, 33
  spray insulation, 34
  tankless water heaters, 33
  tubular skylights, 33
  window films, 34
entry halls, 84
environmental inspection, 234
  asbestos, 239
  carpenter ants, 243
  carpenter bees, 242
  lead-based paint, 241
  mold, 242
  septic tanks, 240
  termites, 243
  underground oil tanks, 240
  water wells, 241
  wet basements, 242
environmental issues, radon, 239-240
environmental remediation documents, 12
epoxy, leaving behind, 252

escalation clause, 164
escrow account
  deposit money, 216
  seller liability after closing, 269-270
estate sales, 173
  dispersing proceeds of sale, 174
  family roles, 174
  marketing, 174
  taxes, 175-176
  value of estate, calculating, 176-177
exceptions, commission, 53-54
exclusive agency listing agreement, 51
expensive materials in improvements, 26
exterior upkeep, 6

F

fair market value, 175
falling market, 132
family photos, staging, 86
features sheet, 110
fees
  administrative, 268
  attorney, 267
  closing, 267-268
  overnight delivery, 268
  recording costs, 267
final mortgage commitment, 16
financing, flipping homes, 193
financing letter for offer, 230
finishing basement, 21
fireplace, 86
  showings, 123
firewood, 253
first impressions, 84
fixtures, attention during showings, 126
flag poles, 251
flat-fee listing agreement, 52
flipping homes, 191
  architecture love, 193
  buyer expectations, 193
  contractors, 193, 200
  décor love, 193
  financing, 193

first project, 204
flip test, 195
location, 194-195
market cycles, 202
market knowledge, 192
marketing
    contractors, 206
    leading information, 206
overview, 192
partners, 201
personality type, 193
reasons to get into, 192
ROI (return on investment), 204-205
safety nets, 202
skills needed, 192-194
taxes, 201
timeline, 202-204
upgrades, 195-196
    cosmetic improvements, 198
    diamond in the rough, 198
    restoration, 197
    structural overhaul, 196-197
flooring, 86, 247
    hardwood floors, 22
    kitchen, 89
    showings, 126
flow of information at deal time, 138
flower boxes, 24
    taking, 251
flyers, 110
folding brochures, 110
forms, FSBO, 62
freezers, second, 254
French drains, 22
fruit, showings, 123
FSBO (For-Sale-By-Owner), 55
    appraisals, 58
    attorney guidance, 65
    buyers
        locating, 62
        Realtor, 56, 60
    canvassing neighborhood, 63
    CMA (competitive market analysis), 56
    comps, 56
    contracts, 62

describing home, 61
    amenities, 62
    architecture, 62
    condition, 61
    location, 61
    size, 61
description, 56
follow-through with buyer, 60
forms, 62
open houses, public, 64
pricing home, 56-58
    appraiser, 58
    Internet, 57
professional guidance, 65
Realtor drop-ins, 60
Realtors, contacting, 63
showing home, 58
    appointments, 59
    pre-information, 59
    security, 59-60
sign on property, 64
full price, offer at, 213-214

G

garage sale, 276
garages, staging, 94
garbage, showings, 123
garbage disposal, showings, 125
gardening tools, 254
general contracting of renovations, 31
geothermal heat pump, 33
getting home ready, 13
good renovations
    central air-conditioning, 21
    deck/patio, 23
    dormer, 23
    finished basement, 21
    flower boxes, 24
    French drains, 22
    hardwood floors, 22
    landscaping, 23
    main floor powder room, 21
    portico, 23

shutters, 24
updating bathroom, 21
updating kitchen, 20

H

handouts, 110-111
hangers, 254
hardwood floors, 22
    hidden, 126
hazardous materials, 276
highlight sheets, 44
holiday weekends to introduce home, 112
home on market too long, 143-144
home value, trading up, 5
home warranty insurance, 12
homeowner's insurance, 12
homeowner present for showing, 121
hunter buyers, 135-136

I-J

improvements. *See also* renovations
    over-improving, 6, 25
        additions, 25-26
        expensive materials, 26
income from property, calculating, 186-187
income of Realtor, 49-50
income-producing homes. *See* investment
  properties
information flow at deal time, 138
insects
    carpenter ants, 243
    carpenter bees, 242
    termites, 243
inspection, 14, 16. *See also* environmental
  inspection
    environmental, 234
    items listed in contract, 235
    items negotiated, 236
    items required by law to fix, 235
    negotiation, 236
        buyer's request for repairs, 237-238

offer, 219-220
    pest, 234
    systems, 234
    what is inspected, 234
    when is it done, 234
inspection company, questions for, 14
instruction manuals and warranties, 13
insurance, moving, 280
Internet, 139
    pricing home, 57
introduction date, 112
investment properties
    1031 exchange, 181
    attached rental units, 188-189
    attraction of, 187-188
    boarder apartments, 188
    cons of selling, 181-182
    income
        calculating, 186-187
        potential, 185
    long-term real estate investment, 182
    marketing, 185-189
    mother/daughter layout, 188
    passive income, 180
    pros of selling, 180-181
    renters, 182
        continuing lease, 184
        making deals with, 184
        meeting with, 183
        obstacles, 182-184
        showings, 184
    showing, 189
    types, 180

K

key pickup, 120
keys, 269
kitchen
    flooring, 89
    second, 24
    staging, 88-89
    updating, 20

L

landscaping, 23
lawn, 248
lawn and garden, staging, 94-96
lawn mowers, 254
lawn signs, 111
lawsuits, seller liability after closing, 270
lead-based paint, 241
leaving things behind, 254
LED lighting, 34
lifestyle, staging, 86
light fixtures, 249
lighting, showings, 122
linen boxes, 277
list price, 68
    instincts of Realtor, 74
    offer above, 214
    offer below, 212-213
    reducing, 77-79
        when to do, 79-80
    setting, 68, 75
        amenities, 76-77
        appraisals, 72-73
        architecture, 75
        comparables, 70-71
        largest home in community, 77
        local market trends, 71-72
        location, 75
        most valuable home in community, 77
        relevant data, 70
        tax assessments, 72-73
    suggested list price, 43
listing agreement, 51
    commission section, 52
    exceptions, 53-54
    exclusive agency, 51
    flat-fee listing, 52
    net listing, 51
    open listing, 51
    relocation clause, 172-173
    sections, 52
    term of, 52

listing presentation, 42-46
listing sheets, showings, 122
living room, staging, 85-86
local market trends, list price, 71-72
local moving, 274-275
location
    describing, 105
    flipping homes, 194-195
    list price and, 75
lockboxes, 120
long-term real estate investment, 182
losing money when selling, 6
lowball offers
    defining, 149
    negotiating, 150-152
    overpriced homes, 149
    responding to, 149-150
luxury taxes, 265

M

mail, showings, 124
mailboxes, 251
main floor powder room, adding, 21
market
    buyer's market, 6-8
    down, buyers' beliefs, 146
    falling market, 132
    home on too long, 143-144
    knowledge of, flipping homes, 192
    seller's market, 9-11
    transitional market, 9
market cycles, flipping homes, 202
market trends, list price, 71-72
marketing
    estate sales, 174
    flipped homes
        contractors, 206
            leading information, 206
    investment properties, 185-189
    target marketing, 134
marketing plan, 43
    advertising, 44
    highlight sheets, 44

introducing home to other Realtors, 44
offers, handling, 45
photo brochures, 44
presentation, 43
pricing strategy, 43
reaching buyers, 44
showings, 44
staging, 43
when to go on the market, 44
marketplace, Realtors and, 48
mirrors, 85
MLS's (Multiple Listing Services), 62
cycle-one buyers, 140
delaying showings after, 140-141
describing home, 61
entering home, 113
modifying use of home, 25
mold, 242
monitoring showings, 78
mortgage, 12
final mortgage commitment, 16
offer, 217-219
cash, 219
payoff at closing, 260-261
preapproved, 218
prequalified, 218
mother/daughter layout, 188
moving
back health, 276
garage sale, 276
local, 274-275
movers
estimates, 278-279
insurance, 280
paying, 281
selecting, 278
terminology, 281-282
tipping, 281
your role, 280
out-of-state, 275
pre-moves, 276
multifamily dwellings, 180
multipage brochures, 110

multiple offers, receiving/reviewing, 162-165
multiple renovations simultaneously, 31
multiple showings
conducting, 127
as positive, 128
music, showings, 122
myth that buyers have gone away, 152-153

N

negotiated inspection items in contract, 236
negotiations
emotions, 150
inspection, 236
buyer's request for repairs, 237-238
lowball offers, 150-152
overpriced homes, 148
neighborhood amenities, 127
neighbors, 128
net listing agreement, 51
nonresident sellers, 264

O

offers
above list price, 214
accepted, 15
accepting
other offers after, 231
what to do afterward, 231
backup, 166
below list price, 212-213
buyers, 220-221
closing dates, 215
counteroffer, 151
second counteroffer, 151
deposits, 216-217
first few days, 141-142
full price, 213-214
handling, 45
inspection, 219-220
lowball
defining, 149
negotiating, 150-152

overpriced homes, 149
    responding to, 149-150
mortgage, 217-219
    cash, 219
    preapproved, 218
    prequalified, 218
multiple, receiving/reviewing, 162-165
presentation
    contract, 223
    copies of earnest money checks, 230
    cover letter, 221-222
    disclosure forms, 230
    financing letter, 230
presenting, 165
selecting best, 165-167
source, 220-221
terms, buyer selling property before
    buying, 215
oil tanks, underground, 240
one-page flyers, 110
one-step bidding process, 162-163
open houses
    FSBO, 64
    public, 115-116, 142-143
    Realtor open house, 113
    Realtors, 141
open listing agreement, 51
out-of-state moves, 275
outperforming the market, 132
over-improving, 6, 25
    additions, 25-26
    expensive materials, 26
overnight delivery fees, 268
overpriced homes
    buyers, 148-149
    lowball offers, 149
    negotiations, 148
    reducing price, 148
    "what's wrong with it" perception, 148
    withdrawing property, 149
overpricing, 77
owing too much on home, 7

P

packing
    boxes
        book cartons, 277
        dish packs, 277
        linen boxes, 277
        picture cartons, 277
        utility boxes, 277
        wardrobe boxes, 277
    collecting boxes, 276
    nonbreakables, 275
    one room at a time, 275
    order of rooms, 275
    tall items, 276
packing materials
    blankets, 278
    boxes, 277
    bubble wrap, 278
    paper pads, 277
paint
    chips in, 85
    lead-based, 241
paint cans, leaving behind, 252
pantry, staging, 89
paperwork, 11-12
    showings, 124
partners in flipping homes, 201
passive income, 180
patio/deck, 23
patios, staging, 96-98
payments, commission, 49
peak selling season, 112
pediment, 23
personality type for flipping homes, 193
pest inspection, 234
pets, showings, 123-124
photo brochures, 44
photographing home, 107
    importance of good photos, 107-108
    landscaping photos during winter, 127
    photography mistakes, 108-109
    professional real estate photographers, 107
    purpose of good photos, 107-108

photos, staging and, 86
picture cartons, 277
points, 157
poorly executed renovations, 25
porch swing, 251
porches, staging, 96-98
portico, 23
powder room on main floor, adding, 21
power of attorney, 177
pre-moves, 276
premiums, buyers paying, 158-159
presale inspection, 14
presentation of home, 43, 47
presentation of offer, 165
    contract, 223
    copy of earnest money checks, 230
    cover letter, 221-222
    disclosure forms, 230
    financing letter, 230
price
    driving up, 158-159
    fair market value, 175
    full price, offer at, 213-214
    list price, 68
        instincts of Realtor, 74
        offer above, 214
        offer below, 212-213
        reducing, 77-80
        setting, 68-77
    sale price, 68
    suggested list price, 43
price reduction, 148
prices
    rising
        buyers missing market, 157
        changes caused by, 157-158
pricing, 133
    aggressive, reasons for, 134
    importance of, 67
    overpriced homes, buyers and, 148-149
    overpricing, 77
    Realtors, 47
pricing own home, 56-58
    appraiser, 58
    Internet, 57

pricing strategy, 43
problem areas, anticipating, 139
professional real estate photographers, 107
profit and loss on sale, calculating, 268
prominent Realtors in neighborhood, 38
public open houses, 115-116, 142-143

Q-R

questions to ask Realtor, 45-46

radiant heat, 33
radon, 239-240
readying home, 13
real estate companies
    claims, 40-41
    global reach, 41
real estate photographers, 107
Realtor open house, 113
Realtors
    buyers', FSBO, 60
    communication, 38
    contacting, FSBO, 63
    drop-ins on FSBOs, 60
    evaluation of renovation ideas, 26
    friends, 39-40
    income, 49-50
    interviewing, 38
        at first walk-through, 42
        listing presentation, 42-46
        marketing plan, 43
        questions to ask, 45-46
    introduction day, 112
    listing Realtor hosts showings, 121
    managing deal, 45, 48
    marketplace, 48
    open houses, 141
    out-of-pocket expenses, 50
    presentation of home, 47
    pricing homes, 47
    prominent in neighborhood, 38
    relatives, 39-40
    seller education, 47

showings, 48
staging, 47
teaming with, 104
trust, 38
reasons for selling, 4
recording costs, 267
reducing list price, 77-79, 148
when to do, 79-80
refrigerators, second, 254
relocations, 170
relocation clause, 172-173
relocation packages, 171-172
removing items for staging, 85
renovations. *See also* improvements
bad
changing style of home, 24
converting bedroom, 24
converting yard, 25
modifying use, 25
poorly executed, 25
second kitchen, 24
budget creation, 29-30
contractors, finding and interviewing, 27
cost-saving
footprint of home, 30-31
general contracting, 31
moving appliances, 32
multiple simultaneously, 31
planning, 32
stay in home during renovation, 31
supervision, 32
delays in, 28
energy-saving, 32
geothermal heat, 33
LED lighting, 34
radiant heat, 33
spray insulation, 34
tankless water heaters, 33
tubular skylights, 33
window films, 34
footprint of home, 30-31
general contracting of home, 31

good
central air-conditioning, 21
deck/patio, 23
dormer, 23
finished basement, 21
flower boxes, 24
French drains, 22
hardwood floors, 22
landscaping, 23
main floor powder room, 21
portico, 23
shutters, 24
updating bathroom, 21
updating kitchen, 20
increasing value through, 20-24
moving appliances, 32
multiple simultaneously, 31
planning, 32
Realtor evaluation, 26
schedule, 28-29
supervision, 32
rental units. *See* investment properties
renters, 7
continuing lease, 184
making deals with, 184
meeting with, 183
obstacles to selling, 182-184
showings, 184
repairs, buyer's request for, 237-238
repairs prior to sale, 13
repairs required by law to make, 235
replacing appliances for walk-through, 250
restoration, flipping homes, 197
return on investment (ROI), flipping homes, 204-205
right time to sell, 6-11
rights, withdrawing from market, 5
rising prices
buyers missing market, 157
changes caused by, 157-158
ROI (return on investment), flipping homes, 204-205
rugs, 86

S

safety nets, flipping homes, 202
sale
    stages
        appraisal, 16
        attorney review, 15
        closing, 16
        deposits, 15
        final mortgage commitment, 16
        inspection, 16
        offer accepted, 15
        walk-through, 16
sale price, 68
scents, showings, 124
schedule for renovations, 28-29
scheduling appointments for showings, 118-119
second counteroffer, 151
second kitchen, 24
secret comps, 71-73
seller's disclosure, 111-112
seller's market, 9-11
seller's responsibilities at closing
    buyer's credits, 266-267
    certificates for use, 258-260
    commission and fees, 267-268
    pay mortgage and liens, 260-261
    settlement statement, 266
    taxes, 261, 265
sellers
    commission, 52
    educating, Realtor, 47
    nonresident sellers, 264
    present for showing, 121
sense of urgency in buyers, 146-147
septic tanks, 240
settlement statement, seller's responsibilities, 266
sheds, 251
short-time ownership, 7
showers, 248

showings, 44
    appliances, 124
        hidden, attention during showing, 126
    architect's blueprints left for viewing, 125
    beds, unmade, 125
    brochures, 122
    buzz, creating, 113
    candy dish, 123
    contact person, 118
    controlling from afar, 125-127
    cooking smells, 124
    delaying, 140-141
    dishes in sink, 125
    fireplace, 123
    first weekend on the market, 119
    fixtures, hidden, attention during showing, 126
    fruit, 123
    FSBO, 58
        appointments, 59
        pre-information, 59
        security, 59-60
    gaining entry to home, 119
        key pickup, 120
        lockboxes, 120
    garbage, 123
    garbage disposal, 125
    guidelines, 118
    hardwood floors, hidden, 126
    homeowner present, 121
    hours for, 119
    investment properties, 189
    lighting, 122
    listing Realtor hosts, 121
    listing sheets, 122
    mail, 124
    monitoring, 78
    multiple
        conducting, 127
        as positive, 128
    music, 122
    neighborhood amenities, 127
    paperwork, 124

pets, 123-124
preparing for, 122-123
Realtors, 48
renters, 184
scheduling appointments, 118-119
sickness during, 122
smells, 124
smoking, 124
suspending during illness, 122
temperature of home, 123
tracking, 128
valuables, 124
winter, landscaping photos, 127
shutters, 24
taking, 251
sign on property, FSBO, 64
signs, 111
sinks, 248
staging, 89
size, describing, 105-106
smells, showings, 124
smoke certificate, 259
smoking, showings, 124
sold comps, 71
source of offer, 220-221
spray insulation, 34
spring market, 112
stages of sale
appraisal, 16
attorney review, 15
closing, 16
deposits, 15
final mortgage commitment, 16
inspection, 16
offer accepted, 15
walk-through, 16
staging, 43, 47, 133
attics, 94
basements, 94
bathroom, 90-91
bedroom, 91-92
closets, 92
decks, 96-98

dining room, 86-87
family photos, 86
first impressions, 84
garages, 94
kitchen, 88-89
lawn and garden, 94-96
living room, 85-86
pantry, 89
patios, 96-98
porches, 96-98
professional stagers, 98-99
removing items, 85
sink, 89
vacant homes, 98
windows, 93
stain cans, leaving behind, 252
stale homes, 148
stove/oven, 248
structural overhaul, flipping homes, 196-197
style of home, changing, 24
suggested list price, 43
sump pump, 22
supervision of renovations, 32
supply and demand, 143
survey, 12
swing sets as negotiable item, 251

T

tall items, packing, 276
tankless water heaters, 33
target marketing, 134
tax assessments, list price and, 72-73
taxes
closing
seller's responsibilities, 261, 265
estate sales, 175-176
flipping homes, 201
luxury taxes, 265
temperature of home at showings, 123
term of listing agreement, 52
termites, 243
terms of offer, buyer selling property before
buying, 215

things to leave behind, 254
time to sell, 6-11
timeline for deal, 138
    setting, 11
timeline for flipping homes, 202-204
tire-kicker buyers, 137-138
toilets, 248
townhouse, 6
tracking showings, 128
trading down, 6
trading up, drop in value, 5
transactions, number of, 5
transfer of ownership, 268
transitional market, recognizing, 9
trash cans, 254
tubs, 248
tubular skylights, 33
two-step bidding process, 164

U

underground oil tanks, 240
updating bathroom, 21
updating kitchen, 20
upgrades, flipping homes, 195-196
    cosmetic improvements, 198
    diamond in the rough, 198
    structural overhaul, 196-197
upgrades sheet, 110
use and occupancy agreements, 271
use of home, modifying, 25
utility boxes, 277

V

vacant homes, staging, 98
validation, 147
valuables at showings, 124
value
    creating, 69
    fair market value, 175

W

walk-through, 16, 246
    appliances, replaced, 250
    broom-clean condition, 249
    ceilings, 247
    debris, 249
    dishwasher, 247
    floors, 247
    lawn, 248
    showers, 248
    sinks, 248
    stove/oven, 248
    toilets, 248
    tubs, 248
    walls, 247
    washer/dryer, 247
wall light fixtures, 249
walls, 247
wardrobe boxes, 277
washer/dryer, 247
water heaters, 33
water wells, 241
wells, 241
wet basements, 242
what sells a home, 132
    leading the deal, 138-139
    pricing, 133-138
    staging, 133
    whole buyer pool, exposure to, 139-142
"what's wrong with it" perception, 148-149
why homes sell, 132
window films, 34
windows, staging, 93
winter sales, landscaping photos, 127
withdrawing from market, 5, 149
workshop tools, 254

X–Y–Z

yard, converting, 25

zoning certificate, 259

Fulton Co. Public Library
320 W. 7th Street
Rochester, IN 46975